Assemblage, Enactment, and Agency

Assemblage, Enactment, and Agency offers an exploration of the emerging shift in policy research towards the notion of policy enactment, namely, the creative recontextualization and translation of policy ideas into social realities by policy actors in education. Bringing together recent work on the intersections between assemblages, enactments, and agencies in educational policy analysis, the authors call attention to issues of subjectivity, practice, power, and relationality as they offer critical perspectives that challenge linear/instrumentalist views of policy processes. In doing so, they not only interrogate conventional understandings of policy design, implementation, and evaluation, they also recognize the role of agency, interpretation, sense-making, translation, embodiment, and meaning throughout policy processes. They also explore the contested nature of policy, situating educational policies as sites of conflict and negotiation between actors, highlighting the uncertainty, fragility, and instability of policy work. By offering a nonlinear and heterogeneous account of education policy, the collection furthers contemporary conversations on the nature and goals of education reform. This book was originally published as a special issue of *Discourse: Studies in the Cultural Politics of Education*.

Melody Viczko is an Assistant Professor of Critical Policy, Equity and Leadership Studies at Western University, Canada. Her research takes a relational approach to educational policy analysis, looking at how actors assemble around policies and how these assemblages influence democratic governance practices in education. Her current research focuses on the engagement of higher education institutions with other government and non-state actors through internationalization policies. She is the editor of *Assembling and Governing the Higher Education Institution: Democracy, Social Justice and Leadership in Higher Education* (with Lynette Shultz, 2016).

Augusto Riveros is an Assistant Professor in the Faculty of Education at Western University, Canada. His research explores the intersections of philosophy, educational administration, and education policy analysis, and his recent work looks at the enactment of standards and competencies for leadership practice in the context of globalization. His work has been published in numerous journals, including *Discourse: Studies in the Cultural Politics of Education*, *Educational Philosophy and Theory*, *Education Policy Analysis Archives*, the *International Journal of Leadership in Education*, the *Journal of Educational Administration,* and *Studies in Philosophy and Education*.

Assemblage, Enactment, and Agency

Educational policy perspectives

Edited by
Melody Viczko and Augusto Riveros

LONDON AND NEW YORK

First published 2017
by Routledge
2 Park Square, Milton Park, Abingdon, Oxon, OX14 4RN, UK

and by Routledge
711 Third Avenue, New York, NY 10017, USA

Routledge is an imprint of the Taylor & Francis Group, an informa business

© 2017 Taylor & Francis

All rights reserved. No part of this book may be reprinted or reproduced or utilised in any form or by any electronic, mechanical, or other means, now known or hereafter invented, including photocopying and recording, or in any information storage or retrieval system, without permission in writing from the publishers.

Trademark notice: Product or corporate names may be trademarks or registered trademarks, and are used only for identification and explanation without intent to infringe.

British Library Cataloguing in Publication Data
A catalogue record for this book is available from the British Library

ISBN 13: 978-1-138-22901-3

Typeset in TimesNewRomanPS
by diacriTech, Chennai

Publisher's Note
The publisher accepts responsibility for any inconsistencies that may have arisen during the conversion of this book from journal articles to book chapters, namely the possible inclusion of journal terminology.

Disclaimer
Every effort has been made to contact copyright holders for their permission to reprint material in this book. The publishers would be grateful to hear from any copyright holder who is not here acknowledged and will undertake to rectify any errors or omissions in future editions of this book.

Contents

Citation Information vii
Notes on Contributors ix

Introduction–Assemblage, enactment and agency: educational policy perspectives 1
Melody Viczko and Augusto Riveros

1 'Where you stand depends on where you sit': the social construction of
policy enactments in the (English) secondary school 7
Meg Maguire, Annette Braun and Stephen Ball

2 Re/assembling spaces of learning in Victorian government schools:
policy enactments, pedagogic encounters and micropolitics 22
Dianne Mulcahy

3 Faciality enactments, schools of recognition and policies of difference (in-itself) 37
P. Taylor Webb and Kalervo N. Gulson

4 The enactment of professional learning policies: performativity and
multiple ontologies 55
Augusto Riveros and Melody Viczko

5 When things come undone: the promise of dissembling education policy 70
Jill Koyama

6 Teaching without faculty: policy interactions and their effects on the
network of teaching in German higher education 82
Alexander Mitterle, Carsten Würmann and Roland Bloch

7 Producing calculable worlds: education at a glance 100
Radhika Gorur

CONTENTS

8	The sociomateriality of education policy *Paolo Landri*	118
9	Symbolic power, politics and teachers *Aspa Baroutsis*	132
	Index	141

Citation Information

The chapters in this book were originally published in *Discourse: Studies in the Cultural Politics of Education*, volume 36, issue 4 (August 2015). When citing this material, please use the original page numbering for each article, as follows:

Introduction
Assemblage, enactment and agency: educational policy perspectives
Melody Viczko and Augusto Riveros
Discourse: Studies in the Cultural Politics of Education, volume 36, issue 4 (August 2015)
pp. 479–484

Chapter 1
'Where you stand depends on where you sit': the social construction of policy enactments in the (English) secondary school
Meg Maguire, Annette Braun and Stephen Ball
Discourse: Studies in the Cultural Politics of Education, volume 36, issue 4 (August 2015)
pp. 485–499

Chapter 2
Re/assembling spaces of learning in Victorian government schools: policy enactments, pedagogic encounters and micropolitics
Dianne Mulcahy
Discourse: Studies in the Cultural Politics of Education, volume 36, issue 4 (August 2015)
pp. 500–514

Chapter 3
Faciality enactments, schools of recognition and policies of difference (in-itself)
P. Taylor Webb and Kalervo N. Gulson
Discourse: Studies in the Cultural Politics of Education, volume 36, issue 4 (August 2015)
pp. 515–532

Chapter 4
The enactment of professional learning policies: performativity and multiple ontologies
Augusto Riveros and Melody Viczko
Discourse: Studies in the Cultural Politics of Education, volume 36, issue 4 (August 2015)
pp. 533–547

CITATION INFORMATION

Chapter 5
When things come undone: the promise of dissembling education policy
Jill Koyama
Discourse: Studies in the Cultural Politics of Education, volume 36, issue 4 (August 2015) pp. 548–559

Chapter 6
Teaching without faculty: policy interactions and their effects on the network of teaching in German higher education
Alexander Mitterle, Carsten Würmann and Roland Bloch
Discourse: Studies in the Cultural Politics of Education, volume 36, issue 4 (August 2015) pp. 560–577

Chapter 7
Producing calculable worlds: education at a glance
Radhika Gorur
Discourse: Studies in the Cultural Politics of Education, volume 36, issue 4 (August 2015) pp. 578–595

Chapter 8
The sociomateriality of education policy
Paolo Landri
Discourse: Studies in the Cultural Politics of Education, volume 36, issue 4 (August 2015) pp. 596–609

Chapter 9
Symbolic power, politics and teachers
Aspa Baroutsis
Discourse: Studies in the Cultural Politics of Education, volume 36, issue 4 (August 2015) pp. 610–618

For any permission-related enquiries please visit:
http://www.tandfonline.com/page/help/permissions

Notes on Contributors

Stephen Ball is a Professor of Sociology of Education at the Institute of Education, UCL, UK. He is the cofounder and managing editor of the *Journal of Education Policy*. His main areas of interest are in sociologically informed education policy analysis and the relationships between education, education policy, and social class. He is the author of *How Schools Do Policy: Policy Enactments in Secondary Schools* (with Meg Maguire and Annette Braun, 2012) and *Foucault, Power and Education* (Routledge, 2013).

Aspa Baroutsis is a Postdoctoral Research Fellow in the School of Education at Queensland University of Technology, Brisbane, Australia. She completed her Ph.D., on the politics and perceptions of newspapers' coverage of teachers, at the University of Queensland, Australia.

Roland Bloch is a researcher in the Institute of Sociology at Martin Luther University, Halle-Wittenberg, Germany. His research focuses on stratification in German graduate education, study reform, and the career conditions for academics.

Annette Braun is a Lecturer in the Sociology of Education at the Institute of Education, UCL, UK. Her main areas of interest centre on gender and social class, trajectories from education to work, professional identities, and critical policy analysis. She is the coauthor of *How Schools Do Policy: Policy Enactments in Secondary Schools* (with Meg Maguire and Stephen Ball, 2012).

Radhika Gorur is a Senior Lecturer at Deakin University, Australia, and a Director of the Laboratory of International Assessment Studies. Her research focuses on contemporary social policy, and in particular on the rise of quantification and the proliferation of numbers in education policy. Using material-semiotic approaches, she seeks to understand how some policy ideas begin to cohere, stabilize, gain momentum, and make their way in the world.

Kalervo N. Gulson is an Associate Professor in the Faculty of Arts and Social Sciences at the University of New South Wales, Sydney, Australia. His current research focuses on the relationship between education policy and calculative spaces, and what kind of life is possible within and through these calculative spaces. His recent publications include *Education Policy, Space and the City: Markets and the (In)visibility of Race* (2011) and *Policy, Geophilosophy, Education* (with T. Webb, 2015).

Jill Koyama is an Associate Professor in the College of Education at the University of Arizona, USA. Her work covers three strands of inquiry: the productive social assemblage of policy, the controversies of globalizing educational policy, and the politics of language

NOTES ON CONTRIBUTORS

policy and immigrant and refugee education. She is the author of *Making Failure Pay: High-Stakes Testing, For-Profit Tutoring, and Public Schools* (2010).

Paolo Landri is a Senior Researcher in the Institute of Research on Population and Social Policies of the National Research Council (CNR–IRPPS), Rome, Italy. His main research interests concern educational organizations, professional learning, and educational policies.

Meg Maguire is a Professor of Sociology of Education at King's College London, UK. Her research is in the sociology of education, urban education, and policy, and she has a long-standing interest in the lives of teachers and issues of class, race, gender, and age in teachers' social and professional worlds.

Alexander Mitterle is a researcher in the Department of Sociology at Martin Luther University, Halle-Wittenberg, Germany. His work has appeared in the *Review of Education* and *Discourse: Studies in the Cultural Politics of Education*. His research focuses on field stratification in German higher education.

Dianne Mulcahy is based in the Graduate School of Education at the University of Melbourne, Australia. Her research interests lie in theoretical and empirical work on knowledge, identities, and professional practice in the context of secondary and tertiary sectors of education. She is currently researching aspects of the materiality of learning, and their implications for pedagogy and professional practice.

Augusto Riveros is an Assistant Professor in the Faculty of Education at Western University, Canada. His research explores the intersections of philosophy, educational administration, and education policy analysis, and his recent work looks at the enactment of standards and competencies for leadership practice in the context of globalization.

Melody Viczko is an Assistant Professor of Critical Policy, Equity and Leadership Studies at Western University, Canada. Her current research focuses on the engagement of higher education institutions with other government and non-state actors through internationalization policies. She is the editor of *Assembling and Governing the Higher Education Institution: Democracy, Social Justice and Leadership in Higher Education* (with Lynette Shultz, 2016).

P. Taylor Webb is an Associate Professor in the Department of Educational Studies at the University of British Columbia, Canada. His work examines and critiques how education rationalizes and produces 'governable subjects' within liberal and neo-liberal normative architectures. His books include *Teacher Assemblage* (2009) and *Policy Science 3.0: Policy Geophilosophy and Education* (with Kalervo N. Gulson, 2014).

Carsten Würmann is a Research Fellow in the Centre for School and Education Research at Martin Luther University, Halle-Wittenberg, Germany. His work and research focus on the structure of academic teaching in German universities, the cultural history of teaching, and the career conditions of academic researchers.

INTRODUCTION

Assemblage, enactment and agency: educational policy perspectives

The idea for this special issue emerged after a panel held at the *7th International Conference on Interpretive Policy Analysis* in 2012 in Tilburg, the Netherlands. Our goal for the panel was to bring together recent work around the notions of *assemblage, enactment and agency* in educational policy analysis, with particular attention to issues of subjectivity, practice, power, and relationality. After the conference, we invited other papers to form a special issue on these topics. The collection of papers in this issue aims to explore the emerging shift in policy research towards analyses embracing the notion of policy enactment, and specifically, theorizations that attend to the:

> creative processes of interpretation and translation, that is, the recontextualisation – through reading, writing and talking – of the abstractions of policy ideas into contextualised practices. (Braun, Ball, Maguire, & Hoskins, 2011, p. 586)

These new approaches offer innovative and exciting opportunities for exploring the complexity of policy processes in educational fields.

The authors in this issue share an interest in critiquing linear views of policy processes for their limitations in understanding complexity in policy research. Such linear views of policy have a tendency to separate processes of policy-making into discrete categories of design, implementation, and evaluation that privilege the agential actor as instrumental decision-maker. The interpretive turn in policy analysis (Yanow, 2000) has been critical of these approaches, arguing that their focus is on policy goals aimed a pre-defined problems with pre-defined outcomes. As Shore and Wright (2011) argued, instrumentalism still dominates much of the policy analysis research, particularly in the field of educational policy. Within the interpretive turn in policy analysis, the notion of policy enactment not only poses challenges to linear conceptualizations of policy design, implementation and evaluation, but also questions the instrumentalist view of actors, recognizing the role of agency, interpretation, sense-making, translation, embodiment, and meaning throughout the policy process. The scholarship in this area draws upon notions of assemblage (Rizvi & Lingard, 2010); enactment (Ball, Maguire, & Braun, 2012), networks (Fenwick, 2010; Nespor, 2002; Resnik, 2006; Vidovich, 2007), materiality (Sørenson, 2009), and performativity (Mulcahy, 2011), these approaches to policy analysis share a commitment to examine the ways in which policy as a process emerges out of interactions between diversely conceptualized heterogeneous actors.

The analytic of 'process' is important here for our purposes, for as Hernes (2014) argues, 'process thinking invites reflections on the relationships between the given state of affairs and the multiple possibilities for things to turn out otherwise' (p. 3). Indeed, as Landri (2015) illustrates, engagements with policy are productive; they perform new realities that might never have existed without the moments of resistance, problem definition and change. Similarly, in their essay for this issue, Maguire, Ball and Braun

(2015) illustrate the fragility and instability of policy work, and that these uncertainties mean openness for what could be performed in the enactment of policy. The aim in this issue is to interrupt the technocratic, instrumentalist view of policy in education, and instead, offer potentialities for democratic thinking in educational policy analysis. But what is democratic in these studies of policy? Webb and Gulson (2015) remind us that the promise of emancipatory practices needs our attention in the enactment of policies aimed at transforming educational spaces. Examining what comes to be performed through policy is an important step in understanding the realities for those affected by policies and conceptualizing the ways in which things might be differently performed.

In their contribution, Meg Maguire, Annette Braun, and Stephen Ball (2015) offer an exploration of the multifaceted ways in which educational policies are contextualized in schools. They draw on their study on policy enactments in English secondary schools (Ball, Maguire, & Braun, 2012) to show how contextual factors such as policy type, power and positionality, space and time constraints, as well as different subjectivities, are critical for understanding the ways in which policies are translated into practices in schools. Their proposal looks beyond the conventional accounts of 'policy implementation' in which policy is generally treated as a finished object crafted at the higher levels of the bureaucratic structures. These conventional accounts portray schools as decontextualized and homogeneous organizations where policies are merely transferred and applied. In contrast to this functionalist conception of policy processes, Maguire, Braun and Ball argue that policies are better seen as enacted through creative processes of interpretation and translation (Braun et al., 2011). The authors examined the enactment of two policies: 'Behaviour Management' and 'Standards and Attainment' to find out that enacting a policy is a process fraught with fragility and instability. Not all policies are adopted in the same way, as each policy carries different significance for different people. Issues of power and positionality also influence the way in which policies are performed into existence, as well as the time of the year and the particular spaces in which those performances take place. They conclude by noting that '"where you stand" in terms of subject department, pedagogical values, the time of the year and a range of other biographical factors such as length of service, plays powerfully into "where you sit"' (Maguire, Braun, & Ball, 2014).

In her paper, Dianne Mulcahy (2015) uses the analytic of assemblage to trace the ways in which learning spaces and pedagogical practices emerge as sociomaterial arrangements in the process of enacting a policy initiative in the state of Victoria in Australia. She analyses the multiple, and sometimes contradictory, ways in which the 'Building the Education Revolution' (BER) programme was constituted as a heterogeneous assemblage of social and material entities. In her analysis, Mulcahy identifies the micropolitics of the learning spaces as a key factor in the processes of territorialisation (Deleuze & Guattari, 1987) that take place as the policy makes its way into the classroom. In the dynamic of the territorialisation, new assemblages are configured by the rearrangement of the pedagogical and the material in the school. Policies play a fundamental role in the materialization of these new spaces. In Mulcahy's view, the BER initiative could be seen as a 'performative agent with interventionist possibilities regarding schools' spatial and pedagogic outcomes and goals' (Mulcahy, 2015). The deployment of the analytic of assemblage in policy analysis reveals the open and contested nature of policy enactments in schools. It offers an alternative to rationalist approaches to educational policy that looks beyond the conventional linear and bureaucratic characterizations of policy work. Mulcahy's work characterizes policy as a much more complex process, one that is fluid, emergent and mutable, a sociomaterial practice that produces, reproduces and transforms the multiple realities of the school.

In their contribution, Taylor Webb and Kalervo Gulson (2015) use Deleuze and Guattari's (1987) analytics of *difference-in-itself* and *faciality* to discuss the idea of difference applied to *schools of recognition*. These are 'public choice schools ... that enunciate a culturally focused curriculum, identity of brand' (2015). In their study, Webb and Gulson investigate the development of the Africentric Alternative School in the Toronto District School Board, showing how neoliberal discourses on multiculturalism engender particular forms of difference and identity within a politics of representation. Their analysis reveals that when neoliberal policies on multiculturalism are enacted, various codings and decodings of racial identity are produced. They note that these new significations emerged in a process of marketization and commodification of education through school choice policies. In their view, the particular iterations of identity and recognition, produced and reproduced by neoliberal multiculturalism, fail to deliver on their emancipatory promise. Instead, it creates a system of grouping and sorting that reaffirms difference while denying the possibility of educational equity. In Webb and Gulson's (2015) words 'schools of recognition are the disciplinary and reproductive machine of self-selected and entrepreneurial significations – the *sine qua non* of neoliberal education policy'.

Melody Viczko and Gus Riveros (2015) articulate a conceptual challenge to the formalized structures of professional learning to argue more attention is needed to understanding the idiosyncratic ways in which policy discourses are enacted in schools. Drawing upon the notion of multiple ontologies (Mol, 1999), the authors argue for considering teacher learning its sociomaterial entanglements in order to see the multiple yet simultaneous realities of its performance that exist in schools. They show how teacher learning is brought into reality through assemblages of many actors: administrative techniques, policies, artefacts and people. In doing so, they aim to influence how policy-makers think about and construct strategies for educational reform that specifically target teachers changed teaching practices. The significance of this work for this issue is that it challenges the singularity with educational institutions often conceive of educational reform. The authors' conceptual argument challenges instrumentalist policy theories focused on implementation with a linear process resulting in one outcome to show that the sociomaterial world in which policies are enacted opens the realm of possible realities for teaching learning is configured in schools.

Jill Koyama (2015) uses the concept of controversy to explore the assemblage formed when curriculum change, school reform and vulnerable populations of refugee students come together in one school in the USA. Drawing upon actor-network (AN) theories of assemblage, Koyama reports on ethnographic data collected over 26 months in schools in the USA looking at the No Child Left Behind policy network. In this article, she features a case of one school's turnaround plan related to a mandated curriculum aimed at improving the academic achievement of refugee students. She frames policy enactment as a socio-material process best described as meshwork (Heimans, 2012), whereby 'practice is both always discursive and material ... reimpose[s] the messiness of bodies into accounts of practice' (p. 318). Koyama's approach to policy weaves both material and social actors: various material elements of the turnaround plan, ideologies and discourses, school administrators and teachers and other human actors working in the school. Using interview and other qualitative data, the author describes the controversies, that is, the tensions and inconsistencies among the policy enactments, within the way the turnaround plan is brought into existence in the school through various actions. She shows how these controversial enactments exist simultaneously and produce different effects in how the curriculum for the turnaround plan unfolds within the school. Such assemblage thinking highlights the turnaround plan an entity in multiplicity, showing how actors located outside of the school, such as community organization and refugee resettlement agencies, become assembled and effect change. In conclusion, Koyama argues for assemblage thinking in policy studies to show the agency of policy 'as cultural mediator rather than passive artifact that required actors to respond to it'. Studying how policy things come together and come undone reveals a novel and broadening understanding of the totality of policy enactment.

Alexander Mitterle, Carsten Würman, and Roland Bloch (2015) provide a complex but thorough account of contemporary teaching in German higher education by detailing the entanglements of present and past policies at one university. What began as an initial research project aiming to understand university teaching structures by comparing course catalogues and teaching personnel data, Mitterle, Würman and Bloch set out to further understand a puzzling finding: discrepancies between the texts indicated instances in which some professors were actually teaching more than they ought to. Drawing on Actor Network Theory, the authors describe the administrative ordering and policy interactions that bring teachers, students and funding together to make such circumstances happen. The significance of their approach is the focus is on 'figures normally left in the dark' such as instruments for calculating teaching load, staff planning charts, standardised faulty/student ratios, capacity law and funding schemes. By tracing the networks that both historically and currently assemble around these actors, they show how institutional actors are administratively assembled so that the network of teaching and research activities appears stable. However, what the authors' analysis shows is that such stability functions in practice through the result of complex processes of negotiation through the bureaucracy of instruments, charts and laws. The end result, the authors explain: 'what remains are administratively visible courses, taught by teachers that are not associated within the teaching faculty ... teaching takes place without faculty' (Mitterle, Würman, & Bloch, 2015).

The interest of this intriguing tale for the special issue is the way the authors show how stability in the organization of the university's administrative practices comes to be produced not through the orderly dictions of policies but rather through the complexity of the messy practices that emerge as these policies are translated into action. Tracing the messiness is challenging but doing so illuminates how material actors perform organizational realities.

Radhika Gorur (2015) argues that a focus on the performative nature of policy illuminates the political and ontological project of policy work. Drawing on Science and Technology Studies (STS) and the sociology of measurement, Gorur invokes the concept of assemblage to trace the ways in which scientific indicators, presented as facts, are produced through the interactions of social actors so that prescriptive policy directives can be formulated into national policy goals and reform. In her article, she examines the production of the indicators in the *Education at a Glance* (EAG) annual report from the Organisation for Economic Cooperation and Development (OECD). Using both historical texts written by and interviews with key actors involved with the OECD, Gorur tells 'the story of the OECD indicator development project'. Here, she shows how the differing interests are negotiated between assessment specialists, social scientists, psychometricians and policy-makers in the production of the report. The work of these actors is the site of translation, where indicators become political projects of evaluation and measurement for ordering educational systems on a global scale through interactions with the EAG. As Gorur states, 'the two projects – the scientific project and the governance project – are impossible to keep apart'. For Gorur, there is a moral imperative to develop 'an understanding of measurement as a productive rather than a descriptive practice'. The significance for policy studies in Gorur's argument is the connections made between the science and governance of policy through the study of the everyday negotiations between policy actors.

Paolo Landri (2015) examines an elaborate case study that highlights the complex reassembling of humans and non-humans in the enactment of a state reform for education in a Provinica in South Italy. Landri shows how the newly instituted initiative, titled 'zones for the improvement of education provision', instigates the creation of new policy spaces. In presenting the case, he asks how this new policy space materializes in practice and whether multiple instantiations of the space emerge in the enactment of this policy reform. Drawing on sociomaterial notions of the materialization of space (Mol & Law, 1994), Landri traces how objects enrolled into the reform, such as texts, information systems, maps and politically shaped spaces (such as parliament), 'are mobilized to enact the zone' by performing different manifestations of this space. Contrary to instrumentalism that views reform producing a single result, the author details the multiplicity of space created through the reform: as a bounded region, a network for deliberation and a fluid zone where relationships change. Landri's point in this work is to empirically illustrate the socio-material argument that materialisations are not representative of the social world but that the interactions between human and non-human actors in an instance of policy reform reconfigure the spaces in which such change emerges and come define what the policies are as they are performed in multiple ways. Furthermore, his work rejects the deterministic view of the certainty of linear policy processes to show moments of failure, resistance and change, arguing that policy actors traditionally seen at the margins of policy-making emerge as powerful in their engagements with the materiality of educational reform.

In conclusion, this issue examines how the notions of assemblage and enactment are used to study how processes of policy emerge in educational contexts, whereby policies are not seen as static entities of unity but rather as multiple and heterogeneous in nature. The authors invited to this issue are also interested in exploring the agential nature of policy processes, situating educational policies as sites of contestation, conflict and negotiation between actors. As the articles in this issue show, social and material entities form assemblages that perform particular educational contexts, that is, political environments in the doing of educational policy through dynamic processes of micropolitical contestation (Mulcahy), policy definition through material and discursive practices (Koyama), measurement and evaluation (Gorur) and organization of pedagogical environments (Mitterle, Würmann, & Bloch). The analytical contexts are diverse in this issue; however, the concern for policy processes is common to the authors' interest in understanding the work of educational policy.

Melody Viczko and Augusto Riveros
Western University in London, ON, Canada

References

Ball, S. J., Maguire, M., & Braun, A. (2012). *How schools do policy. Policy enactments in secondary schools*. London: Routledge.

Braun, A., Ball, S. J., Maguire, M., & Hoskins, K. (2011). Taking context seriously: Towards explaining policy enactments in the secondary school. *Discourse: Studies in the Cultural Politics of Education, 32*, 585–596. doi:10.1080/01596306.2011.601555

Deleuze, G., & Guattari, F. (1987). *A thousand plateaus: Capitalism and schizophrenia*. (B. Massumi, Trans.). Minneapolis and London: University of Minnesota Press.

Fenwick, T. (2010). un(Doing) standards in education with actor-network theory. *Journal of Education Policy, 25*(2), 117–133. doi:10.1080/02680930903314277

Gorur, R. (2015). Producing calculable worlds: Education at a glance. *Discourse: Studies in the Cultural Politics of Education, 36*(4), 578–595.

Heimans, S. (2012). Coming to matter in practice: Enacting education policy. *Discourse: Studies in the Cultural Politics of Education, 33*, 313–326. doi:10.1080/01596306.2012.666083

Hernes, T. (2014). *A process theory of organization*. Oxford: Oxford University Press.

Koyama, J. (2015). When things come undone: The promise of dissembling education policy. *Discourse: Studies in the Cultural Politics of Education, 36*(4), 548–559.

Landri, P. (2015). The sociomateriality of education policy. *Discourse: Studies in the Cultural Politics of Education, 36*(4), 596–609.

Maguire, M., Braun, A., & Ball, S. (2015). 'Where you stand depends on where you sit': The social construction of policy enactments in the (English) secondary school. *Discourse: Studies in the Cultural Politics of Education, 36*(4), 485–499.

Mitterle, A., Würman, C., & Bloch, R. (2015). Teaching without faculty: Policy interactions and their effects on the network of teaching in German higher education. *Discourse: Studies in the Cultural Politics of Education, 36*(4), 560–577.

Mol, A. (1999). Ontological politics. In J. Law & J. Hassard (Eds.), *Actor network theory and after* (pp. 74–89). Oxford: Blackwell.

Mol, A., & Law, J. (1994). Regions, networks and fluids: Anaemia and social topology. *Social Studies of Science, 24*, 641–671. doi:10.1177/030631279402400402

Mulcahy, D. (2011). Assembling the 'accomplished' teacher: The performativity and politics of professional teaching standards. *Educational Philosophy and Theory, 43*(suppl. 1), 94–113. doi:10.1111/j.1469-5812.2009.00617.x

Mulcahy, D. (2015). Re/assembling spaces of learning in Victorian government schools: Policy enactments, pedagogic encounters and micropolitics. *Discourse: Studies in the Cultural Politics of Education, 36*(4), 500–514.

Nespor, J. (2002). Networks and contexts of reform. *Journal of Educational Change, 3*, 365–382.

Resnik, J. (2006). International organizations, the 'education-economic growth' black box and the development of world education culture. *Comparative Education Review, 50*, 173–195. doi:10.1086/500692

Rizvi, F., & Lingard, B. (2010). *Globalizing education policy*. London: Routledge.

Shore, C., & Wright, S. (2011). Conceptualising policy: Technologies of governance and the politics of visibility. In C. Shore, S. Wright, & D. Pero (Eds.), *Policy worlds: Anthropology and the analysis of contemporary power* (pp. 1–26). New York, NY: Berghahn.

Sørenson, E. (2009). *The materiality of learning: Technology and knowledge in educational practice*. Cambridge: Cambridge University Press.

Viczko, M., & Riveros, G. (2015). The enactment of professional learning policies: Performativity and multiple ontologies. *Discourse: Studies in the Cultural Politics of Education, 36*(4), 533–547.

Vidovich, L. (2007). Removing policy from its pedestal: Some theoretical framings and practical possibilities. *Educational Review, 59*, 285–298. doi:10.1080/0013191070142723

Webb, T., & Gulson, K. (2015). Faciality enactments, schools of recognition and policies of difference (in-itself). *Discourse: Studies in the Cultural Politics of Education, 36*(4), 515–532.

Yanow, D. (2000). *Conducting interpretive policy analysis*. Thousand Oaks, CA: SAGE.

'Where you stand depends on where you sit': the social construction of policy enactments in the (English) secondary school

Meg Maguire[a], Annette Braun[b] and Stephen Ball[b]

[a]King's College London, London, UK; [b]Institute of Education, London, UK

> Drawing on a study of education policy enactments in four English secondary schools, this paper argues that different 'types' of policies call-up different forms of enactments, and that teachers and others who work in schools will have different orientations towards some of these possible ways of 'doing' school. Through exploring the ways in which two main policies are being enacted, 'Behaviour Management' and 'Standards and Attainment', we argue that policy type, power and positionality, space and time constraints, as well as different subjectivities, render policy enactment a more fragile and unstable process than is sometimes documented in policy analysis and implementation studies. Thus, in policy enactment terms, 'where you stand depends on where you sit'.

From policy implementation to enactment in schools

In much writing on education policy, the meaning of policy is frequently either just taken for granted and/or seen as an attempt to 'solve a problem' – what Colebatch (2006a, p. 2) refers to as the 'established ways of thinking about policy'. This form of 'normative' policy analysis

> rests on an unspoken presentation of government as a problem-solving being, separate from the society over which it rules ... Government recognises problems and chooses courses of action to deal with them: these courses of action are 'policy'. (Colebatch, 2006a, p. 3)

The problem is that if policy is seen only in these terms, then all the other moments in the processes of policy and policy enactments that go on in schools, and other organisations, become marginalised or go unrecognised. The jumbled, sometimes ambiguous, messy process that is experienced on the ground by policy actors, what Colebatch (2002) calls the 'policy activity' of negotiations and coalition-building that work to enact various policies, become displaced, invisible and risk going unrecognised in policy analysis.

Even though policy work in social welfare settings has been revitalised through attempts to generate 'joined up thinking' and incorporate more policy actors, policy making at the legislative level is still characterised by instrumentality and hierarchy. In these sorts of accounts, the teacher and 'other adults' working in and around schools, are bleached out of the policy process or positioned as 'implementers'. However, while many policies 'done' in schools are produced by government elites, legislators and sometimes by influential stakeholders, policy making in all its levels and in all its sites also involves 'negotiation, contestation or struggle between different groups who may lie outside the formal machinery of official policy-making' (Ozga, 2000, p. 113). Policy enactment is a process of social, cultural and emotional construction and interpretation – and not all of these processes are reported or interrogated in outcomes-driven studies of policy implementation. Yet, recognising that policy enactments are multi-layered and messy may help in understanding the complicated relationship between making policy and practising policy in complex situated contexts like schools (Colebatch, 2006a).

Policy is detailed and circulated through texts and artefacts and it is interpreted in equally complex and sophisticated ways. Spillane (2004, p. 7) has argued that in what he calls 'conventional accounts' of policy implementation, very often implementation failure gets blamed on policy actors who, it is alleged, choose not to enact the policy reform or who ignore it. His point is that policy work is more complicated and involves what he calls a process of sense-making. That is, policy actors 'use the lenses they have developed through experience to filter their awareness' (p. 7) and interpret these signals. Policy actors' interpretations account for disruptions in practice. In this article, we are taking interpretation to mean the way in which policy actors initially 'read' and respond to policy. This will be situated and contextualised. Does the policy have to be done? Who will enact it? What does it really mean in practical terms? In our view, policy enactment involves creative processes of interpretation and recontextualisation – and this process sometimes involves 'interpretations of interpretations' (Rizvi & Kemmis, 1987). These interpretations of interpretations are undertaken in senior leadership meetings (the school managers), in department meetings and sometimes by individual teachers. In all this, the space for 'interpretation' varies from policy to policy and sometimes, from person to person, as we shall see. Policies rarely tell you exactly what to do, they rarely dictate or determine practice, but some more than others narrow the range for imaginative responses.

In many of the school-based policy implementation studies, the focus is with implementation as a way of describing how a single policy reform from the centre/top is worked out in practice in schools. These approaches, useful though they are, do not necessarily help with understanding how it is that certain policies, or strands within policies, are selected and who selects them and what alternatives are discarded along the way. They do not illuminate the ways in which policies can be clustered together to form new policy ensembles that can have unintended, or unexpected consequences in schools. They also do not help us understand how and why school leaders and schoolteachers negotiate with, manage and put sometimes conflicting policies into practice simultaneously. Spillane (2004, p. 6) suggests that what he calls more 'conventional' policy models are often based on rational choice theory. Choices are made based on personal assumptions and 'utility maximization'. Spillane's argument is that if this approach is taken, then where policies do not get fully implemented, this is frequently explained as due to the policy being 'muddled or weak, or because it does not fit with the interests of utility-maximizing local officials' (Spillane, 2004, p. 6). He argues that conventional implementation studies conceive of the school itself as a somewhat homogenous and de-contextualised organisation, an undifferentiated 'whole' into which various policies are slipped or filtered into place. Even more crucially, many of these studies assiduously filter out the ways in which policy actors co-generate different policy possibilities (Forester,

2012), particularly in low-stakes policy areas where there may be a little more space for creative attempts at alternative policy enactments.

In this article, we argue that 'enactments' is a theoretically richer concept which better captures the multifaceted ways in which policies are read alongside/against contextual factors, by different sets of policy interpreters, translators and critics (Ball, Maguire, & Braun, 2012). For example, taking enactment, rather than implementation, as our approach to understanding policy work allows us to recognise the ways in which different schools attempt to realise policy through activities such as in-service sessions for teachers or the circulation of assessment data. These policy-driven activities can both fashion and constrain the possibilities of interpretation and the social construction of policy practices within each individual school. Enactments are illustrated by and come out of the 'micro-politics of policy practices through the diverse accounts of situated and entangled practitioners themselves' (Forester, 2012, p. 23). Policy is not 'done' at one point in time, it is always a process of 'becoming'. It is reviewed and revised as well as sometimes dispensed with or sometimes simply just forgotten. There will be multiple subjectivities and positions that will shape how policies are understood, and differences will occur in enactments over time and in different spatial contexts. Enactment then is messy, incomplete and a form of interpretation and intersubjectivity in action.

Heterogeneity and divergent enactments

In this paper we want to try out some further ideas about policy enactments. Writing is a form of 'thinking aloud' and in this paper, drawing on some of our interview data, we want to elaborate on enactments both theoretically and empirically. As we have said already, a great deal of attention has been paid to how well policies are realised in practice, 'implemented', and less attention has been paid to the ways in which different policy actors in schools, interpret policies in practice in ways that make sense to themselves (Spillane, 2004) but which may not be congruent with other enactments. There may be dominant or official enactments co-existing with informal, less visible and undocumented policy practices. As we have already claimed, some policies are more dominant than others, non-negotiable high-stakes policies that command attention and even compliance, other policies are more fluid. These are different types of policies; they are sometimes fore-grounded, and at other times they are almost invisible. For example, schools may have behaviour policies that are monitored and enforced at the start of the school year but fall away after an initial spurt of activities of monitoring and policing. The wearing of school uniforms would be one example of this type of policy.

Enacting policies is a process and not a one-off event and in this process some policy actors are more dominant than others; some teachers may be less influenced by particular policy shifts than others. Time and space and positionality and commitments all play a part in the different workings (or not) of policy interpretations in action. As we have argued elsewhere, schools are not of a piece; schools are highly complex and internally differentiated organisations (Braun, Maguire, & Ball, 2010). This heterogeneity lends itself to divergences in the various interpretations of and attention paid to different policies, as we shall see. Quite simply, our point is that depending on the perspectives, values and positions of different types of policy actors and different types of policies, as well as grounded factors of time and place, enactments are contingent, fragile social constructions. Hence 'where you stand depends on where you sit' (Colebatch, 2006b, p. 10) – at least to some extent!

The education policy context – in England

One of the drivers for our work has been the proliferation of education policy in the English context. To a great extent, education policy making in England has been driven by wider international policy imperatives. The international measurement of children's attainments, the production of national league tables and the ranking of education systems by various global institutes (Mortimore, 2013) have fuelled a sense of educational 'crisis' and an international policy reaction that has concentrated on raising standards (Mansell, 2007). This policy move has been in flow for more than the last 20 years or so. In many nation states, attention has been paid to policy work such as curriculum reform, assessment reform and the reform of pre-service teacher education with a view to raising academic attainment. Although it is evidently the case that global education policy has been characterised by dominant discourses of both regulation, standardisation, and somewhat contradictorily, diversity and individualism (Gewirtz & Cribb, 2009, p. 164), nevertheless, these reforms and restructurings have taken different forms in different national settings.

For instance, in the English setting, there has been a constant steer from central governments towards 'constant improvement in examination results and other performances' (Ball et al., 2012, p. 9). As different political parties have come and gone, each administration has produced its own plethora of education policies designed by the central state and passed down to schools. These have covered a wide range of in-school matters, from the safeguarding of children to healthy eating, reducing school exclusions, reforming the content of the curriculum and the examination system as well as the governance and organisation of schools. There is an assumption that schools will respond quickly to all these demands and policy requirements. However, the complex setting of school life means that schools that are charged with enacting a wide range of policies may have to prioritise what they do. In the classroom, teachers may well be driven by a range of concerns and demands of their own; policies that seem remote may become discarded.

The study

This paper draws on a study of policy enactments in four English secondary schools,[1] which aimed to provide a grounded account of the complexities of the relations between policy and practice in schools in a period of incessant change and policy shifts. The study had two main objectives: to develop a theory of policy enactment, and to provide a critical exploration of the differences in the enactment of policy in 'similar' contexts. The study focused on four main issues: (1) the localised nature of policy actions, that is the adjustments and accommodations and conflicts which inflect and mediate policy; (2) the ways in which many different (and sometimes contradictory) policies are simultaneously in circulation and interact with, influence and inhibit one another; (3) the interpretational work of policy actors; and (4) the role of resource differences in limiting, distorting or facilitating responses to policy.

The fieldwork was conducted in four co-educational, non-denominational and non-selective secondary schools, what we have termed 'ordinary schools'. We recognise the challenge of identifying 'ordinary' schools in a time when English schools are under considerable pressure to fabricate themselves as 'extraordinary' – as 'strong' or 'outstanding' in various respects and as 'successful' as far as is possible (Maguire, Perryman, Ball, & Braun, 2011). The schools are moderately successful with a sound track record of academic achievement, performing at around the national average. They are located in different Local Authorities, including one that is in inner-London (Atwood school), two in different parts of outer-London (George Eliot and Wesley schools) and the fourth in a county town (Campion school). In selecting 'ordinary' schools we sought to avoid 'outstanding' schools or schools that were less pressured to respond to aspects of policy requirements. We also sought to avoid schools that had been identified as having shortcomings; these schools would be under tight scrutiny and would be likely to be concentrating on raising their performance.

In a short paper, it is difficult to provide an adequate contextualisation of each school, and every school is a unique institution. The schools were all co-educational and were still under the control of their local authorities at the time when we were collecting data. That is, they had not become academy schools. Our inner-city case study school (Atwood) has a multi-ethnic, socially mixed student body. One of the outer-London schools (George Eliot) sits in an area where there is a large community of families of 'South Asian' heritage, and this is reflected in the school's intake. The other suburban school (Wesley) is ethnically more diverse, although the school is seen as a destination for the 'less academic' children in the area. The school in the county town (Campion) is located in a white, lower-middle and working-class neighbourhood and this is reflected in their intake. The four schools are all in some way 'typical' for their locality with regards to income levels. Taking the proportions of students on free school meals (FSM) as a proxy for poverty, the FSM percentages in the two suburban schools (George Eliot and Wesley) are broadly in line with the national average of around 15%. In Campion, FSM is lower and in Atwood, the percentage of FSM students is roughly twice the national average.

We collected four kinds of data: contextualising information from each school; policy texts and artefacts – national, local and school-centred; observations of meetings, training etc.; and semi-structured interviews. In terms of our criteria for data collection of texts and artefactual materials, we collected the key documents that related to our three key policies under investigation (see below) as well as any other texts that seemed relevant or were being used in the schools such as Governing Body Reports on performance, school exclusion data, student diaries, staff briefings, etc. We also collected general school brochures, newsletters to parents and regularly scrutinised each school's website.

We attended a wide range of school meetings such as professional development sessions for staff, governors meetings and department meetings where the researchers wrote up unstructured field notes of what they observed. Interviewees included the head teachers, members of the senior leadership teams, heads of departments and other middle managers, classroom teachers, teaching assistants and non-teaching staff such as bursars and mentors, as well as local authority representatives and relevant 'outsiders' with a link to the school. Questions included topics such as their career trajectories, their views on what policies were high profile in their schools and their perceptions and experiences of our three core policies. Due to time and cost constraints, we concentrated on the perceptions and experiences of adult workers in education, although we acknowledge the policy roles that are played by parents, school governors and school students. The research generated a data set of 93 digitally recorded and transcribed interviews, together with a wide range of documentary and observational data. The study focused on three substantive policies: personalised learning; performance demands in English and mathematics; and behaviour management. These policies were chosen to represent differences such as: (1) their national high-profile; (2) their specificity (particularly in terms of being target-related); (3) their whole school or departmental focus; and (4) their social, achievement or equity goals.

A great deal of data coding and analysis took place in extended team meetings where we shared our interpretations of the data set. We were looking for and attending to examples of different forms of engagement with different kinds of policies. We were looking for discrepancies between different policy actors in our schools as well as differences and similarities between our schools. We also concentrated on the 'role of authoritative actors in producing "pre-emptive readings"' (Ball et al., 2012, p. 15).

In the next part of this paper we will explore how different 'types' of policies call-up different forms of enactments, and, how those who work in schools may have different orientations towards some of these possible ways of 'doing' school. Enacting policy is context specific and thus, time and place play a part in shaping complex ways in which policies get dealt with – or not! Depending on the type/ level of policy, depending on the social actors who are centrally involved, depending on how policy translations are 'practised', different forms of enactments take place, sometimes within the same departments illustrating Colebatch's (2006b, p. 10) claim that 'where you stand depends on where you sit' so that policy actors are themselves situated as well as being 'sense-makers'.

Different orientations – different positions

One of the policies that we had selected for exploration was behaviour management in school. In England, student's behaviour, classroom management and 'control' have always been a focus of action by 'policy-makers, schools and their teachers' (Powell & Tod, 2004, p. 1). Not surprisingly, policy approaches from governments of all political persuasions endorse the need for effective classroom control. Head (2007, p. 1) explains that currently 'there is an assumption that if teachers deal with difficult pupil behaviour as a first step, then the young people will learn better'. 'Fixing' behaviour will 'fix' learning.

> This new angle is different from that of the more traditional concern with the moral implications of behaviour and the teaching of traditional values through stern discipline ... poor behaviour is emphasised as a significant cause of educational failure. (Wright, 2012, p. 288)

In England, parental anxieties about school discipline, frequently ratcheted up by the media, continue to be a significant driver for continued action (Steer, 2005, 2009). In consequence, behaviour management has always been a key policy zone for government attempts at micro managing schools – and the churning out of successive reports, strategies and behaviour 'challenges' to schools (Department for Children, Schools and Families [DCSF], 2009; Gove, 2012) signal the longevity of this policy imperative. No government can afford to look 'weak' on discipline, and successive governments may want to look tougher than their predecessors. Each school is required to make its own decisions about how they will construct a 'whole school' attempt at enacting 'behaviour for learning' and this aspect of the school is an important part of the school inspection framework. Schools have to be compliant with this policy demand.

However, in the process of enacting disciplinary policies, there are tensions, due in some part to the different orientations and different roles/positions of policy actors in schools. For example, what is commended in one subject area (say, Drama or Physical Education) may not be seen as appropriate behaviour in other classes. What is regarded as acceptable at one stage/age might be less appropriate in a different phase of schooling. Individual teachers in the same departments may hold contrasting beliefs and values (for example, about the need to support student autonomy and encourage creativity). In one of our schools, George Elliot School, the professional orientations of some members of staff led to different interpretations and practices in enacting behaviour management. This was evidenced in contrasting approaches towards punishment as well as a need to manage consensus within the school community, sometimes at the expense of the students.

> I think there is a bit of a discrepancy between members of staff as to what the role of managing behaviour is. Some staff would like, if a student offends, you know, does something wrong, wants to see an instant punishment while other staff are more in favour of rehabilitation and the idea of restorative justice ... And I think that's probably the biggest difficulty with behaviour is trying to make sure that everybody's happy with what takes place. I think some of the sanctions that are given out to students probably aren't in the students' best interests. (Sunny, Pastoral HOD, qualified teacher, George Elliot School)

Reena, a senior pastoral leader (non-teacher) in the same school who had a professional background in counselling and psychotherapeutic approaches to working with young people, had constructed an interpretation and practices that were influenced by her specialist training. Her approach was based on a need for self-awareness and the links between cognition, feelings and actions (Corrie, 2009; Goleman, 1996). She was more concerned to help students understand and 'own' their actions and feelings, rather than 'fixing' any learning difficulties:

> The main challenges, I would say, in my experience, anger management, lack of anger management for a better word. It's sort of, the inappropriate responses of young people, which leads them to make the wrong choice and get into a conflicting situation ... The greater contents of my work is around managing, sort of, temperaments and emotions and, sort of, finding alternative ways of responding, especially to adults. (Reena, Pastoral Head of Year, George Elliot School)

Her work involved encouraging greater self-knowledge and awareness, all which may take longer to develop and may not seem as immediate as more punitive sanctions to some classroom teachers, as she also recognises:

> You know, working with them together to resolve the conflict. And I could turn round to a young person and say, you know, 'These things that you've said have really upset this person', you know, 'Can you understand and empathise?' ... I think you find, you know, again I have, sort of, sometimes may have been in people's bad books because of my philosophy on how to work with young people, you know. And I know a lot of teachers, sort of, they want sanctions, sanctions, sanctions. I understand that and, yes, children do have to learn consequences. But, for me, it's not the sanction, it's trying to understand why you've done something and how not to do it again and the sanction would be a part of that, you know. (Reena)

Behaviour policies are differently interpreted and enacted by Reena, in part because of the meanings and commitments that she brings to bear in her practice – her professional knowledge and values and emotional response; her situated and subjective professional identity (Forester, 2012; Zembylas, 2007). In practice, 'behaviour for learning' is a key plank of policy and has to be directly addressed in school documentation for auditing and inspection purposes. Senior leadership teams in schools have little choice but to do this – non-compliance is not possible and their responses will be bound up with their roles as school managers. The orientation is to outcomes and achievement, not to personal growth and development.

> We deal with behaviour if it's inappropriate or interfering with a student's achievement, *but the focus is all about achievement. We don't want to turn out well-behaved individuals, we want to turn out individuals* who have got the skills, qualifications to be able to go on and lead a successful life. (Hazel, Deputy Head of Wesley School)

All four schools in our study 'translate' state policy into institutional policy, and what results is a mix of practical and performative responses. However, other levels and different forms of interpretation and practices were being enacted in teams, departments and classrooms. In some subjects, discipline may be more relaxed because of the subject and its environment (the drama studio, for example) while in other settings (perhaps a more hazardous environment such as a science laboratory) control and management may be more overt. Classroom teachers with more day-to-day contact with students may have more time/space in which to negotiate and co-generate behaviour and conduct policy with the students; senior managers are responsible to ensure that the school is compliant with overt (legislated) policy requirements. Thus, behaviour for learning may get enacted in different ways because of different personal and professional orientations as well as because of the different posts of responsibility held by various policy actors in the school. Aspects of behaviour management, that some teachers may regard as petty or less important (dress codes, for instance) may be differently enforced; the ways in which behaviour for learning are enacted may be stronger at the start of the school year or with younger students, and more relaxed in the days towards the summer holidays and after examinations have taken place. The point is that the enactment of behaviour policies will be heterogeneous, context dependent and differently evidenced. Enactment of policies of behaviour in rhetoric and policy documentation will have to have a high visibility, particularly in terms of performance/inspection demands; in practice, enactments may be less high profile, contradictory and sometimes hardly in evidence at all. To a large extent, those policy actors on the ground will construct their enactment practices from their professional commitments, value and pedagogic beliefs, that is, from 'where they stand' (Colebatch, 2006b, p. 10) although divergences may be more possible in the policy area of behaviour management than standards and attainment, a high-stakes policy, for instance.

High stakes policies

A second policy arena that we had selected for exploration in our project was the 'raising standards' agenda. To explain the English context briefly, children are tested at key points throughout their schooling. When they are 16 years old and at the end of compulsory schooling, they sit various tests in a range of secondary school subjects. Success can determine which pathway students will follow (academic or vocational) as well as provide an 'indication' of alleged school effectiveness and performance as results are 'sorted' into published league tables that show how well each school performs. Initially the 'measure' of success was the percentage of students who achieved five of these

General Certificates of Secondary Education (GCSEs) at grades of between A* and C. When politicians discovered that this target could be achieved by various forms of 'gaming' (for example, entering students for different examinations that had the equivalence of two or more of these GCSEs), the targets were ratcheted up. In the period when we were in the field, policy was changed to demand that the five GCSEs now included English and Mathematics (Department for Education [DfE], 2010).[2] This policy shift made English and Mathematics the most important subjects at GCSE level – particularly in 'ordinary' schools like ours. It certainly made them the most visible in enactment terms:

> This is going to sound terrible but there's a pecking order of subjects these days ... I know that what I'm saying is as head of maths, and that's quite a key role in the school now and that's carrying weight ... you can't escape the fact that maths and English have got certain responsibilities which they have to carry out and sometimes need to be a bit more equal than the other subjects, I think. (Adrian, Head of maths, Campion)

This visibility was 'obvious' to everyone in the school (Ball et al., 2012). The consequences of this policy prominence meant that, in our schools at least, these core departments were under a great deal of pressure and concomitantly, were in a 'good' situation in their schools in terms of attracting additional resourcing, additional staff and favourable time-tabling slots. For example, in George Elliot, where the pressure was on for the mathematics team to raise their game, the school timetable had been changed to allow all the examination cohorts to be taught at the same time each day. This management shift meant that the department could target small groups of students as well as focus on specific mathematical topics with particular students in order to achieve the scores they were after. All the other departments knew that this timetabling arrangement (even if it disadvantaged them) was essential; the school needed to achieve in this subject area.

> Senior management, and the students know for themselves that maths and English are now the subjects. Do you know what I mean? ... that suddenly maths and English are elevated to a completely different status. (Martin, Head of maths, George Eliot)

> I think government knows what it wants, it says English and maths because that's fundamental to learning so we, as a school, we're sort of being pushed in that direction. (Philip, Headteacher, Wesley)

The high visibility and the relentless pressure on these two departments (Perryman, Ball, Maguire, & Braun, 2011) were intense.

> You know, Maths, English and science, there's a huge pressure on them because, obviously, being core subjects, you know, if they don't get their 70% A to C, then it has a big impact on the school's results overall. (Wendy, Head of Social Science, Wesley)

> And there's enormous pressure put on us: can they (the students) get a C grade? And the whole school's reputation is based on [the] percentage of the students, can they get to a C grade and also how that relates to how many students we're expected to get to a C grade. (Neil, Deputy Head of English, Wesley)

In this policy arena, there was a direct responsibility for raising standards with which the heads of subject departments were charged with achieving. For the teachers in these departments and for the senior school managers, to some extend there is no-where else to 'stand' except in relation to 'doing' standards better and better! In these high stakes policy arenas, there may be very little choice in terms of the agenda although creative and imaginative responses and leadership may make this work more engaging and pedagogically valuable.

In contrast, this high visibility sometimes meant that other 'parts' of the school and other departments were able to go under the radar to some extent. In some departments, different commitments and values shaped practice in action; some teachers in some subjects were more able to highlight the centrality of their intrinsic disciplinary concerns rather than test grades.

> The (new head of department) sees the only purpose of the art department now is to get As to Cs at GCSE ... whereas I always believed we didn't get as good results – we got reasonable results but we didn't get as good results as he thinks he's going to – but, between you and me, I mean, I believed that kids needed to be able to explore, develop and be artists. (Dave, Art Teacher, Cavendish)

> We really want life-long participation ... we have to think about what our kids want because we do want them to play sports after (they leave) school. (Rachael, Head of PE, George Elliot)

One more point – policy enactments are also more/less visible depending on where the departments and staff are physically located in the school campus. For example, many of the centres for supporting students with 'learning difficulties' were tucked away in less accessible and less obvious parts of the building, behind the dining rooms or in a lower level of the school. In another school, the sixth form students were housed in a separate building away from the main campus. Physical 'invisibility' can sometimes remove the pressures to enact policies – or at least some of the minor and less high stakes policies. High visibility in some areas can lend a 'cloak of invisibility' to other less central parts of school life. These 'lower-stake' policy settings may also be less susceptible to implementation studies and policy analysis more generally, a point that may well be worth further research.

Policy actors: power, positionality and perspectives

In our study on policy enactments in secondary schools (Ball et al., 2012, p. 49) we have argued that 'participants and institutions, and agency and interpretation, are all typically undifferentiated' in many of the policy interpretation and implementation studies. In contrast, we found that some teachers are not deeply invested in the policy process at all; they do not take an active part in interpreting and translating policy. Their concerns lie elsewhere. Schools may well be busy enacting a wide number of policies, but this process may simply pass some teachers by – a case of 'now (some of you) see policy and now (some of you) don't'. In cases like this 'where you stand' may simply refer to matters of experience and day to day priorities rather than any more broader issues of values and/or ethics.

Not surprisingly, most junior and newly qualified teachers (NQTs in the English school system) in their first year of teaching, and at times even more experienced teachers, exhibit a form of 'policy dependency' and high levels of compliance. They are looking for guidance and direction. For them, coping in their classroom is the reality that influences the constructions of the meanings of school, policy, teaching and learning. They rely heavily on 'interpretations of (policy) interpretations' (Rizvi & Kemmis, 1987).

They are also to some extent 'shielded' and 'buffered' from policy by more senior colleagues, although this is subject and person dependent. In the secondary school, the subject department is their primary reality and the place where policies become interpreted and conveyed to them:

> I think the first term, the Christmas term, was really very difficult to get through, you know. The terms were long and then you start to get to know your students, your students were testing the boundaries and all this lesson planning, behaviour management, everything. (Mai, NQT mathematics, George Elliot)

Different policies and their enactments usually seemed distant from the immediate concerns and perspectives of beginning teachers. The first year in particular was described as a 'blur', a matter of getting by from day to day, and getting very tired. Morgan, Ludlow, Kitching, O'Leary, and Clarke (2010, p. 191) found that 'while remote structural factors may heavily influence teaching, it is the perception of events at micro-level that impinge most strongly on motivation'. From this position policy is something that comes from 'them' – either the senior leadership team in the school or 'government' or both. Policy work at this level is a matter of muddling through, although almost all of the NQTs reported being well supported by their colleagues and were determined and resilient. National, institutional and 'classroom' policies and priorities, became a veritable 'mash-up' of bits and pieces, suggestions for practice, key government discourses and tips from their mentors.

On the one hand, we observed attempts to recruit all teachers as active and creative participants in processes of translating and enacting certain policies, through in-service activities, meetings, observations and 'sharing'. On the other, there was the reliance of new teachers on local policy texts and artefacts and other forms of guidance that could lead to standardisation.

> The school's been a lot better, you know, in terms of telling us what you should be doing, you know, on a day-to-day basis and these are the things that we need to prioritise and these are the things we need to focus on. (Aabid, Social Sciences, George Elliot)

Most beginning teachers focus on day-to-day survival and getting their classroom 'right', and responding to what they see as what is expected of them, 'you just kind of follow exactly what you're told to do' (Naomi, Religious Education, Atwood). Furthermore, new teachers in England have undertaken their teacher training in a particular regime of accountability constraints, and may not be able to imagine a different way of being a teacher. Gillian, an NQT science teacher in Atwood school found it difficult to remember many of the policies that were being enacted in her school.

> Gillian: I'm not massively aware of many policies. Except for the behaviour one. And the homework policy. Which, actually, the homework one slightly – the department homework policy and the school policy possibly slightly contradict each other.
>
> Interviewer: What's the idea of the school's policy?
>
> Gillian: Well, I don't … I don't really know, actually, I just follow the department one. There has been something about that, about putting grades onto kids' work, like effort grades. I think the school policy is you have to and I don't know what our department policy is, but there was massive discussion about whether we should record them in our planners and not put them on the work. But I don't know what the answer was.

The subject department plays a key role for the beginning teacher, although departments do vary in their coherence and supportiveness and centrality to policy. Departments vary in degrees of their 'earned autonomy' and institutional confidence (see Braun et al., 2010), often in relation to their 'output' performances, and being seen as 'well performing' or even 'outstanding'. This cultural status and reputation within the school can have implications for the junior teacher's experience of and engagement with policy. Some subjects, like English, 'carry' well-established subject cultures, and all departments are to an extent 'different worlds' (Siskin, 1991, p. 156) and important organisational sub-structures in the socio-cultural terrain of secondary school. For the beginning teacher, and the more junior members of staff, much policy may simply not be recognised or be visible at all. Much policy may seem distant and unrelated to the pressures of their everyday life; they do not enact policy, they 'follow what they are told' and hope to survive to teach another day. These teachers are at the sharp end of policy delivery, although they may only have a very partial or hazy appreciation of what is entailed. As Gillian says, 'I'm not massively aware of many policies' beyond those that impact her day-to-day life in the classroom. In what she says, we see the way in which the social world of the new teacher renders some policies more/less visible, and more/less meaningful – a highly specific, subjective and situated construction of policy enactment.

In this section, we have argued that some policy actors are typically much less invested in policy enactment in the wider school setting as their concerns are driven by their level of experience, their position and their engagement with their classrooms and students on a day-to-day basis. However, as a point of comparison and also to illustrate the impact of positionality, it is useful to consider what some of the more senior school managers have to say about policy work. What comes across is their understanding of the wider context as well as their decision-making capacity – their capacity to interpret and define.

> One of the staff said, 'Well this is something that I've been talking to (the local school authority/district) about. What do you think? And we said, 'Hold it! Great idea but if we get into that we'll start to crumble at the edges'. (Graeme, Headteacher, Campion)

And what must not be forgotten is that it is not only teachers who interpret and translate policy in schools and have some influence in enactments:

> We were talking this morning, the head and I, if it really became difficult in terms of staffing. And his view is that you do need a teacher in every classroom ... One of the interesting things obviously is that non-teaching staff cost an awful lot less than teaching staff. (Alicia, School Business Manager, Wesley)

Discussion

In this article, we have argued that the way in which policies are enacted in schools is made more complex by a range of contextualising factors. One over-riding influence relates to the 'type' of policy that is being explored and whether it is mandated or merely recommended. Another aspect that plays into policy enactment is the different positions and perspectives of the local actors. Spillane (2004, p. 6) has argued that conventional policy accounts frequently position local actors as 'interpreting policy to fit their own agenda', and while some of them may do this, others will have a different set of concerns altogether from those enshrined in dominant policy imperatives. In practice, they may well look to other more experienced local actors for guidance and a policy steer. It could be useful for future researchers to explore the ways in which positionality, experience, the allegiances and disciplinary commitments of teachers, as well as loyalties and in-school relations play out in how policies are interpreted and enacted. As Spillane (2004, p. 181) has noted, policy makers need to address the 'tension between the external representations – the new ideas – and local policymakers' and teachers internal representations'. In this paper we have concentrated on one key aspect of what is involved in policy enactment. In some ways, it might be argued that we have simply utilised Spillane's (2004) notion of policy work as a 'sense-making' process; and in many ways, this is what some of our data certainly suggests. However, this sense making is multi-dimensional and other aspects such as biography, teacher identity and positionality, disciplinary cultures and political perspectives all make-up who teachers are and where they stand (Colebatch, 2006b, p. 10).

In addition, in the school setting, there are always constraints of time and space that influence what happens and the ways in which policy is sometimes left to one side; time and space also shape, to some extent, where it is that teachers 'stand'. Rituals and rites of passage, such as the start and end of each year, the examination period, the annual arrival and departure of staff and students lend a pattern and rhythm to the annual cycle of the school. Thus, it is not surprising that enacting policy is a complicated and sometimes inchoate process. It is both contingent and specific, situated in time/space and seen as less/more important by different policy actors in schools. Time and space play a crucial role in the when, how and why of policy enactment. For instance, some policies become very 'tied' to a particular senior leader; when they leave the school, so does their policy portfolio and their particular approach. Some policies start the year as high profile, foregrounded by school leaders; by the end of the year they have faded away and become forgotten. In studies of policy work, this very real dimension of the way schools are actually constructed, performed and produced is sometimes forgotten.

In coming to understand how things are the way they are, Haidt (2012) argues that reason does not always drive social matters; intuitions and emotions can often be just as useful in explaining how and why things get done. In schools, different policy actors have different loyalties, different projects of the self and different sets of personal and professional values and some of this is mediated by their positionality in school. Senior policy actors and middle managers in key departments (English and mathematics) certainly have to be compliant with dominant forms of policy imperatives and have to be able to demonstrate how this is being implemented; other more junior policy actors often have different and more immediate (policy) concerns in their daily life, as we have discussed in this article.

However, and sometimes this is another often forgotten fact in policy studies, there is more to teaching and school life than policy. There are 'discretionary spaces' (Fenwick & Edwards, 2010, p. 126) in and beyond policy, corners of the school where policy does not reach, bits of practice that are made up of teachers' good ideas or chance or simply the time of the year and the nature of the subject/ discipline. For example, the end of the last term of the year in the English secondary school is always a time for celebration, relaxation after examinations and outings and festivities like sports days and swimming galas. Time is a key factor in realising policy enactments – or not; and at certain times policies are high profile (discipline at the start of the school year) and then move to the background at other times. In periods where the school is more 'relaxed', this will be reflected in classrooms where students will be engaged in creative or 'fun' activities rather than preparing for examinations. Enactment is about policy realisation, but unlike much policy rhetoric, schools are 'real-time' places where people get tired and where they inevitably pay different kinds of attention to different kinds of policies at different times of the year. For all these sorts of reasons then, 'where you stand' in terms of subject department, pedagogical values, the time of the year and a range of other biographical factors such as length of service, plays powerfully into 'where you sit' (Colebatch, 2006b, p. 10) and renders policy enactment a more fragile and unstable process than is sometimes imagined.

Notes
1. 'Policy enactments in the secondary school: theory and practice', ESRC reference: RES -062-23-1484.
2. As we were finishing our fieldwork, the new Conservation Coalition Government changed the attainment goalposts for GCSE; students can now 'gain' an English Baccalaureate (Ebac) if they achieve GCSEs in English, mathematics, sciences, a language and a humanities subject (see Perryman et al., 2011). The inclusion of a language requirement has placed strains on schools, as modern foreign languages are not compulsory in English schools after the age of 14 years.

References
Ball, S. J., Maguire, M., & Braun, A. (2012). *How schools do policy. Policy enactments in secondary schools*. London: Routledge.
Braun, A., Maguire, M., & Ball, S. J. (2010). Policy enactments in the UK secondary school: Examining policy, practice and school positioning. *Journal of Education Policy, 25*, 547–560. doi:10.1080/02680931003698544
Colebatch, H. K. (2002). *Policy* (2nd ed.). Buckingham: Open University Press.
Colebatch, H. K. (Ed.). (2006a). *Beyond the policy cycle: The policy process in Australia*. Sydney: Allen & Unwin.
Colebatch, H. K. (2006b, November–December). *Thinking about policy: Finding the best way*. Paper given at GovNet International Conference, Australian National University, Canberra.
Corrie, C. (2009). *Becoming emotionally intelligent* (2nd ed.). London: Network Continuum.
Department for Children, Schools and Families (DCSF). (2009). *Behaviour challenge strategy*. Retrieved from http://www.dcsf.gov.uk/pns/DisplayPN.cgi?pn_id=2009_0171
Department for Education (DfE). (2010). *The importance of teaching*. London: HMSO.
Fenwick, T., & Edwards, R. (2010). *Actor-network theory in education*. London: Routledge.
Forester, J. (2012, July). *On the theory and practice of interpretive policy analysis: From the micro-politics of practice to interpretive analysis and theorizing in action*. Paper presented at the Interpretive Policy Analysis Conference, Tilburg.
Gewirtz, S., & Cribb, A. (2009). *Understanding education: A sociological perspective*. Cambridge: Polity Press.
Goleman, D. (1996). *Emotional intelligence: Why it can matter more than IQ*. London: Bloomsbury.
Gove, M. (2012). *Improving behaviour and attendance in schools*. Retrieved from https://www.gov.uk/government/news/new-powers-for-teachers-to-improve-discipline-in-schools
Haidt, J. (2012). *The righteous mind*. New York, NY: Pantheon Books.
Head, G. (2007). *Better learning, better behaviour*. Edinburgh: Dunedin Academic Press.
Maguire, M., Perryman, J., Ball, S., & Braun, A. (2011). The ordinary school—What is it? *British Journal of Sociology of Education, 32*(1), 1–16. doi:10.1080/01425692.2011.527718
Mansell, W. (2007). *Education by numbers*. London: Politico.
Morgan, M., Ludlow, L., Kitching, K., O'Leary, M., & Clarke, A. (2010). What makes teachers tick? Sustaining events in new teachers' lives. *British Educational Research Journal, 36*, 191–208. doi:10.1080/01411920902780972

Mortimore, P. (2013). *Education under siege. Why there is a better alternative*. Bristol: Policy Press.
Ozga, J. (2000). *Policy research in educational settings: Contested terrain*. Buckingham: Open University Press.
Perryman, J., Ball, S., Maguire, M., & Braun, A. (2011). Life in the pressure cooker – School league tables and English and mathematics teachers' responses to accountability in a results-driven era. *British Journal of Educational Studies, 59*, 179–195. doi:10.1080/00071005.2011.578568
Powell, S., & Tod, J. (2004). A systematic review of how theories explain learning behaviour in school contexts. In *Research Evidence in Education Library*. London: EPPI-Centre, Social Science Research Unit, Institute of Education.
Rizvi, F., & Kemmis, S. (1987). *Dilemmas of reform*. Geelong: Deakin University Press.
Siskin, L. S. (1991). *Realms of knowledge: Academic departments in secondary schools*. London: Falmer Press.
Spillane, J. (2004). *Standards deviation; How schools misunderstand education policy*. Cambridge, MA: Harvard University Press.
Steer, A. (2005). *Learning behaviour: The report of the practitioners' group on school behaviour and discipline*. London: DfES.
Steer, A. (2009). *Learning behaviour: Lessons learned. A review of behaviour standards and practices in our schools*. Nottingham: DCSF.
Wright, A. (2012). Fantasies of empowerment: Mapping neoliberal discourse in the coalition government's schools policy. *Journal of Education Policy, 27*, 279–294. doi:10.1080/02680939.2011.607516
Zembylas, M. (2007). Emotional ecology: The intersection of emotional knowledge and pedagogical content knowledge in teaching. *Teaching and Teacher Education, 23*, 355–367. doi:10.1016/j.tate.2006.12.002

Re/assembling spaces of learning in Victorian government schools: policy enactments, pedagogic encounters and micropolitics

Dianne Mulcahy

Melbourne Graduate School of Education, The University of Melbourne, Melbourne, VIC, Australia

> The significant public investment that has been made over the past decade in the educational infrastructure of universities, colleges and schools has prompted increasing interest in the re-consideration of learning and the spaces in which learning takes place. Set within policy interest in Australia in how spaces can contribute to the broader policy agenda of achieving an 'Education Revolution', this article takes as its context the Building the Education Revolution (BER) infrastructure programme. Promoting the idea of twenty-first century learning in open, flexible learning spaces, this programme embeds a particular view of pedagogic practice and the spaces in which it is performed. Deploying data from video case studies of how government schools within the state of Victoria are utilising these spaces to improve teaching and students' learning, I trace education policy in action utilising an analytic of assemblage. In the empirical complexity of the passage of BER policy in schools, learning spaces emerge as open and closed, flexible and contained, heterogeneous and homogeneous; pedagogic practices are similarly seemingly paradoxical – learner-centred and teacher-centred, individualised and directly instructional or whole-group. The argument is made that this ontological variability is a site of micropolitics through which the predilections of BER policy are substantially challenged.

Introduction

It has been argued that the architectural practice of 'classroom-as-container' is a dominant discourse in educational research on the relationship of learning to space and that this discourse 'functions as an "imagined geography" of education, constituting when and where researchers and teachers should expect learning to "take place"' (Leander, Phillips, & Taylor, 2010, p. 329). The significant public investment that has been made in a number of countries over the past decade in the educational infrastructure of universities, colleges and schools has prompted increasing interest in the re-consideration of learning and the spaces in which learning takes place. In policy discourses on the relationship of learning to space, learning is now no longer expected to take place in self-contained classrooms but rather in an expanded geography of open, flexible, twenty-first century learning spaces within which different spaces can be assigned to different student groups and different types of learning (Department of Education and Early Childhood Development, 2009; Ministerial Council on Education Employment Training and Youth

Affairs [MCEETYA], 2008). The notion of twenty-first century learning is used to signify the kind of learning thought to be required for life in the twenty-first century. Students are no longer expected to be passive recipients of knowledge, rather, they are encouraged to actively construct knowledge. Advocates of this learning emphasise the centrality of skills such as collaboration, communication, critical thinking, problem-solving and digital literacy (see for example, http://atc21s.org/). Twenty-first century learning spaces are thought to afford the development of these skills, along with related kinds of learning such as collaborative learning, personalised learning and self-directed learning.

Sitting under the broad umbrella of twenty-first century learning, ideas such as collaborative, personalised and self-directed learning[1] now drive the infrastructural arrangements for Australian school education. As Newton and Gan (2012) have it:

> during the past decade innovative school design has focused on student-centred learning within rich digital learning environments. Many schools are shifting from the 'cells and bells' environment of classroom teaching into larger, more fluid spaces with a range of furniture settings. Rather than having one subject-specific teacher in an individual classroom, increasingly students work in a way that brings together learning across disciplines supported by teams of teachers. (p. 76)

In a re-imagined geography of education, government policy-makers advocate models of learning which are more distributed and responsive to the needs of numerous stakeholders. For example, when looking to release a *Learning Spaces Framework*, an Australian policy-making body commented:

> 21st century learning requires new spaces that connect school, home and community learning, increasing flexibility and supporting learning outside the boundaries of school buildings and beyond the conventional school day. (MCEETYA, 2008, p. 4)

It is clear in these policy formulations that learning spaces need to support learning and institutional activity; these spaces are not framed however, as playing a *constitutive* role in this activity. Thus, writing on new approaches for school design that are being taken up in the USA, Lackney (2011) claims that:

> educational leaders and decision makers need to recognize that school facilities are, in effect, a policy statement on the relative importance a community places on education and students. School buildings are cultural artifacts that reflect the values of the community long after the original stakeholders who envisioned, planned, designed, and built them are gone. (p. 353)

Going beyond this 'culturalist' perspective on school facilities, an assumption that I take into the study reported here concerns the participatory role that these artefacts play in teaching and learning. Further to connecting school, home and community learning and serving as a policy statement on the value of education, they *enact* – are performative agents in – the everyday knowledgeable practice of schools and elsewhere. New approaches for school design such as open, flexible learning spaces can be considered to participate in learning and knowledge production: 'they shift action; and, like machines, they perform tasks and are endowed with certain competencies' (Shore & Wright, 2011, p. 3). In various fields such as science studies (Latour, 1987; Law, 2000),[2] organisation studies (Gherardi, 2006; Orlikowski, 2002) and increasingly in education (Fenwick,

2012; Nespor, 1994; Sorensen, 2009), knowledge and learning are understood as a constitutive enactment of the cultural *and* the material.

The intended contribution of this paper lies in foregrounding the critical role that material objects such as school facilities play in policy work and, in so doing, offering a view of policy *matters*. This perspective on policy forms part of shifts in policy research towards analyses that take in notions of policy enactment (Ball, Maguire, & Braun, 2012; Braun, Maguire, & Ball, 2010; Singh, Thomas, & Harris, 2013) and policy assemblage (Koyama & Varenne, 2012; Li, 2007; Mulcahy, 2011; Nielsen, 2011; Prince, 2010). Bypassing the binary between the social – for example, social constructivist[3] approaches to pedagogy and spatiality – and the material – for example, 'new materialist' (Coole & Frost, 2010) renderings of these processes – prompts focusing on their co-constitution and raises issues that are significant for understandings of policy research, educational policy and educational politics. Policy *matters matter*, not as discrete objects such as school facilities with properties of openness and flexibility, but as effects of *materialising processes* in which people and objects take part, and through which power is purveyed.

The paper has two broad parts. First, I examine what the theoretical literature says about policy research, drawing principally on sociological and science studies accounts. Among other things, these accounts challenge the idea that policy can be conceived in terms of an untrammelled transfer of its contents and form from one policy setting to another. Second, I turn to actor-network theory (ANT) (Latour, 2005; Law, 2009) and poststructuralist theory that invokes the work of Deleuze and detail the analytical approach of assemblage whereby strictly human-centred categories of knowing and decision-making are challenged. Subsequently, I discuss how the assemblage approach can be put to work and present 'close-up' accounts of learning spaces and pedagogy in practice, attending specifically to the sociomaterial work involved in this practice. Giving attention to this work, I claim, can help make more visible what is often invisible in both policy and pedagogic practice and help renew ways of supporting policy-makers and school practitioners. It can also raise new questions and invite consideration of new methodological approaches to policy research.

Background and context

Begun in 2009, and not unlike Labour's school renovation programme, Building Schools for the Future, in the UK,[4] The Building the Education Revolution (BER) programme was a $16.2 billion capital building programme initiated by the Australian Federal Government in response to the global financial crisis and included an economic stimulus package of construction and refurbishment of schools. A major policy initiative, it saw funding distributed through State Governments to schools to develop new learning spaces and facilities (Loughlin, 2013). While the BER's primary goal was to support the economy, in the Victorian context, it was utilised to provide Victorian government schools with twenty-first century learning spaces for current and future students. Hybrid designs were developed which could accommodate traditional classroom-based approaches to teaching and learning as well as approaches such as team teaching and inquiry learning which the new learning spaces are deemed especially well-suited to support.

ASSEMBLAGE, ENACTMENT, AND AGENCY

Policy enactments: orthodoxies and other stories

Having a long-standing interest in interstitial spaces, I am drawn to researching the workings of policy as it is mobilised, or not, in 'small-p' policy settings such as schools and their communities and the political potential that these spaces can provide. In this section, I articulate how we can think educational policy and its movements from governments to schools by briefly outlining three approaches to policy processes. These processes tend to be mutually informing rather than mutually exclusive.

'Rationalist' approach to educational policy: policy as a problem-solving device

Underscored by a positivist view of science, this approach:

> assumes that there are 'objective entities' out there called 'policies' that are the result of decisions made by some rational authority (e.g., a government, committee, management board or chief executive) and which reorganise bureaucratic action to solve particular 'problems' and produce a 'known' (or desired) outcome. (Shore & Wright, 2011, p. 4)

Thus, in the empirical context under study here, the particular problem that was deemed by the Australian government as in need of a solution concerned not only the global financial crisis of 2009 but also twenty-first century learning. Commonly, this approach prescribes 'a number of determinate steps, from an analysis of the policy context and the elucidation of a range of policy options to the processes of policy selection, production, implementation and evaluation' (Rizvi & Lingard, 2010, p. 1). For example, the policy process under consideration here can be thought to have started with a programme, the BER infrastructure programme, which could mobilise the idea of twenty-first century learning and turn it into a material object such as a new school facility or 'new generation' learning environment to be handed on for use in schools. Structured using a linear logic, this rationalist approach to the policy process assumes that governments initiate policy and that the people towards whom a policy is directed such as school principals and staff implement it in intended ways. However, as Shore and Wright (2011, p. 3) claim: 'a key quality of policies is that, once created, they often migrate into new contexts and settings, and acquire a life of their own that has consequences that go beyond the original intentions'.

'Enacting' approaches to educational policy: policy as people making sense and putting this sense 'into' practice

An enacting approach to policy processes 'resists the tendency of policy science to abstract problems from their relational settings by insisting that the problem can only be understood in the complexity of those relations' (Grace, 1995, p. 3). It signals an emerging shift in policy scholarship towards analyses that consider theories of enactment (Ball et al., 2012; Braun et al., 2010; Maguire, Ball, & Braun, 2010).

> Policy enactment involves creative processes of interpretation and recontextualisation – that is, the translation through reading, writing and talking of text into action and the abstractions of policy ideas into contextualised practices. (Braun et al., 2010, p. 549)

As used by Braun et al. (2010), the term enactment reflects 'an understanding that policies are interpreted and translated by diverse policy actors as they engage in making meaning of official texts for specific contexts and practices' (Singh et al., 2013, p. 466). They are never simply implemented. Enacting policy literally means using diverse processes to put policy 'into' practice – 'in relation to history and to context, with the resources available' (Ball et al., 2012, p. 3). Importantly, policy actors are diverse; they can comprise people as well as meetings, plans, tactics, texts, talk, technology and objects. In this enactments research however, they tend to present as 'social actors' (Ball, Maguire, Braun, & Hoskins, 2011, p. 637) rather than material agents. A residual representational idiom[5] of policy appears to play out in the use of terms like interpretation and translation. I maintain that in the rationalist and enacting accounts of policy processes, policy is largely conceived as 'outside' practice rather than as fully immersed in and immanent to it – policy *as* practice. Policy is accommodated or 'spoken' to practice (Ball et al., 2011).

An enacting approach to a policy object such as the BER infrastructure programme, and its newly built products – new generation learning spaces – assumes that while policy and practice inter-relate, they are nevertheless, ontologically disjunct. It presupposes an interactional approach which, as Dewey and Bentley (1949) commented over 50 years ago, relies upon *pre-existing* elements or entities and on accounts of the process of interaction in terms of a particular relationship between these entities (for discussion of this approach, see Vanderstraeten & Biesta, 2001). This approach tends to play out in the empirical research on learning spaces, for example: 'Learning takes concrete shape ... within its social-material surround. A school site should therefore support dynamic learning processes' (Gislason, 2007, p. 6) and:

> In an analysis of school renovation processes, it is essential to evaluate, on the one hand, the changes in educational practices, including the changing characteristics, roles and attitudes of the social actors directly and indirectly involved, and on the other, the mechanisms of appropriation of the space by these actors. (Marques, Veloso, & Sebastiao, 2013, p. 2)

Here, space is taken to be given in advance – a 'social-material surround' – and appropriated by social actors. It is not taken to come into existence or 'become' with these actors. As argued in the section following, the notion of policy enactment can, with profit, go beyond understanding that policy discourses are written onto bodies and spaces and that policy is represented, interpreted and translated. The term enactment is somewhat differently inflected in ANT and Deleuzian-inspired work; it not only carries the idea of making up – taking form – rather than 'simply' appropriating, but also of doing again and again and again. A more experimental/improvisatory/lively (Bennett, 2010) note is struck.

Policy assemblage: policy as a sociomaterial practice
Originating in actor-network theory and poststructuralist theory that invokes the work of Deleuze, an assemblage analytic affords thinking policies as processes rather than entities and impels one to ask 'What can a policy (or a policy object such as a "flexible" learning space) *do*' and 'for what and for whom?' Linking directly to practice, it signals that, as policy analysts, we are not in the realm of human volition – neither education policy makers' plans *for* practice and preferences with regard to executing these plans, nor practitioners' translations of these plans. 'Assemblages are composed of heterogeneous elements that may be human and non-human, organic and inorganic, technical and natural' (Anderson & McFarlane, 2011, p. 124). They flag agency and power relations,

'the hard work required to draw heterogeneous elements together, forge connections between them and sustain these connections in the face of tension' (Li, 2007, p. 264).

In an assemblage framing, policy is understood as heterogeneously assembled – arranged – rather than articulated in texts and then interpreted or appropriated (Nielsen, 2011). This framing emphasises emergence and indeterminacy and draws new attention to the role of things in policy and practice. Here, the term enactment is used in 'more than human' ways. It is less a matter of (human) interpretation than of material practice. As Anderson and McFarlane (2011, p. 125) claim, 'the most obvious reference points for assemblage as a concept include an "after" actor-network theory literature' (Hetherington & Law, 2000; Hinchliffe, 2007; Latour, 2005) and the emphasis in Deleuze and Guattari on the event of 'agencement' – 'a process of *connecting*, gerund rather than noun' (Bradley, Sumsion, Stratigos, & Elwick, 2012, p. 142, original emphasis). In an actor-network rendering, the term assemblage is often used to emphasise circulation (Latour, 1999) and coming into being, rather than fixed arrangements. Thus, Law (2004) describes assemblage as:

> a process of bundling, of assembling ... in which the elements put together are not fixed in shape, do not belong to a larger pre-given list but are constructed at least in part as they are entangled together. (p. 420)

In the empirical context of this paper, this 'larger pre-given list' can be thought to refer to open learning spaces, traditional closed classrooms and even Victorian government policy's 'hybrid designs'. Following Deleuze and Guattari (1987, p. 85), there are:

> two overall kinds of assemblage elements: the discursive forms of expression (system of signs, language, non-corporeal effects) and the non-discursive forms of content (material practices and systems of things, actions and passions). (Nielsen, 2011, p. 83)

I maintain that by adopting an analytic sensitive to mobility and materiality, different kinds of things that are happening or things that are happening differently (Coleman & Ringrose, 2013) in policy processes can be brought into view.

A methodological note: deploying an analytic of assemblage in policy work

The concept of the *assemblage* forwarded by Deleuze and Guattari (1987) is akin to the notion of *actor-network* in actor-network theory and directs attention to the many, diverse and contesting actors, agencies and practices through which human subjects and material objects take form. Deploying an assemblage approach affords consideration of the concrete material-discursive arrangements that constitute the local conditions of the assemblage and challenges the idea of policy as inevitably centre stage, inviting attention to other actors and agencies. In both actor-network theory and Deleuzian philosophy, material practices have an agency that can be as consequential as any human agency. ANT's 'notion of sociomateriality represents an attempt to overcome the social/material dualisms ... by refusing to introduce predefined categories when analysing any assemblage' (Postma, 2012, p. 142). In Deleuzian philosophy, the term assemblage refers to the coming together of different kinds of entities, in order to produce something new (Deleuze & Guattari, 1987). It takes in the terms *territory* and *territorialisation*, which give an assemblage form, stability and relative fixity (or not, as the further term, deterritorialisation, implies). '(T)he assemblage is fundamentally territorial' (p. 323). It is a reconfiguration of territory and the transformations of a territory take place as heterogeneous elements come together and make room for something more. In addressing the question of what a policy object can *do*, the concept of territorialisation affords attention to the normalising potential of policy, how it can claim territory (e.g. the 'new normal' of open, flexible spaces of learning in schools), and provide us with identities (e.g. twenty-first century learner). It also affords attention to micropolitics (Deleuze & Guattari, 1987) which 'does not begin with, or come to a full stop at the edge of the human world, the conscious human subject, but weaves the entire register (social, mental, natural/material) into the political' (Houle, 2011, p. 107). The micropolitical is a potency, a constitutive force, which can provoke a *rupture* or *break* (p. 110).

In these process-oriented perspectives on policy, it is assumed that what policy *is* depends on how participants in it accomplish it as a practice and that policy participants are people and otherwise. Policy is always *in the making* and in order for it to be transported from one point to another, it must be materialised in discourses such as twenty-first century learning, or objects such as physical facilities, or practices such as team teaching and inquiry learning. In other words, it must be performed and importantly, performed time and again, in order to 'stick' as an assemblage with the power to effect sustained change to teaching and learning in schools. For when these discourses, objects and practices change direction or shift shape, policy too changes – is formed within differing sets of relations. It becomes plastic (Murdoch, 1998, p. 358, citing Forer, 1978).

Data and methods

The project being reported here is a small-scale, one-year study (2012–2013) sponsored by the author's University in collaboration with a state government Department, the Victorian Department of Education and Early Childhood Development, which is committed to research on learning space design and its 'real-world' practice. Utilising a stratified sampling strategy, data were collected from school Principals, teachers and students located in (1) a large, outer suburban, government secondary school in a low socio-economic area; (2) a large, suburban, government secondary school in a high socio-economic area; (3) a medium size, government primary school in a relatively affluent suburb of a regional Victorian city; and (4) a medium size, government primary school in the western suburbs of Melbourne servicing a low socio-economic and immigrant community. All schools sampled have a reputation for innovative pedagogic practice with regard to the take-up of new learning spaces. For the purposes of this paper, I will concentrate my analysis on the two primary schools.

Video-based case studies of 'naturally' occurring interactions in middle and senior learning units at these schools are storied. The video-recordings were made during a one-day fieldwork study at each school, and accompanied with interviews conducted with school principals (and in one case an assistant principal as well), participating teachers (four altogether) and participating students (four altogether). Quantitative and qualitative methods were used to analyse the video data. Quantitative analysis involved creating 'lesson tables' such that simple descriptive analysis by frequency could be undertaken of 'lesson events' (e.g. introduction to the lesson, student group work) demonstrated in each learning space; qualitative analysis involved semiotic methods towards showing the ways in which these events are produced in socio-material relations. Analyses were undertaken using the methodological approach of tracing the sociomaterial (Fenwick, Edwards, &

Sawchuk, 2011; Mulcahy, 2013). My use of this approach is guided by the categories of a typology first put forward by Shapin and Schaffer (1985) when describing the origins of experimental science. Proposing the categories of sociality, materiality and textuality as the means of scientific knowledge making, these categories equally afford understandings of learning (defined minimally as growth in knowledge) and the practices that produce it. Variously social, material and textual, it is these practices that were studied primarily. In working the data fragments below, I draw largely on the teacher data set. Artefacts and images (e.g. wall displays) were video-recorded as the students led the research team on an 'ethnographic walk' of their learning spaces and documentary data were collected (e.g. floor plans, teacher unit planners).

Practices of assembly: policy objects at work

Enactment 1: 'it's more about what's happening within the spaces than ... the spaces themselves'

We are at Wattle Park Primary School, a medium size, government school in a relatively affluent part of a regional city, in the 'middle learning unit' which consists of seven year three out of four teachers and approximately 170 students. As indicated in Figures 1, 2 and 3, the physical learning space under study contains two classes of 50 or so students and two teachers who 'work together as a team', sometimes in combination (see Figure 2) and, at other times, separately and in 'focus groups' (see Figure 3), such that 'a bit more one-on-one time' can be given to selected children. As one of the teachers, Johanna, comments, across the course of any class, 'one of us generally has a smaller group, whether it's needs-based or whether it's goal-focused'.

The practice of giving selected students 'a bit more one-on-one time' involves withdrawing them to a more enclosed space, a 'room' at the rear of the larger physical learning space (see again Figure 3). A practice of assembly, it is produced as bodies, spaces, subjectivities and the differentiated curriculum (activities targeted at meeting the needs of members of the focus group) are entangled together.

A further and rather telling practice of assembly, most evident in the introduction to this literacy lesson, concerns the seating plan or black, marked-out space that is evident in Figure 2 and acts to contain the children when taught as a whole class group. As Johanna's team teaching partner, Rose, comments at interview: 'you can see we've got that big black square on the floor that all the kids come and sit in'. The material

Figure 1. A panorama still of the learning space under study: 'free-range' learning.

Figure 2. Combined class at commencement.

pedagogical practice of 'that big black square on the floor that all the kids come and sit in', mobilises teacher agency and teacher power, and brings disciplined student bodies into effect. The big black square claims a teaching territory. The transformation of the larger learning community as it is referred to locally, takes place as multiple elements (human bodies, the big black square, interactive whiteboard) come together, to make a new territory, or better perhaps, reassemble an old territory, in a process of reterritorialisation. Here, I suggest, the political is integral to the pedagogic and the material; a process of micropolitics is in play, a *break* with or an *intervention* in the spatial order of things.

Not unlike the 'room' in which children are withdrawn when they require learning support, this micropolitical space mimics a more traditional classroom and signals that 'new generation' learning spaces (as shown in Figure 1) can assume the form of a

Figure 3. Class occupying two 'room' locations.

traditional classroom. Johanna reflects at interview on spatial and pedagogic configurations:

> And the layout of the space, having the other end, which was my former classroom ... being able to sort of withdraw and work with a group down there, it just separates us so it's not all happening in the one space where you've got some kids trying to listen to you and other kids trying to work and they are still chiming in on what you're saying.

As Deleuze and Guattari (1987, p. 312) claim, 'sometimes one leaves the territorial assemblage for other assemblages, or for somewhere else entirely: interassem-blage, components of passage or even escape'. Contrary to policy preference where practices of student-centred learning and decentralised decision-making are promoted, and learning spaces which are thought to accommodate these practices are preferred, these practices and spaces emerge as ontologically indeterminate. Their forms flex as do the teachers 'within' them. Shifting easily between a discourse of open learning community and classroom, Rose reports:

> I started here at the start of last year, okay, so this is my second year, I'm a grad. So, and I came straight into this learning community, and I was in this classroom last year and I moved into the opposite one this year. So I've started teaching in the open learning communities.

When education practices are imagined as 'spatialised knowledge-building practices' (Edwards & Clarke, 2002, p. 157), no hard and fast distinction between open and closed learning spaces needs to be drawn. As the Principal of Wattle Park Primary has it, 'it's more about what's happening within the spaces than actually the spaces themselves'.

The critical significance of the material pedagogical practices traced here can be found in the way in which ontological assumptions behind policy that urges teachers to make the most of flexible learning spaces (Department of Education and Early Childhood Development, 2011) are deflected, certainly over the course of a lesson's introduction. The material enactment of the 'big black square on the floor' is consequential inasmuch as the practice of enclosing spaces goes against the grain of government policy. A type of micropolitics is playing out in which one kind of assemblage (a contained, homogeneous, 'micro' one), is held against another (a flexible, heterogeneous, 'macro' one), in a process of rupture, at least for a time.

Enactment 2: *'It's the way that you operate, ... actually live the twenty-first century pedagogies'*

Servicing a low socio-economic and immigrant community, Gum Park Primary School is a medium size, government school in the western suburbs of Melbourne. Filming was undertaken in the senior learning community[6] with its five 'learning advisors' and 130 children. The numeracy and measurement activity filmed concerns the concept of area and the children gather initially as a whole cohort in the 'community space' before being dispersed into two learning spaces towards engaging in a series of activities involving forming the concept of area and measuring it. A strong social constructivist thread runs through the interview data collected, with the Assistant Principal of Gum Park commenting that 'learning isn't done in isolation, it's done together', leading to the view that:

if those spaces out there were treated like classrooms, they wouldn't be socially constructed because all of the doors would be shut, the middle space would be empty, or … it would serve different purposes. So, you know, you look at what are the purposes of those spaces, and one of our strong beliefs is socially constructed, and so therefore our spaces I think reflect that really well.

Learning spaces must be fit for purpose:

So the spaces are divided into – you know, we've got our classroom library in one of them. Like I said, the other one is one of a maths room. We've got a community space where we all come together and it's where we collaborate and we share, and then we've got … they are constantly changing. So our community space used to be in the middle where all classes would meet, and now our community space is in one of the other rooms because we've used our larger area as our science space because we needed more room. (Ariana, year 5/6 teacher, Gum Park Primary)

We decided 130 kids in one place is really hard, and you'll find some kids are just tuning out and not listening. So we have kind of split it up a bit more to two home rooms each, and one for direct instruction. It's much easier that way to manage the kids academically, but then you do break up in small groups sometimes for reading, and do workshops for even more direct (instruction), whilst other kids are on independent tasks. (Mona, year 5/6 teacher, Gum Park Primary)

Just as the purposes of learning change, so too do learning spaces. As the Assistant Principal attests: 'You never go into a space that's fixed for a number of weeks because the teachers will change those spaces according to the purposes of the learning'. She adds:

It can't just be the bricks and mortar of a school that makes a contemporary learning space because you can have a contemporary learning space in a traditional school … It's the way that you operate; it's the way that you group students and teachers together; it's the way that you actually live the twenty-first century pedagogies through everything that you do from top level planning down to … the planning of students in small groups. It's all of those levels that all work hand in hand to actually link the contemporary spaces, rather than the bricks and the mortar and the set up I think.

While subscribing fully to the notion of twenty-first century learning which for this Assistant Principal concerns 'student voice and choice', the policy link between pedagogy and space is loosened, or in the terms of actor-network theory, it is translated, inasmuch as 'you can have a contemporary learning space in a traditional school'. The contemporary learning space has a variable geography, and, as the Assistant Principal recounts, for certain students at Gum Park Primary, a variable ontology. Living twenty-first century pedagogies such as inquiry learning and social constructivist learning means reconfiguring 'a big open space' towards making 'my space':

So some students need to go to their caves, and in a big open space, it can be quite daunting. So a lot of them, furniture moving is making those nooks and crannies where they can go and sit, and you'll see kids pulling all the ottomans around them to make that physical boundary of 'this is my space, and this is where I'm working'.

Clearly, in 'making those nooks and crannies' and 'pulling all the ottomans around them', policy *matters matter* to students. This 'making' and 'pulling' is a *materialising process* in and through which territory can be reclaimed; it can be considered a further form of micropolitical work.

Re/assembling spaces of learning in Victorian government schools

Promoting the idea of twenty-first century learning in open, flexible learning spaces, the BER infrastructure programme embeds a particular view of pedagogic practice and the spaces in which it is performed. It can be considered a performative agent with interventionist possibilities regarding schools' spatial and pedagogic outcomes and goals. In the complexity of the passage of BER policy into schools however, learning spaces are contingent upon context and situation and open to change. They take form materially and socially:

> It can't just be the bricks and mortar of a school that makes a contemporary learning space – and each of these assemblage elements allows for the making and potential unmaking of policy. They are both open and closed, flexible and contained, heterogeneous and homogeneous; pedagogic practices are similarly seemingly paradoxical – learner-centred and teacher-centred, individualised and directly instructional or whole group. As the Principal of Gum Park Primary states: 'the more open we are, the more planned and focused we are'.

Learning spaces and pedagogies have a history and traditional practices persist:

> Just the spaces where the students can work allows them to do so many different things – pooling any of the resources we have and using them in different ways and allowing the kids the opportunity to go between classes and get knowledge from different places – there's so many different ways that it's just not traditional any more. They're not sitting at their desk the whole time or sitting on the floor the whole time—they're learning from each other and using a community of teachers as well. (Johanna, year 3/4 teacher, Wattle Park Primary)

Students still sit at their desks or on the floor, at least for part of the time. Contrary to policy and popular accounts of the traditional classroom which is commonly claimed to be fixed and inflexible with regard to the pedagogies it affords (Department of Education and Early Childhood Development, 2009, 2011), an assemblage rendering of space credits the idea that spaces, like persons, are in-the-making; their ontology is variable – they shift their identity or shape. They can be seen as relational products (albeit provisional) of practices of assembly. Contemporary learning spaces are constituted, in part, by the lines of their engagement with elsewhere (Massey, 2007). They are *syncretic* or non-coherent (Law et al., 2013) because they display both open and other – 'closed' or traditional – features that characterise quite different school architectural traditions. For Law et al. (2013, p. 4), syncretism is a way of talking of spatial coherence that is also non-coherent (which is not to say incoherent). The analyses undertaken here acknowledge that 'policy' and 'intervention' such as contemporary learning spaces and twenty-first century learning are never singular terms but always entail an array of meanings and practices.

When deploying an analytic of assemblage in policy research, the focus is not whether a particular concept of space (open, flexible, contained, traditional) is 'true' but whether it works, and whether it opens up possibilities in a given situation and for what and for whom it does this. Tracing practices of assembly of spaces of learning challenges the idea of a predetermined policy outcome – that flexible spaces are necessarily good for teaching and learning. Whether the new learning spaces cater to the needs of all students and student groups remains an open question. As a secondary teacher involved in the study reports, 'I think the spaces are more set up for creativity, more set up for unpredictability, more set up for engagement' than for students who struggle. 'It is through policy that governments seek to reform educational systems' (Rizvi & Lingard, 2010, p. 5) and their framings of how the reform process can be undertaken are of consequence. In the cases reported here, education policy and practice are largely aligned: 'I love it here with the big open spaces, it's fantastic, it really is. It's just easier, I don't know, to work together as a team' (Rose, three out of four teacher, Wattle Park Primary). This alignment however, can be otherwise: '(Y)ou can have a contemporary learning space in a traditional school'. Focusing up new flexible learning spaces as government policy does can obscure moments where these policy objects take 'an unexpected turn to become part of an unforeseen and/or novel policy assemblage' (Prince, 2010, p. 172). A fully performative idiom of policy through which its materialising processes, including its power relations, can be traced, allows other(ed) forms of learning space to come into view. Room is made for something more. And, this 'something more' takes in the concept of policy as an open system, a process, rather than a totalising structure or a programme that policy-makers and practitioners must carry out.

Notes

1. Reference is also made in policy material to terms like constructivist learning, active learning, inquiry project based learning and individualised learning each of which can be considered to also sit under this broad umbrella.
2. Science studies runs under a number of labels including 'science and technology studies', 'the sociology of scientific knowledge', 'science, technology and society' and 'social studies of science and technology'.
3. Social constructivism is a theory of knowing and knowledge premised on the idea of *human* sense-making. It is a broad church and takes in cultural, sociological and psychological perspectives.
4. This programme was controversially scrapped in July 2010, two months after the general election in the UK.
5. In contrast, a *fully* performative (or enactments) idiom would provide the idea that policy has 'no ontological status apart from its various acts which constitute its reality' (Butler, 1990, p. 337).
6. In Victorian Primary schools, 'seniors' comprises children at the top-end of Primary school – years 5/6. These children are commonly aged ten and eleven.

References

Anderson, B., & McFarlane, C. (2011). Assemblage and geography. *Area, 43*(2), 124–127. doi:10.1111/j.1475-4762.2011.01004.x

Ball, S., Maguire, M., & Braun, A. (2012). *How schools do policy: Policy enactments in secondary schools*. London: Routledge.

Ball, S., Maguire, M., Braun, A., & Hoskins, K. (2011). Policy actors: Doing policy work in schools. *Discourse: Studies in the Cultural Politics of Education, 32*, 625–639. doi:10.1080/01596306.2011.601565

Bennett, J. (2010). *Vibrant matter: A political ecology of things*. Durham, NC: Duke University Press.

Bradley, B., Sumsion, J., Stratigos, T., & Elwick, S. (2012). Baby events: Assembling descriptions of infants in family day care. *Contemporary Issues in Early Childhood, 13*(2), 141–153. doi:10.2304/ciec.2012.13.2.141

Braun, A., Maguire, M., & Ball, S. (2010). Policy enactment in the UK secondary school: Examining policy, practice and school positioning. *Journal of Education Policy, 25*, 547–560. doi:10.1080/02680931003698544

Butler, J. (1990). *Gender trouble*. London: Routledge.

Coleman, R., & Ringrose, J. (Eds.). (2013). *Deleuze and research methodologies*. Edinburgh: Edinburgh University Press.

Coole, D., & Frost, S. (Eds.). (2010). *New materialisms: Ontology, agency, and politics*. Durham, NC: Duke University Press.

Deleuze, G., & Guattari, F. (1987). *A thousand plateaus: Capitalism and schizophrenia* (B. Massumi, Trans.). Minneapolis and London: University of Minnesota Press.

Department of Education and Early Childhood Development. (2009). *Pedagogy and space: Transforming learning through innovation*. Melbourne: State of Victoria (Department of Education and Early Childhood Development).

Department of Education and Early Childhood Development. (2011). *Making the most of flexible learning spaces: A guide for principals and teachers*. Melbourne: Author.

Dewey, J., & Bentley, A. F. (1949). *Knowing and the known*. Boston, MA: Beacon Press.

Edwards, R., & Clarke, J. (2002). Flexible learning, spatiality and identity. *Studies in Continuing Education, 24*, 153–165. doi:10.1080/01580370220000020965

Fenwick, T. (2012). Matterings of knowing and doing: Sociomaterial approaches to understanding practice. In P. Hager, A. Lee, & A. Reich (Eds.), *Practice, learning and change: Practice-theory perspectives on professional learning* (pp. 67–83). Dordrecht: Springer.

Fenwick, T., Edwards, R., & Sawchuk, P. (2011). *Emerging approaches to educational research: Tracing the sociomaterial*. London and New York, NY: Routledge.

Gherardi, S. (2006). *Organizational knowledge: The texture of workplace learning*. Malden, MA: Blackwell.

Gislason, N. (2007). Placing education: The school as architectural space. *Paideusis, 16*(3), 5–14.

Grace, G. (1995). *School leadership: Beyond education management—An essay in policy scholarship*. London and Washington, DC: Falmer Press.

Hetherington, K., & Law, J. (2000). After networks. *Environment and Planning D: Society and Space, 18*(2), 127–132. doi:10.1068/d216t

Hinchliffe, S. (2007). *Geographies of nature: Societies, environments, ecologies*. London: SAGE.

Houle, K. (2011). Micropolitics. In C. J. Stivale (Ed.), *Gilles Deleuze: Key concepts* (pp. 103–115). Durham, NC: Acumen.

Koyama, J. P., & Varenne, H. (2012). Assembling and dissembling: Policy as productive play. *Educational Researcher, 41*, 157–162. doi:10.3102/0013189X12442799

Lackney, J. A. (2011). New approaches for school design. In F. W. English (Ed.), *The SAGE handbook of educational leadership* (2nd ed., pp. 353–381). Thousand Oaks, CA: SAGE.

Latour, B. (1987). *Science in action: How to follow scientists and engineers through society*. Cambridge, MA: Harvard University Press.

Latour, B. (1999). *Circulating reference: Sampling the soil in the Amazon forest. Pandora's hope: Essays on the reality of science studies* (pp. 24–79). Cambridge, MA: Harvard University Press.

Latour, B. (2005). *Reassembling the social: An introduction to actor-network-theory*. Oxford and New York, NY: Oxford University Press.

Law, J. (2000). Comment on Suchman, and Gherardi and Nicolini: Knowing as displacing. *Organization, 7*, 349–354. doi:10.1177/135050840072009

Law, J. (2004). *After method: Mess in social science research*. London and New York, NY: Routledge.

Law, J. (2009). Actor-network theory and material semiotics. In B. S. Turner (Ed.), *The new Blackwell companion to social theory* (3rd ed., pp. 141–158). Chichester and Malden, MA: Wiley-Blackwell.

Law, J., Afdal, G., Asdal, K., Lin, W.-Y., Moser, I., & Singleton, V. (2013). Modes of syncretism: Notes on non-coherence. CRESC working paper number: 119. Retrieved from http://www.cresc.ac.uk/publications/modes-of-syncretism-notes-on-non-coherence

Leander, K. M., Phillips, N. C., & Taylor, K. H. (2010). The changing social spaces of learning: Mapping new mobilities. *Review of Research in Education, 34*, 329–394. doi:10.3102/0091732X09358129

Li, T. M. (2007). Practices of assemblage and community forest management. *Economy and Society, 36*, 263–293. doi:10.1080/03085140701254308

Loughlin, J. (2013). How photography as field notes helps in understanding the building the education revolution. *The Australian Educational Researcher, 40*, 535–548. doi:10.1007/s13384-013-0112-1

Maguire, M., Ball, S., & Braun, A. (2010). Behaviour, classroom management and student 'control': Enacting policy in the English secondary school. *International Studies in Sociology of Education, 20*, 153–170. doi:10.1080/09620214.2010.503066

Marques, J., Veloso, L., & Sebastiao, J. (2013). How to rebuild a secondary school: Space, knowledge and education. In B. Boufoy-Bastick (Ed.), *Cultures of educational policy* (pp. 59–101). Strasbourg: Analytrics.

Massey, D. (2007). *World city*. Cambridge and Malden, MA: Polity Press.

Ministerial Council on Education Employment Training and Youth Affairs. (MCEETYA). (2008). *Learning spaces framework: Learning in an online world*. Carlton South: Author.

Mulcahy, D. (2011). Assembling the 'accomplished' teacher: The performativity and politics of professional teaching standards. *Educational Philosophy and Theory, 43*(Suppl. 1), 94–113. doi:10.1111/j.1469-5812.2009.00617.x

Mulcahy, D. (2013). Turning around the question of 'transfer' in education: Tracing the sociomaterial. *Educational Philosophy and Theory, 45*, 1276–1289. doi:10.1080/00131857.2013.763592

Murdoch, J. (1998). The spaces of actor-network theory. *Geoforum, 29*, 357–374. doi:10.1016/S0016-7185(98)00011-6

Nespor, J. (1994). *Knowledge in motion: Space, time, and curriculum in undergraduate physics and management*. London and Washington, DC: Falmer Press.

Newton, C., & Gan, L. (2012). Revolution or missed opportunity. *Architecture Australia, 101*(1), 74–78. Retrieved from http://architectureau.com/articles/revolution-or-missed-opportunity/

Nielsen, G. B. (2011). Peopling policy: On conflicting subjectivities of fee-paying students. In C. Shore, S. Wright, & D. Però (Eds.), *Policy worlds: Anthropology and analysis of contemporary power* (pp. 68–85). New York, NY: Berghahn Books.

Orlikowski, W. (2002). Knowing in practice: Enacting a collective capability in distributed organizing. *Organization Science, 13*, 249–273. doi:10.1287/orsc.13.3.249.2776

Postma, D. (2012). Education as sociomaterial critique. *Pedagogy, Culture & Society, 20*, 137–156. doi:10.1080/14681366.2012.649419

Prince, R. (2010). Policy transfer as policy assemblage: Making policy for the creative industries in New Zealand. *Environment and Planning A, 42*, 169–186. doi:10.1068/a4224

Rizvi, F., & Lingard, B. (2010). *Globalizing education policy*. Abingdon: Routledge.

Shapin, S., & Schaffer, S. (1985). *Leviathan and the air-pump: Hobbes, Boyle, and the experimental life*. Princeton, NJ: Princeton University Press.

Shore, C., & Wright, S. (2011). Conceptualising policy: Technologies of governance and the politics of visibility. In C. Shore, S. Wright, & D. Però (Eds.), *Policy worlds: Anthropology and analysis of contemporary power* (pp. 1–25). New York, NY: Berghahn Books.

Singh, P., Thomas, S., & Harris, J. (2013). Recontextualising policy discourses: A Bernsteinian perspective on policy interpretation, translation, enactment. *Journal of Education Policy, 28*, 465–480. doi:10.1080/02680939.2013.770554

Sorensen, E. (2009). *The materiality of learning*. Cambridge: Cambridge University Press.

Vanderstraeten, R., & Biesta, G. J. J. (2001). How is education possible? Preliminary investigations for a theory of education. *Educational Philosophy and Theory, 33*(1), 7–21. doi:10.1111/j.1469-5812.2001.tb00251.x

Faciality enactments, schools of recognition and policies of difference (in-itself)

P. Taylor Webb[a] and Kalervo N. Gulson[b]

[a]Faculty of Education, University of British Columbia, Vancouver, BC, Canada; [b]Faculty of Arts and Social Sciences, The University of New South Wales, Sydney, NSW, Australia

> This article discusses the idea of *difference* in relation to *schools of recognition*. The analysis is based on a three-year study that mapped the development of the Africentric Alternative School in the Toronto District School Board. Within, we review the concept of difference and juxtapose it with Gilles Deleuze's concept of *difference-in-itself* as a way to think about educational policy enactments. In order to understand how difference and recognition were enacted – and enacting – we examine how the idea *faciality* positioned eight key people in the development of the school.

> Parents didn't think it was "Black" enough, and it really caused a lot of damage ... It was like a mini cultural war again, over "Blackness." (TDSB Trustee)

What constitutes "acceptable" educational difference in neoliberal and multicultural school markets (Baker, 2002; Hale, 2005; Melamed, 2006)? If parental choice and school markets are the premises on which neoliberal education policy is enacted, how and why are some schools marked as different from others? In what ways do "[n]eoliberal policy engender new racial subjects, as it creates and distinguishes between newly privileged and stigmatized collectivities" (Melamed, 2006, p. 1)?

This paper discusses the ideas of *difference* and *difference-in-itself* in relation to *schools of recognition*. For our purposes, schools of recognition are public choice schools, such as charter schools in the USA, forms of "alternative schools" in Canada, or government-funded private schools in Australia, that enunciate a culturally focused curriculum, identity, or brand (i.e., racial, ethnic, linguistic, religious, gender, dis/ability; see also Wells, Lopez, Scott, & Holme, 1999). Rizvi and Lingard (2010, p. 159) noted that "the struggle of recognition is fast becoming the paradigmatic form of political conflict" and our schools of recognition locate a specific policy site where such politics occur in education. Additionally, there are political and policy lineages to schools of recognition, evident in the independent Black schooling movement of the UK and the USA (Gerrard, 2013; Shujaa, 1988, 1992; Shujaa & Afrik, 1996). However, in the contemporary policy environment that emphasizes school choice, the mainstream media reported that ideas of recognition have prompted, and converged with, the development of culturally focused schools and largely framed these schools as attempts at educational equality through the practices of "re-segregation" (Anonymous, 2013; Cavanagh, 2012; Cohen, 2012; Galloway, 2012).

Part of what this article examines are the limits of difference and recognition in education markets within multicultural countries. In other words, this article examines the precariousness of schools of recognition as the marketized and provisional granting of collective rights in multicultural countries. Here, we examine how difference and recognition are enacted in education policy in two ways: (1) through the "limited spaces opened up by neoliberal multiculturalism" (Hale, 2005, p. 11) and (2) through the idea of *faciality* (Deleuze & Guattari, 1987) that suggests that racial identity is an effect of machines that code and decode for it *in relation to the White Man*. Deleuze and Guattari (1987, p. 178) explain:

> If the face is in fact Christ, in other words, your average ordinary White Man, then the first deviances, the first divergence-types, are racial: yellow man, black man ... They must be Christianized, in other words, facialized ... Racism operates by the determination of degrees of deviance to the White-Man face.

For our purposes, the "machines" coding and decoding racial identities are the colonial legacies of schooling that have emerged into the contemporary machines of school markets and neoliberal education policy. While we discuss the idea of faciality in greater detail in just a moment, our analysis illustrates the provisional status of collective rights produced in neoliberal education policy that code and decode racial identities in school markets. Thus, we use *faciality* to illustrate how education policy perpetuates racial codings and decodings in relation to the "White Man" (Deleuze & Guattari, 1987, p. 178; see also, Gillborn, 2005); and, further, we develop the idea of *faciality enactments* to illustrate how educational neoliberalism positions and animates people to perform racial de/re/codings within the "new" commodifications of racial difference in contemporary school markets.

The analysis is based on a three-year study that mapped the development of the Africentric Alternative School (AAS) in the Toronto District School Board (TDSB). This small school-within-a-school opened in September 2009 with an aim to teach a Black education focus into the mandated provincial curriculum, alongside an emphasis on providing students with access to the political, cultural, social, and economic aspects of Afrocentricity. The school was the outcome of nearly 20 years of activism by parents and community members in Toronto that sought an education that would address the problem of Black student disadvantage in Toronto schooling, including a 40% drop-out rate compared to 23% for non-Black students (James, 2011).

Prior to the AAS, many options were proposed to address Black student disadvantage, and at times, put in pilot form, including several curricula options (Dei, 1996). In the 1990s, these pilots were conducted in concert with an explicit antiracist and ethno-cultural foci at the provincial and school board level – alongside a broader focus on the intersecting notions of recognition and identity. Conversely, the political activism that produced the AAS occurred within, and material support from, an amalgamated Toronto Board of Education. After the amalgamation of this board into a megaboard with surrounding suburban cities (the current TDSB) and the closure of a provincial government antiracist unit, the micropolitics of antiracism education were enacted in relation to broader debates about the role of identity politics in education and within a more managerialist and market-focused policy environment (McGaskell, 2005; Zine, 2001).

In the early 2000s, a variety of programs were proposed, organized around the idea to integrate "the histories, cultures, experiences and contributions of people of African descent and other racialised groups into the [TDSB] curriculum, teaching methodologies and social environment of the schools" (Toronto District School Board, 2008, cited by James, 2011, p. 191). Related to this recognitive politics and under the theme of "Improving the success of Black students," the AAS was proposed in 2007, ratified by the board in 2008, and opened in September 2009.

The AAS, then, represents an important event of racial recognition in the multi-cultural registers of Canada, perhaps even a moment of "strategic essentialism" (Danius, Jonsson, & Spivak, 1993). In this paper, we review the concept of *difference*, notably in the work of Charles Taylor, and juxtapose it with Gilles Deleuze's concepts of "difference-in-itself" as a way to think about and understand school enactments of racial identification and categorization. In order to understand how difference and recognition were enacted – and enacting – our analysis examines how *faciality* and assertions of difference arranged the school choice environment of Toronto during 2008–2009 and positioned eight key people in the development of the AAS, including several TDSB Trustees.

Difference and recognition: the faces of (neo) liberal multiculturalism

Difference makes distinctions between things (states, conditions, people) that are assumed to be equivalent or identical. Difference is also used to illustrate distinctions over a period of time. In either case, difference refers to variations between groupings and invokes processes of comparison (Stagoll, 2010). Importantly, difference is implicated within ideas of recognition. This point may seem obvious, in that difference is perceived in some way; however, the relationships between difference and recognition are not so obvious.

Perhaps no other quote represents the contemporary multicultural politics of recognition than Charles Taylor's (1994, p. 27) proclamation that:

> our identity is partly shaped by recognition or its absence, often misrecognition of others, and so a person or group of people can suffer real damage, real distortion, if the people or society mirror back to them a confining or demeaning or contemptible picture of themselves.

Taylor's statement locates the idea of recognition within representations (i.e., pictures) of people and groups that align – or not – with ideas of identity. In this sense, difference is associated with ideas of multiculturalism when identities are cast within a politics of representation. Ideas of difference emerge when misrecognition is done *to* persons and/or groups but can also surface when persons and groups recognize themselves with representations of identity (West, 1990).

We can consider mis/recognition in reference to Canadian multiculturalism in three ways. First, multiculturalism can be both a strategic and an institutional way for governments to manage and control difference. Strategically, multiculturalism:

> allows the state to set the terms of the "difference debate." These terms are highly individual: they are concerned with individual rights and preferences – the right to choose and display difference with respect to individual identity. (Mitchell, 2003, p. 391)

Institutionally, multiculturalism permits "minority" groups to be included so long as they follow certain carefully prescribed rules about how this is to be undertaken (Mitchell, 2003). The second way mis/recognition is evident in Canadian multiculturalism is that it overlaps with what has been identified as the "color-blind" premise of Canadian multiculturalism that occludes race and racism altogether (Mackey, 1999). This means, "for the most part, education in Canada is mired in a color-blind and monocultural discourse in terms of vision, content and style that the promise of democracy, inclusivity and equity continue to elude minority students" (James, 2011, p. 192).

Market forms of education, such as school choice, account for the third way to understand mis/recognitions of Canadian multiculturalism. This occurs when identities are articulated and recognized in education markets as a corrective to "color-blind" multiculturalism. Hale (2005, p. 28) stated similarly:

> collective rights, granted as compensatory measures to "disadvantaged" cultural groups, are an integral part of neoliberal ideology. These distinctive cultural policies (along with their sociopolitical counterparts), rather than simply the temporal lapse between classic liberalism and its latter day incarnation, are what give the "neo" its real meaning. To emphasize the integral relationship between these new cultural rights and neoliberal political economic reforms, I use the term "neoliberal multiculturalism."

In this paper, we point to how contemporary educational markets use neoliberal multiculturalism as a form of educational equity that is operationalized as a remedy to Canada's "color-blindness." Additionally, we illustrate this "equity-commodification" as part of an extended analysis on ideas of difference, recognition, and representation *that occur within* the "capitalist axiomatics" of schooling – and not outside of these axiomatics (Deleuze & Guattari, 1987, p. 214). For instance, Gilroy (2000) observed that representations are often developed as intellectual property and placed in the hands of absolutists who treat difference as a:

> piece of intellectual property over which they alone hold effective copyright. Their expositions of it specify the elusive qualities of racialized difference that only they can claim to be able to comprehend and to paraphrase, if not exactly *decode*. (Gilroy, 2000, p. 179, our italics)

In what follows, we discuss how Deleuze (1994) conceptualized the idea of difference, differently. Moreover, we examine how difference is produced through the idea of *faciality* that is not interested in who represents difference, but how identity is an effect of machines that *code* and *decode* for it (Deleuze & Guattari, 1987). In other words, our discussion of *faciality* is related to how neoliberal education policy is enacted, and, for our purposes, racially enacted through various codings and decodings of racial identity.

Difference-in-itself

The AAS is a signification of difference that was produced through school choice policies that created and depended on the idea of differentiation within neoliberal education markets (Gulson & Webb, 2013a, 2013b; Webb, Gulson, & Pitton, 2014; Youdell, 2004). Borrowing from Henri Bergson, Deleuze (1991, p. 23) observed that positing difference that presumes an identity as a sufficient cause (rather than contingent effect) is a "difference by degree." Borrowing from Bergson again, Deleuze (1991, p. 23) distinguished *difference by degree* with *difference in kind*; whereas the latter marks the endless qualitative differences that resist categorization. Deleuze (1994) would claim that all *differences by degree* are ultimately reduced to *differences in kind* when assumptions of identity are examined. Cornell West (1990) argued likewise when he stated that *difference by degree* "presuppose[s] the very phenomena to be interrogated, and thereby, foreclose the very issues that should serve as the subject matter to be investigated" (p. 104). Deleuze (1994) would eventually elaborate upon these ideas with his idea about *difference-in-itself* or the *intensive multiplicity* – which we discuss in just a moment.

Deleuze (1994, p. 138) argued that, "difference [by degree] becomes an object of representation always in relation to a conceived identity, a judged analogy, and imagined opposition or a perceived similitude". In this sense, difference by degree is a perception applied as a "difference between" (things, objects, states, people, etc.) and involves grouping things that are purportedly the same and noting distinctions between them. Initially, and in contrast to "difference between," readers might consider "difference within" as a way to understand difference-in-itself. In order to compare, difference by degree invokes universals or transcendent understandings (e.g., standards) to denote coherent and different classifications. "Signification" is the term Deleuze used to refer to the representations between transcendental concepts and particular objects and is entirely related to the politics of representation discussed above. This point is evidenced in the quote that introduced this paper – the transcendental "Blackness" – and we return to it later in our analysis (and, which are related to several transcendentalisms in Whiteness studies; see, for example, Leonardo, 2009). For now, the idea of difference-in-itself is a foil for how neoliberal multiculturalism capitalizes on difference by degree to enact educational markets – the presupposition of identity that is commodified, marketized, and enacted.

Difference-in-itself is an idea that does not presuppose identities. Instead, *difference-in-itself* is an affirmation of the "singularity" of each moment, thing, state, etc., a "particularity that is" and an "indetermination, newness which creates itself" (p. 48). *Difference-in-itself* extends the idea of distinctions to the point where notions of "the same" are seriously questioned if not entirely dismissed. Deleuze (1994, p. 225) would argue that *difference-in-itself* "does not negate difference: on the contrary, it recognizes difference just enough to affirm that it negates itself, given sufficient extensity and time." Here, *difference-in-itself* assumes an intensive multiplicity that is constantly effected by indeterminacies and chance over a period of time. Difference, then, is re-articulated as the constant changes in a singularity that are constantly becoming and not able to be grouped or organized in relation to universals or transcendentals.

Édouard Glissant (1989) and his version of "creolization" is an important illustration of *difference-in-itself* (and particularly germane in its location of the Caribbean as a contrasting signification of African "Black" – i.e., Africentric – in this study). Rejecting hybridity and intersectionality, Glissant argued that creolization was a process of constant becoming and, specifically, a creative becoming away from fixed identities and toward states of constant flux. Glissant (1989) argued:

> creolization demonstrates that henceforth it is no longer valid to glorify "unique" origins that the race safeguards and prolongs … To assert that people are creolized, that creolization has value is to deconstruct in this way the category of "creolized" that is considered a half way between two "pure" extremes. (Glissant, 1989, p. 140)

Glissant (1989) rearticulates hybrid notions of creolizations by operationalizing *difference-in-itself* in order to demarcate a becoming "into another people" that experience "the constantly shifting and variable process of creolization (of relationship, or relativity)" (p. 15). For our purposes, Glissant is an example of how *difference by degree* is challenged through his deconstruction of identity based on "uniqueness" and "purity." More importantly, Glissant's idea of creolization is an articulation of *difference-in-itself* when applied to race and the raciologizing of people: "the impossibility of legitimate lineages, pure racial origins, or reified cultured affiliations" (Burns, 2009) – a politics that Elizabeth Grosz (2002) described as "becoming imperceptible."

Faciality and policy enactment

Notwithstanding Glissant's example of creolization, it is precarious to assert *difference-in-itself* as part of a cultural politics in education, and for some, as we will show, life-threatening. In claiming *difference-in-itself* as both an analytic and as a political possibility, dangers of radical exclusion lie beneath attempts at de/identifying – which we note are risks that are disproportionately assumed – if at all – depending on different and unequal social arrangements. For example, Étienne Balibar (2005, p. 28) noted how presumptions of identity and disavowal of the same presumptions run serious risks of radical exclusions. He stated:

> An assertion of singularity, differing from any type, is an ethical imperative which escapes the essentialist categorizing of humans, but it is also, so it seems, the result of what Foucauldians would call bio-political and bio-economic processes, which associate infinite individualizations with social control, therefore at least the possibility of some radical exclusions.

The concept of race continues to function as a transcendental politics that can be "infinitely" signified in relation to – and *for* – radical exclusions. Balibar (2005) suggested that there is differentiation that is used to create a "hierarchic totality" – such as racial typologies – and a differentiation that is premised on the relationship of difference to singularities (i.e., *difference-in-itself*). Balibar (2005) stated:

> how identities always "differ from themselves," or the fact that the most fundamental difference, the one that precisely resists the classifications and typologies, or its own fixation as essential difference, always arises from oneself or to be absolutely *different* is also, indeed to differ from any difference that has been ascribed to the singular by narratives of domination and objectification. (p. 26)

Here, then, race and racism continue to maintain particular (unequal) social orders even if the kinds of possibilities ushered forth by *difference-in-itself* signal an alternative politics – a politics that challenges the assumptions of neoliberal multiculturalism.

The idea of *faciality* signals how race and racism are continually coded and decoded in social and educational life, and an idea that resonates with what Zeus Leonardo (2013) discussed as the "racial contract." *Faciality* signals how race codes everyday life and signals how these codes maintain the colonial (and Christian) racisms that it established by "propagating waves of sameness until those who resist identification have been wiped out (or those who only allow themselves to be identified at a given *degree* of divergence)" (Deleuze & Guattari, 1987, p. 178, our italics). *Faciality* signals how *difference by degree* maintains its historical violence by coding and decoding racial identities (i.e., "sameness") to assert and perpetuate a politics of recognition and representation. Simone Bignall (2013, p. 77) observed, then, that "faciality describes ... a conceptual topography which diagrams the intersection of the two semiotic systems operating as signification and subjectivation." To repeat, Deleuze and Guattari (1987, p. 178) argued:

> If the face is in fact Christ, in other words, your average ordinary White Man, then the first deviances, the first divergence-types, are racial: yellow man, black man ... They must be Christianized, in other words, facialized ... Racism operates by the determination of *degrees* of deviance to the White-Man face. (Our italics)

Policy enactments, then, are positioned within historical legacies dependent on ideas of *difference by degree* – or degrees of deviance from the White Man face. Our contention, and what we will show, is that *faciality*, now, codes and decodes racial identities within the commodified and marketized registers of neoliberal education (Comaroff & Comaroff, 2009; Gilroy, 2000). Thus, faciality functions to map the codings and decodings of racial identity rather than only understanding racial identity as something to be signified, represented, or "phenotyped." Saldanha (2013, p. 19), argued similarly:

> faciality does not simply insist that there are "intersections" of phenotype, sexuality, and power, but holds that the "first" differences created by state-simulated capitalism are racial [e.g., segregated schooling, residential schools]. This is because differences are selected and cultivated against a biopolitical backdrop of colonialism.

Difference-in-itself, then, attempts to counteract *neoliberal faciality* by challenging the assumptions of identity implicit in conceptions of *difference by degree*. Instead, *difference-in-itself* is the affirmation of becomings that constantly differentiate ourselves from ourselves and from each other – a constant creolization, if you will. We think this idea is distinct from other uses of difference in that *difference-in-itself* resists classifying or grouping difference (but simultaneously affirms difference). We also note this idea with the use of one participant's talk below, and we follow this up in the Conclusion and in relation to how, if at all, *difference-in-itself* may be used in attempts at developing ideas about educational equality with the use of schools of recognition.

Methodology

This paper is drawn from a three-year (2010–2013) qualitative study on education policy, curriculum, and difference. Methodologically, our approach was attendant to how issues of power affect the production and subsequent enunciations of different discourses (e.g., equality) and affect the enactments and performances of policy (Ball, Maguire, Braun, & Hoskins, 2011; Simons, Olssen,& Peters, 2009). We understand policy as something "designed to steer understanding and action without ever being sure of the practices it might produce" (Rizvi & Lingard, 2010, p. 5).

Data were generated from over 1000 school, district, and community documents (e.g., Ontario and TDSB policy texts, meeting minutes, newspaper editorials) and other media (such as video footage from school board meetings, documentary films) from 1992–2012. We analyzed how these texts and media signified identity and conceptualized policy. In 2012, we supplemented this archival research with eight semi-structured interviews with stakeholders including community representatives and School Board Trustees. The former were key figures in the development of "alternative schools" (i.e., charters) and who held positions within the Board related to alternative school policy. The latter were elected officials of the school board with a mix of those who voted for and against the school proposal. For reasons of confidentiality, we do not indicate how Trustees voted and we name all as "Trustees," even if they are ex-members.

Semi-structured interviews averaged one- and-a-half hours, with some lasting two-plus hours and one that lasted 12 minutes. All the interviews were audiotaped and transcribed. Data were organized through mentions of markets, choice, difference, race, recognition, and representation – which served as analytic constructs among many examples of participants' talk. In addition, member checks were conducted with participants, asking if the data were accurate and interpretations plausible. No participant revised their respective transcript. All data have been edited. Our interviews attempted and, at times, succeeded in developing rich and challenging conversations. We noted during the interviews that participants and ourselves discussed these issues to help us understand issues of policy, power, and race. In fact, several participants responded at some point during the interview that the discussion had been cathartic for them.

As the very expressions of faciality, that is, "White Men," we did not initiate this study from outside of our own racialized positions. In fact, our racialized positions were an important topic during most of our conversations with participants. Additionally, we invited participants to provide feedback about how our racializations affected our understandings of the case and to correct any errors we may have had. We attempted to develop a reflexive position with regards to race which served as an explicit commitment to participants about our intentions to learn about racialized curriculum policy. Interestingly, and anecdotally, the most engaging conversations with participants about our racialized positions were with participants who had been racialized as Black (in one way or another). In these cases, a fair amount of humor was exchanged during our conversations, particularly when we used our Whiteness as explicit foils to understand the case. For example:

> Interviewer: As a white guy, I'm thinking that it is too dangerous to vote against the school.
> Participant: As a white guy, you can say that, but when you look at it from my perspective, as a Black woman, Black people don't vote. [Both laugh]

This example is not designed to reify subject identities, but to illustrate how we broached our racial positions within the study. Conversely, the least engaging conversations with participants about our racialized positions were with other White participants. In these conversations, we were constantly reminded of our White positions and repeatedly warned about the dangers of talking about race with racialized (non-White) people. In fact, in one interview with White participants, it was suggested that our interest in racialized schools was manifestly racist in intent (which is one way that the "color-blind" nature of Canadian multiculturalism is maintained).

Policy histories: enacting difference and recognition
All participants spoke to the idea that the AAS resulted from Canada's multicultural policies and practices that aligned with Charles Taylor's ideas of difference and recognition discussed above. Specifically, participants discussed the AAS as part of this multicultural

history of recognition of difference, and also in relation to historic formations of prior ethnic-specific schools, namely First Nation schooling, Catholic schooling, and French Immersion. For instance, one Trustee historized the AAS:

> The old Toronto Board of Education had what was originally called the *Wandering Spirit School*, and is now called *First Nation School* which does have a curriculum that I guess you would call First Nation-centric.

Another participant reminded us about Canada's Catholic school system in relation to the AAS: "And don't forget, we have a publicly funded Catholic separate system to begin with." Another participant noted that discussions about difference and recognition in schooling were difficult conversations because of the kinds of histories associated with ethnic and linguistic identities. She sardonically stated, "And it's a very hard conversation because you actually have to bring French immersion into it too. French immersion parents are way scarier [politically adept] than any other parents." One participant observed "there are lots of Jewish schools in Toronto, but they're private." Jewish schools amplified the historical enactments of schools of recognition in Toronto, in the sense that they have been precedents of culturally focused schools, though have been private with no public funding. In our discussions with participants, and more similar to the AAS, were private Islamic schools that were seen as either "safe havens" or "religious ghettos" (Zine, 2007).

The AAS, then, was conceived alongside an equity focus of the TDSB in the 1990s where the positing of *difference by degree* was understood as an acceptable form of cultural politics within the old Toronto Board of Education (the previous, amalgamated Board). This was evidenced following the establishment of the *Wandering Spirit School* and the establishment and short life of a 25 student Black-focused program within a school, called *Nighana* in 1994 (McGaskell, 2005).

The histories of ethnic-specific schooling in Ontario and Canada provided a strong register to develop the AAS. In this sense, Deleuze (1994) was correct when he noted that a politics of representation "conserve or prolong an established historical order, or ... establish a historical order which already calls forth in the world the forms of its representation" (p. 53). More importantly, the AAS was quickly becoming the central focus on a broader set of policy enactments around several schools of recognition in the TDSB proposed around the same time (circa 2005). While we have discussed the disproportionate political and media attention, the AAS received elsewhere (Gulson & Webb, 2013a); here, we note how the historical orders of multicultural representation in Canada – coupled with an intensive neoliberal agenda in the TDSB to marketize schools – provided a rapid increase in the enactments of several schools of recognition, including schools enacted on the basis of gender, sexuality, physical ability (athletes), and an increasing anticipation about the possible enactment of a Muslim-centric school (see Figure 1).

The ideas of *safety* and *violence* were key catalysts in the rapid rise of culturally focused schools in the TDSB, through various choice programs such as the "alternative schools" program (Four-Level Government, 1992; School Community Safety Advisory Panel, 2007). While the Sports Academy falls somewhat outside these registers (and many other of the 44 choice schools in the TDSB), the AAS, First Nation School, Triangle, and the Boys and Girls Academies all utilized the ideas of safety and violence as part of the rationales for their respective enactments in the TDSB school market. Here,

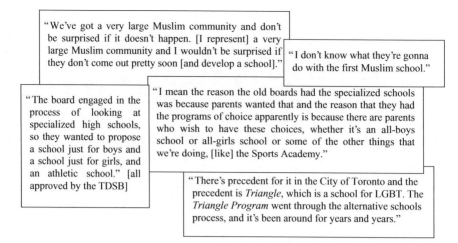

Figure 1. Historical orders of difference and recognition in the TDSB.

then, TDSB Trustees "used a model to separate students" which amounted to using *difference by degree* and alternative school policies to produce school sanctuaries (interview, Trustee). Over time, however, participants noted a commodifying effect produced from these market enactments. A TDSB Trustee remarked:

> So one of the things that came out of that [school choice deliberation] was a discussion amongst a number of us [Trustees] about "so what do we do now because we're making things worse." And, out of the *Boys* schools and the *Girls* schools, those who were deeply opposed to the Africentric School were equally deeply opposed to *Boys* and *Girls* schools. It was about identity. I'm not sure the others would articulate it quite the same way. But I believe we all have the same core fear.

Additional data confirm that participants worried about the possibility that the TDSB school choice market would provide additional commodifications of *difference by degree* for enterprising cultural groups within the TDSB. For instance:

> I understand the focus because it's an Africentric curriculum so it's a focused curriculum which is different from a traditional school. However, there are lots of specialty schools that require focused curriculums, you know, are not called focus schools. And, what's the difference between specialty, boutique, focus, choice? The choice thing is a big deal. Lots of people are really wanting to move away from that term because they don't want to have charter schools because of all the problems that are associated with those (e.g., essentializations, commodifications).

Participants sensed that the educational market multiplied *differences by degree* – "infinite representations." For instance, participants explained how religious ideologies govern representations of gender *and* sexuality – entangling policy within registers of safety, violence, and separation. Policy entanglements provided latent possibilities (i.e., "fear") of developing additional schools of recognition within the TDSB (see Figure 2).

Figure 2 illustrates several ideas. First, schools of recognition were predicated on *faciality* that code and decode historical registers of identity for future policy enactments. More importantly, these histories were woven together within various representations of

ASSEMBLAGE, ENACTMENT, AND AGENCY

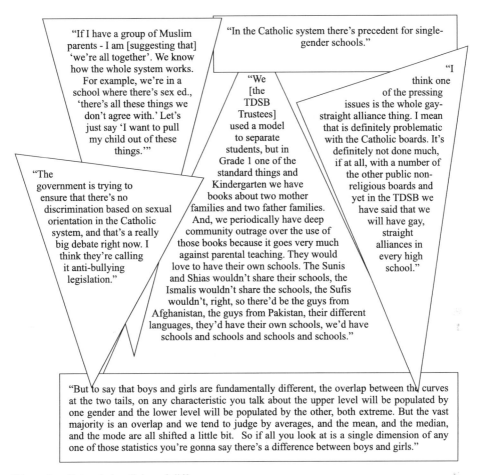

Figure 2. Entangled policies of difference.

difference by degree – girls are categorically not boys, and vice versa; lesbian, gay, bisexual, and transgender (LGBT) are not heterosexual, and vice versa; Sunis are not Shias, and vice versa. However, and our second point, Figure 2 highlights how significations are enacted within the local histories of TDSB policies where "*difference [by degree] becomes an object of representation always in relation to a conceived identity, a judged analogy, and imagined opposition or a perceived similitude*" (Deleuze, 1994, p. 138, italics original). The idea of a "conceived identity" is evidenced in the center triangle of Figure 2 through the discussion of religious difference and the possibility of "infinite representations" of schools. These types of debates have a history in the Toronto school district, such as those in the 1990s over the inclusion of antihomophobia approaches in equity and antiracist materials and initiatives (McGaskell, 2005). In the 1990s, "[a]dvocates for separate policies argued that all forms of difference could not be equated and should be dealt with separately in terms of policy and practice" (Zine, 2001, p. 239).

The bottom box in Figure 2 discusses gender representation through a statistical language of bell curves and averages. Thus, the third point that we wish to highlight from

Figure 2 is that the politics of representation is historical, but enacted within different discourses, registers, or multiple and competing "regime[s] of filiation" (Deleuze & Guattari, 1983, p. 156). Finally, the idea of *difference by degree* is invoked on several occasions in Figure 2. Participants noted how *difference by degree* might be used as political capital in the development of additional schools of recognition, and that would cement *difference by degree* within market logics – the commodification of difference (e.g., Comaroff & Comaroff, 2009). Within these policy enactments, however, we note that *just who is using what* becomes occluded. Are Trustees using *difference by degree* as political capital? Or, is *difference by degree* something only enacted by marginalized groups? Here, then, schools of recognition are a precarious politic that can be undermined as being for "special interest groups," a racialization "double-bind" pertinent to the case of the AAS.

In the final section, we present findings about how participants were arranged and enacted by these policy histories and entanglements. We note how *faciality* positioned participants within the complex and, at times, dangerous enactments of difference, recognition, and for one participant, *difference-in-itself*.

Enacting policy in faciality

The preceding policy landscape – histories, entanglements – positioned participants in relation to the AAS. More importantly, *faciality* affected how participants were treated in relation to the AAS. For instance, evidence of physical threats and physical violence were noted by some participants when they questioned assumptions about identity, difference, and recognition (even when participants voted in favor of the school). One Trustee stated:

> I've gotten so many threats on my life because I didn't support the school. I remember one night very clearly: a woman came up and she made the sign of a gun and said "you should be fuckin' shot." Another time, I was about to leave to go down the stairs and she pushed me. The security guard was behind me, so he had the hood of my coat to pull me back or I would have gone right down on my face. So she was issued a long trespassing order on any Board property.

Another Trustee stated, "phone call after phone call, and email after email. People were furious, angry, sad, and hateful. I started getting threats. I got a couple death threats. I got a lot of hate mail." In fact, the school board meeting that approved the AAS employed security guards due to threats of violence (of differing kinds). Questioning *difference by degree* was difficult because it was fraught with danger depending on where one is located upon the unequal and historical playing-field of identities (i.e., gender, sexuality, class, race, etc.). For instance, a participant who raised questions about identity waxed, "everybody hates me; everybody dislikes me; yes I'm a traitor, I'm a sell-out to the Black race." *Faciality* was a powerful way to analyze how *differences by degree* were organized within the TDSB, and it raised the specter of radical exclusions when questioned.

Notwithstanding violence and threats of violence, participants wrestled with issues of signification as it related to representations of people. Referring to *difference by degree*, the transcendental "Blackness" was invoked when making distinctions among people in Toronto. A current politics of recognition swirling around the AAS concerns the efforts to define and operationalize "Blackness" which, at the moment, is a contest between representations of the "continent" (Africa) and the "islands" (Caribbean) and through this

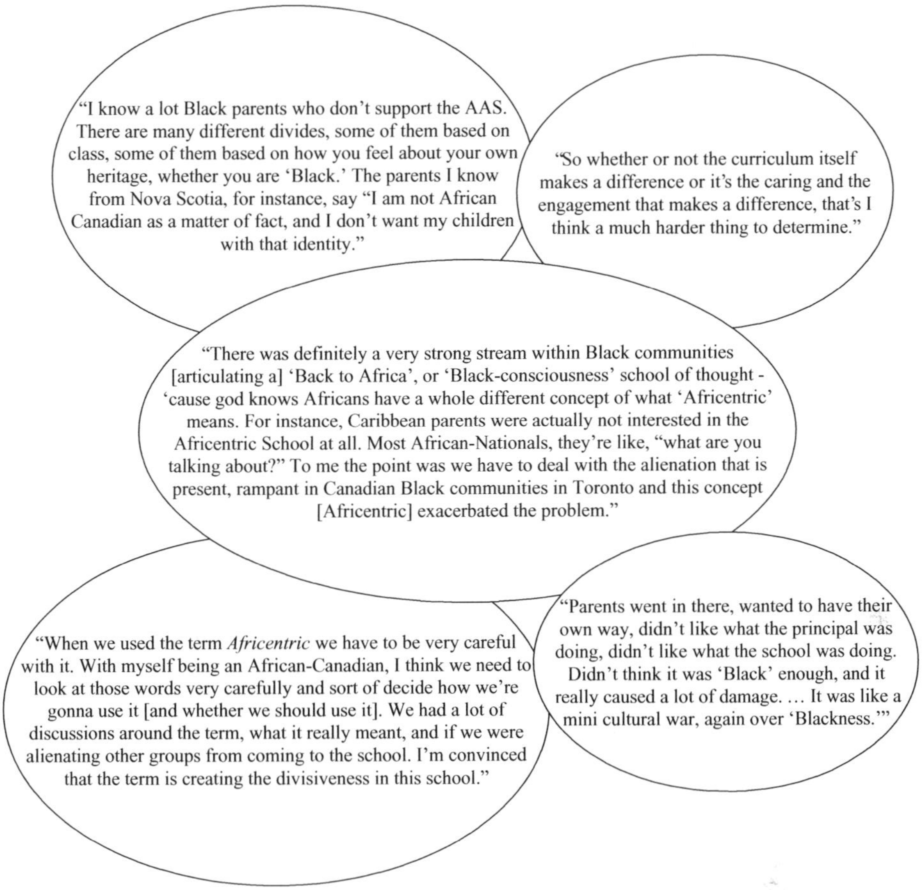

The politics of signifying difference

"I know a lot Black parents who don't support the AAS. There are many different divides, some of them based on class, some of them based on how you feel about your own heritage, whether you are 'Black.' The parents I know from Nova Scotia, for instance, say "I am not African Canadian as a matter of fact, and I don't want my children with that identity."

"So whether or not the curriculum itself makes a difference or it's the caring and the engagement that makes a difference, that's I think a much harder thing to determine."

"There was definitely a very strong stream within Black communities [articulating a] 'Back to Africa', or 'Black-consciousness' school of thought - 'cause god knows Africans have a whole different concept of what 'Africentric' means. For instance, Caribbean parents were actually not interested in the Africentric School at all. Most African-Nationals, they're like, "what are you talking about?" To me the point was we have to deal with the alienation that is present, rampant in Canadian Black communities in Toronto and this concept [Africentric] exacerbated the problem."

"When we used the term *Africentric* we have to be very careful with it. With myself being an African-Canadian, I think we need to look at those words very carefully and sort of decide how we're gonna use it [and whether we should use it]. We had a lot of discussions around the term, what it really meant, and if we were alienating other groups from coming to the school. I'm convinced that the term is creating the divisiveness in this school."

"Parents went in there, wanted to have their own way, didn't like what the principal was doing, didn't like what the school was doing. Didn't think it was 'Black' enough, and it really caused a lot of damage. … It was like a mini cultural war, again over 'Blackness.'"

Figure 3. The politics of signifying difference.

discussion, a politics of recognition and difference were enacted. Here, *faciality* arranged the politics concerned with the transcendental "Blackness" *and* in relation to school markets. Figure 3 shows participants' thinking through the different significations of "Blackness" invoked during the enactment of the AAS. Here, participants enacted policy on the basis of *faciality* that coded and decoded identities.

Figure 3 provides evidence of participants' *faciality* arrangements. Specifically, participants enacted policy from the dual position of signifying the AAS ("Blackness," identity, etc.) and signifying alternatives to such transcendentalisms. Interestingly, one participant attempted to re-think difference – not philosophically or through curriculum policy – but as pedagogy (upper right).

The AAS enacted another participant through his attempt to eliminate difference altogether. This participant signified "humanness" as a way to sidestep the discussion on *difference by degree*. He stated:

> If our fundamental goal is to elevate humanity as the core identity of every person, then we should minimize the religious, cultural, ethnic, genetic, appearance, skill differences, whatever differences. Then that says what we need is a human school.

This statement assumes that schools can have a cosmopolitan function, and that "humanness" is benign. However, as Leonardo (2009) noted, calls for "humanism" has been one way in which whiteness has repudiated the perniciousness and banality of racism – that is, we are all "human" and racism is aberrant, rather than race being an ordering category that has constituted "being" –and classified "not being." Humanist assumptions, however, are predicated on other transcendental significations that problematically eliminates *faciality* (and associated prior histories). A nostalgic return to a democratic or normal school is unlikely given that choice policies are the default mechanism in most discussions about curriculum and schools in the TDSB. The policy histories of identity, recognition, and difference have established the regimes of filiation that will likely be enacted in the production of future choice schools.

Finally, the AAS prompted one participant to seriously consider *difference-in-itself*. She stated:

> You want something for your own kid, right? We all do. However, how do we balance that in our schools? Can we ever come up with a solution in education that embraces the diversity of students, *because they are all different*, but that doesn't divide them. I think this is the hard part. So that's when you get to identity, especially in terms of the worry I think about the *First Nations School* and the *Africentric School*. I think the danger in [schools of recognition] is that it lets the whole system off the hook because it's not really actually doing anything about the problem [of inequality]. (Emphasis added)

Difference-in-itself usurps the idea of schooling based on classifications and sorting due to the immanence of difference or the intensive multiplicity, even though these classificatory practices have persistently endured. We conclude by discussing a few key points.

Conclusion

While we are interested in the differences produced through schools of recognition, our analysis focused on the ways *difference*, *difference-in-itself*, and *recognition* were enacted in educational policy in ways that were not divorced from neoliberal policy practices: school choice, school markets, and ethnic commodifications. Indeed, we propose that schools of recognition depend on economic ideas to articulate notions of educational difference and recognition which subsequently enact (and sediment) school markets and policies that support such arrangements. Participants enacted policy within a complex and politically dangerous ensemble of *faciality* discourses that performed specific policy enactments around racial recognition and school markets in Toronto.

We note that policy enactment "not only recognizes the historical formation of policy but also its constitution as discourse" (Olssen, Codd, & O'Neill, 2004, p. 58). To repeat, a politics of representation, then, "conserve or prolong an established historical order, or … establish a historical order which already calls forth in the world the forms of its representation" (Deleuze, 1994, p. 53). For our purposes, the AAS initiated an array of enactments through historical significations of racial difference and educational equity. Here we can see again the possibilities and limits of neoliberal multiculturalism, in that the AAS both reifies the liberal notion of multiculturalism while repudiating the possibility that multiculturalism leads to cultural transformation. What palpates racial significations is an idea – imaginary, perhaps fantasy – of a democratic and "normal" school. Unfortunately, from our vantage, schooling – whether the historic normal school or the contemporary culturally-focused school – will always resist *difference-in-itself* due its necessary practices of *grouping and sorting* – what Bernadette Baker (2002) asserted as a "hunt" for difference in schools.

An irony of culturally focused schooling is not its attempt at producing educational equality through re-significations of difference, but in assuming that schooling – any schooling – will provide an emancipatory outcome. Another possible trajectory to explore educational equity is through *difference-in-itself* (and as mentioned by one of our participants). In order to affirm *difference-in-itself*, schooling would need to stop the endless "infinite individualizations" brought forth in the name of recognition (Balibar, 2005, p. 28). Stagoll (2010) opined just such a possibility for schooling based on *difference-it-itself*:

> rather than theorizing how individuals might be grouped, it is more important to explore the specific and unique development or "becoming" of each individual. The genealogy of an individual lies not in generality or commonality, but in a process of individuation determined by actual and specific differences, multitudinous influences and chance interactions. (p. 75)

Of course, this is a dangerous gambit which would require educators to affirm difference in the Deleuzean sense (and like one of our participants). Smith (2012) clarified:

> It is not that Deleuze denies subjects and objects have identities – it is simply that these identities are secondary; they are the effect of more profound relations of difference. As Deleuze says, just as there is no "pure" reason but only historically variable processes or "rationalization," so there is no universal or transcendental subject, but only diverse and historically variable forms of "subjectivation," and no object in general, but only variable forms of "objectivation," and so on. (p. 82)

What would schooling look like that aimed at producing "diverse and historically variable forms of 'subjectivation?'" Nevertheless, *difference by degree* is not designed to explore possible or "new" subjectivations. Nor are the practices of difference and recognition utopian escapes from the market even if they utilize transcendental significations of the self, for instance, "Blackness," "Whiteness," and "Jewishness." In fact, as we have argued, *necessary* "radical exclusions" are produced through school markets. Schools of recognition must constantly position themselves within market arrangements that code and decode *differences by degree*. In the end, schools of recognition must care for these arrangements because "neoliberal educational equality" depends on market separations and/or "radical exclusions."

It may be the case that *difference by degree* is intertwined with a politics of nostalgia (Zembylas, 2011) and a politics of melancholia (Gilroy, 2005) that maintain schooling as the disciplinary and reproductive machine that it always has been. But now, schools of recognition are the disciplinary and reproductive machine of self-selected and entrepreneurial significations – the *sine qua non* of neoliberal education policy. As such, the idea of educational equity in culturally focused schools is enunciations for equal opportunities to be subjugated to the discourses of economy (e.g., labor markets), which appears to be a preferable state to being subjugated by White faces. In this sense, schools of recognition are a solace – albeit provisional and tenuous – from *faciality* that explicitly disadvantages groups but does so by reifying *difference by degree* and reify schooling as disciplinary and economic. We don't pretend that *difference-in-itself* is a route to educational equity. However, it is becoming clearer to us that variable forms of subjectivation can confront historical – and contemporary – forms of unequal groupings and bodily categorizations. However, schooling in the TDSB is yet not the place for this particular politics.

Acknowledgments

We would like to thank the two anonymous reviewers for their excellent comments and Viviana Pitton for her extensive archival work on Afrocentric schooling in Toronto.

Funding

This research was supported by a Canadian Social Sciences and Humanities Research Council.

References

Anonymous. (2013). Academy schools are breaking down social segregation not fuelling it. *Conservative Home*. Retrieved from http://conservativehome.blogs.com/localgovernment/2013/01/academy-schools-are-breaking-down-social-segregation-not-fueling-it.html

Baker, B. (2002). The hunt for disability: The new eugenics and the normalization of school children. *Teachers College Record*, *104*, 663–703. doi:10.1111/1467-9620.00175

Balibar, E. (2005). Difference, otherness, exclusion. *Parallax*, *11*(1), 19–34. doi:10.1080/1353464052000321074

Ball, S. J., Maguire, M., Braun, A., & Hoskins, K. (2011). Policy subjects and policy actors in schools: Some necessary but insufficient analyses. *Discourse: Studies in the Cultural Politics of Education*, *32*, 611–624. doi:10.1080/01596306.2011.601564

Bignall, S. (2013). Dismantling the White-man face: Racialisation, faciality and the Palm Island Riot. In A. Saldanha, & J. M. Adams (Eds.), *Deleuze and race* (pp. 73–92). Edinburgh: Edinburgh University Press.

Burns, L. (2009). Becoming-postcolonial, becoming-Caribbean: Édouard Glissant and the poetics of creolization. *Textual Practice*, *23*(1), 99–117. doi:10.1080/09502360802622300

Cavanagh, S. (2012). School choice, and cultural identity, in GOP platform. *Education Week*. Retrieved from http://blogs.edweek.org/edweek/charterschoice/2012/08/school_choice_as_cultural_identity_from_the_gop.html

Cohen, R. (2012). Schools for Jews and Arabs: Separate but definitely not equal. *Haaretz*. Retrieved from http://www.haaretz.com/opinion/schools-for-jews-and-arabs-separate-but-definitely-not-equal-1.443811

Comaroff, J. L., & Comaroff, J. (2009) *Ethnicity, Inc*. Chicago, IL: University of Chicago Press.

Danius, S., Jonsson, S., & Spivak, G.C. (1993). An interview with Gayatri Chakravorty Spivak. *Boundary 2*, *20*(2), 24–50. doi:10.2307/303357

Dei, G.J.S. (1996). The role of Afrocentricity in the inclusive curriculum in Canadian schools. *Canadian Journal of Education*, *21*, 170–186. doi:10.2307/1495088

Deleuze, G. (1991). *Bergsonism*. (H. Tomlinson, & B. Habberjam, Trans.). New York, NY: Zone Books.

Deleuze, G. (1994). *Difference and repetition*. New York, NY: Continuum.

Deleuze, G., & Guattari, F. (1983). *Anti-oedipus: Capitalism and schizophrenia*. Minneapolis: University of Minnesota Press.

Deleuze, G., & Guattari, F. (1987). *A thousand plateaus: Capitalism and schizophrenia*. Minneapolis: University of Minnesota Press.

Four-Level Government/African Canadian Community Working Group. (1992). *Towards a new beginning: The report and action plan of the four-level government/African Canadian community working group*. Toronto: Author.

Galloway, J. (2012). Don't let them resegregate our schools. *Atlanta Journal-Constitution*. Retrieved from http://blogs.ajc.com/political-insider-jim-galloway/2012/10/31/joseph-lowery-in-radio-ads-dont-let-them-resegregate-our-schools/

Gerrard, J. (2013). Self help and protest: The emergence of black supplementary schooling in England. *Race, Ethnicity and Education*, *16*(1), 32–58. doi:10.1080/13613324.2012.733685

Gillborn, D. (2005). Education policy as an act of White supremacy: Whiteness, critical race theory and education reform. *Journal of Education Policy, 20*, 485–505. doi:10.1080/02680930500 132346

Gilroy, P. (2000). *Against race: Imagining political culture beyond the color line*. Cambridge, MA: Harvard University Press.

Gilroy, P. (2005). *Postcolonial melancholia*. New York, NY: Columbia University Press.

Glissant, É. (1989). *Caribbean discourse*. (M. Dash, Trans.). Charlottesville: University of Virginia Press.

Grosz, E. (2002). A politics of imperceptibility. *Philosophy and Social Criticism, 28*, 463–472. doi:10.1177/0191453702028004528

Gulson, K. N., & Webb, P. T. (2013a). "A raw, emotional thing": School choice, commodification and the racialized branding of Afrocentricity in Toronto, Canada. *Educational Inquiry, 4*, 167–187. doi:10.3402/edui.v4i1.22067

Gulson, K. N., & Webb, P. T. (2013b). Education policy racialisations: Afrocentric schools, Islamic schools and the new enunciations of equity. *Journal of Education Policy, 27*, 697–709. doi:10.1080/02680939.2012.672655

Hale, C. R. (2005). Neoliberal multiculturalism: The remaking of cultural rights and racial dominance in Central America. *PoLAR: Political and Legal Anthropology Review, 28*(1), 10–28.

James, C. E. (2011). Multicultural education in a color-blind society. In C. A. Grant & A. Portera (Eds.), *Intercultural and multicultural education: Enhancing global connectedness* (pp. 191–210). New York, NY: Routledge.

Leonardo, Z. (2009). *Race, whiteness, and education*. New York, NY: Routledge.

Leonardo, Z. (2013). The story of schooling: Critical race theory and the educational racial contract. *Discourse: Studies in the Cultural Politics of Education, 34*, 599–610. doi:10.1080/01596306. 2013.822624

Mackey, E. (1999). *House of difference: Cultural politics and national identity in Canada*. New York, NY: Routledge.

McGaskell, T. (2005). *Race to equity: Disrupting educational inequality*. Toronto: Between the Lines.

Melamed, J. (2006). The spirit of neoliberalism: From racial liberalism to neoliberal multiculturalism. *Social Text, 24*(4), 1–24. doi:10.1215/01642472-2006-009

Mitchell, K. (2003). Educating the national citizen in neoliberal times: From the multicultural self to the strategic cosmopolitan. *Transactions of the Institute of British Geographers, 28*, 387–403. doi:10.1111/j.0020-2754.2003.00100.x

Olssen, M., Codd, J. A., & O'Neil, A. M. (2004). *Education policy: Globalization, citizenship & democracy*. Thousand Oaks, CA: SAGE.

Rizvi, F., & Lingard, B. (2010). *Globalizing education policy*. New York, NY: Routledge.

Saldanha, A. (2013). Introduction: Bastard and mixed-blood are the true names of race. In A. Saldanha & J. M. Adams (Eds.), *Deleuze and race* (pp. 6–34). Edinburgh: Edinburgh University Press.

School Community Safety Advisory Panel. (2007). *The road to health: A final report on school safety*. Toronto: Author.

Shujaa, M. J. (1988). Parental choice of an Afrocentric independent school: Developing an explanatory theory. *Sankofa, 2*(1), 22–25.

Shujaa, M. J. (1992). Afrocentric transformation and parental choice in African American independent schools. *Journal of Negro Education, 61*, 148–159. doi:10.2307/2295412

Shujaa, M. J., & Afrik, H. T. (1996). School desegregation, the politics of culture, and the council of Independent Black Institutions. In M. J. Shujaa (Ed.) *Beyond desegregation: The politics of quality in African-American schooling* (pp. 253–268). Thousand Oaks, CA: Corwin Press.

Simons, M., Olssen, M., & Peters, M. (2009). *Re-reading education policies: A handbook for studying the policy agenda of the 21st century*. Boston, MA: Sense.

Smith, D. W. (2012). *Essays on Deleuze*. Edinburgh: Edinburgh University Press.

Stagoll, C. (2010). Difference. In A. Parr (Ed.) *The Deleuze dictionary* (pp. 74–76). Edinburgh: Edinburgh University Press.

Taylor, C. (1994). The politics of recognition. In A. Gutmann (Ed.), *Multiculturalism: Examining the politics of recognition* (pp. 25–73). Princeton, NJ: Princeton University Press.

Webb, P. T., Gulson, K. N., & Pitton, V. O. (2014). The neo-liberal education policies of *epimeleia heautou*: Caring for the self in school markets. *Discourse: Studies in the Cultural Politics of Education, 35*(1), 31–44. doi:10.1080/01596306.2012.739465

Wells, A. S., Lopez, A., Scott, J., & Holme, J. J. (1999). Charter schools as postmodern paradox: Rethinking social stratification in an age of deregulated school choice. *Harvard Educational Review, 69*, 172–205.

West, C. (1990). The new cultural politics of difference. *October, 53*, 93–109. doi:10.2307/778917

Youdell, D. (2004). Engineering school markets, constituting schools and subjectivating students: The bureaucratic, institutional and classroom dimensions of educational triage. *Journal of Education Policy, 19*, 407–431. doi:10.1080/0268093042000227474

Zembylas, M. (2011). Reclaiming nostalgia in educational politics and practice: Counter-memory, aporetic mourning, and critical pedagogy. *Discourse: Studies in the Cultural Politics of Education, 32*, 641–655. doi:10.1080/01596306.2011.620749

Zine, J. (2001). "Negotiating Equity": The dynamics of minority community engagement in constructing inclusive educational policy. *Cambridge Journal of Education, 31*, 239–269. doi:10.1080/0305764012006164

Zine, J. (2007). Safe havens or religious "ghettos"? Narratives of Islamic schooling in Canada. *Race Ethnicity and Education, 10*(1), 71–92. doi:10.1080/13613320601100385

The enactment of professional learning policies: performativity and multiple ontologies

Augusto Riveros and Melody Viczko

Faculty of Education, Critical Policy, Leadership and Equity Studies, Western University, London, Ontario, Canada

> While teacher learning has become a locus of school reform across many international settings, there is relatively little examination of the idiosyncratic ways in which policy discourses on teacher learning are enacted in schools. In this paper, we aim to investigate how these policy discourses are translated and configured into practices and thus, enacted into concrete realities. Using the conceptual notion of *multiple ontologies*, we argue that teacher learning is actualized in a multiplicity of socio-material entanglements, not as a single reality, but as a multiplicity of realities that coexist, simultaneously, in the mesh of assemblages that we call "school." In this study, we describe and trace how particular socio-material configurations of teacher learning produce concrete realities of practice that mobilize and generate specific networked effects. We conclude that the postulation of multiple ontologies of teacher learning prompts a shift in how policy makers could conceive of and develop strategies aimed at transforming teaching practices.

Introduction

Discourses on school reform have positioned teacher learning as a key mechanism for educational change and subsequently, professional development has entered the agenda of educational policy makers in several jurisdictions around the globe (Borko, 2004). The perceived need to align teaching practices with the goals of reform has given visibility to a number of contradictions and tensions between the realities of teaching practices and the realities of educational reform (Hodkinson & Hodkinson, 2005). One of such tensions was explored through an examination of the idiosyncratic ways in which a policy on professional development was enacted in a school in rural Alberta in Canada (Riveros & Viczko, 2012; Viczko, 2009). In this paper, we propose that these different ways to enact learning suggest the existence of *multiple ontologies* of teacher learning in schools. In particular, we argue that these realities of teacher learning emerge through the performances of the different actors, human and non-human, that collide to articulate material contexts of practice.

We suggest that if we want to understand the intricacies of school reform, we require an account of the ways in which policy initiatives are enacted in the school. This requires an account of the ways in which teacher learning is configured as a relational effect, tied to the performances of diverse school actors, humans and non-humans. In this paper, we note that teacher learning in schools is not performed as a single event that occurs in a unique scenario, but instead, we observe that learning is ontologically diverse. The multiple ways in which teacher learning is performed suggest the existence of simultaneous enactments of teacher learning that coexist in schools.

Teacher learning is the concern of many policy initiatives in Canada, as it is included as a priority in many provincial, jurisdictional, and school-level policies (Riveros, Newton, & Burgess, 2012). Many of these policies have echoed calls in the literature for including a more active role for teachers in the processes of *professional development*. For example, Wilson and Berne (1999) have indicated that professional learning should "not be bound and *delivered* but rather *activated*" (p. 194, Italics in original). This suggests that teachers must be seen as active participants in policy initiatives aimed to promote in-service learning instead of passive receivers of information. However, we argue that the idea that teacher learning must be "activated" does not address how learning is enacted in the school, that is, how the learning of teachers is constituted as a reality. Conceptualizing teachers' learning as a process that must be "activated" implies that learning by teachers in schools still depends on the active intervention of powerful actors in control of the learning process, and those actors are not necessarily the teachers. We want to reject conceptualizations of teacher learning that tend to locate learning in a particular space or reduce it to a psychological process that occurs in particular individuals. Instead, we propose that teacher learning is configured in emergent socio-material assemblages that are ontologically diverse and include multiple human and non-human actors. In this paper, we adopt the position that we can study the ontology of teacher learning through policy analysis that considers how the policies on professional development are enacted. In doing so, we draw upon Actor Network Theory (ANT) to focus on the socio-materiality of teacher learning in order to examine how policies on professional development are translated into concrete realities.

We offer a few caveats before we proceed. First, our purpose in this paper is to advance a conceptual consideration for the nature of teacher professional learning in order to engage academic conversations about the future of educational research in this area. While empirical data are drawn on in this paper to give examples of ways in which teachers perform professional learning through both discursive and material means, our goal is to theorize the socio-material aspects of professional learning, that is, the performed realities of professional learning, by enrolling ANT into the network of educational research. By doing so, we hope to appeal to broader conversations about the ways in which policies emerge in practice in schools.

Second, in this paper, we use the term "teacher learning" along with the more traditional moniker of "professional learning." In doing this, we want to shed some light on the use of a somewhat controversial terminology (Dall'Alba & Sandberg, 2006; Nicoll & Edwards, 2012; Popkewitz, 1994; Stronach, Corbin, McNamara, Stark, & Warne, 2002). We suggest the traditional emphasis placed on the "professional" aspects of teacher learning tends to privilege an idealistic image of teachers and their learning (Dall'Alba, 2009; Riveros & Viczko, 2012). This idealization works to obscure the multiple ways in which teacher learning is configured in the school. Indeed, current discourses of school reform have placed teachers and their learning as instrumental to achieve the goals of the school reform movement (Riveros, 2012; Riveros & Viczko, 2012). The appeal to "professionalism" in school reform discourses tends to locate learning processes in idealized subjectivities: the "professional" is presented as the authoritative agent of change in schools and he/she is reintroduced as the site where reform efforts ought to be focused (Popkewitz, 1994; Stronach et al., 2002). We argue that such an instrumentalist characterization of teachers' identities obscures the relational nature of teacher learning. Mindful of the controversies and difficulties surrounding the conventional use of "professional," in this paper we use the term "professional" following Dall'Alba's (2009) characterization of *professional ways of being*. She argued that being professional is a process of becoming:

> Contrary to what prevalent models of professional development would have us believe, this process is unlikely to occur in a predetermined or linear sequence (e.g. as proposed by Benner, 1984; Dreyfus & Dreyfus, 1986) but, rather, to follow a range of possible development trajectories … This unfolding is open-ended and always incomplete. (2009, p. 43)

Adopting professional ways of being means to be immersed in practices that are changing and dynamic. Learning, in this sense, includes embodied processes that are fluid, situated and interconnected, as opposed to static, individualistic and instrumental to the goals of school reform. Furthermore, we recognize that an attempt to define the "professional" dimension of teacher learning requires a critical discussion of issues of knowledge, expertise, power and practice that are beyond the scope of this paper.

We propose that a study of the ways in which teacher learning is configured in the multiple realities of practice would present a challenge to the instrumentalist discourses embedded in contemporary school reform. In order to support this claim, we argue that the notion of policy enactment (Ball, Maguire, & Braun, 2012; Maguire, Braun, & Ball, 2014) offers a situated and context-sensitive account of the idiosyncratic ways in which educational policy is translated in schools. In particular, we contextualize the saliency of examining policy enactment by reflecting on data collected in a study (Viczko, 2009) that examined how a policy on professional learning was enacted in a rural school in Alberta, Canada. We note that these policies were enacted in networked interactions that included human and non-human actors (Riveros & Viczko, 2012). The resultant practices revealed that teacher learning was not a unique event circumscribed to a specific scenario of "professional learning," but a multiplicity of practices that enacted multiple realities. In our analysis of selected examples from Viczko's (2009) study, we describe how there is not one reality of teacher learning but multiple realities – multiple "teacher learnings" that are enacted as relational effects of networked interactions. We echo Mol's (1999, 2003) call for an ontological politics by asking: What privileges some forms of teacher learning over others? How is this selection made? How is this selection legitimized? Our analysis suggests that when professional learning is conceived of in its material multiplicity, that is, the diverse ways in which the material realities are performed in practice, we are better suited to understand the social and material dimensions of how educational policy is translated into concrete realities in the classroom.

Enacting educational policy

Policy has been traditionally understood as a social change mechanism intended to modify people's behaviors in order to achieve certain desired goals (Shore & Wright, 2011). This rationalist approach to policy processes includes a number of steps or stages such as problem definition, design, implementation and evaluation (Rizvi & Lingard, 2010). The underlying assumption is that policy is a "problem-solving" mechanism, an instrument of social change (Bacchi, 1999; Wagner, 2007). However, this traditional understanding of policy overlooked the idiosyncratic ways in which policy is put into practice. Highlighting a shift toward focusing on the enactment of policy, recent work by Ball, Maguire, and Braun (2012), reporting on a study on the enactment of secondary school policies, offered a different picture. One in which policy is brought into existence in complex ways. These scholars showed that policy texts are recontextualized, translated, and adapted in the school. They revealed the creative ways in which policy texts are transformed into practices.

Similarly, Nielsen (2011) looked at a case of conflicting subjectivities between "customer" and "co-owner" of a group of Chinese international students studying at a Danish university. The focus in this study was to use an ethnographic approach to policy analysis to look at how "'peopling' policy with multi-dimensional actors whose subjectivities are created in the intersections or interactions" (pp. 69–70) shows the emergence of policy processes. Nielsen drew upon the work of ANT scholars Latour (1999, 2005) and Law (2009) to argue for a need to pay attention to policy processes as *appropriation*, whereby policy is seen as a series of translations in which ideas and technologies are transformed when they circulate in institutional contexts. By looking at the conflict between the subjectivities of student as consumer and student as co-owner that emerged through the various interactions with policies, agencies and material relations, Nielsen (2011) described the multi-dimensional and interconnected assemblage of actors involved in enacting policy. Furthermore, Neilsen argued that such a study calls attention to how links between policy and subjectivity are enacted in the everyday lives of actors as "a multiplicity of agencies populates the world" (p. 83). The significance of Nielsen's work is the shifting of focus from a linear, rational and instrumental process of policy to one of translation and recontextualization by social actors.

Highlighting the political dimension of policy processes, Shore and Wright (2011) conceptualized policy as a scenario of political contestation, bringing political processes of policy to the fore of the analysis. In their account, actors bring a wide range of resources to the political arena in order to make their discourse prevail. The resources drawn by political actors are both discursive and non-discursive, which means that in order to legitimate their voices, actors construct and contribute to different arrangements or networks constituted by people and objects, thus the policy scenario is constituted by numerous socio-material arrangements that generate contexts of action, deliberation and further practice. This picture of policy processes offered by Shore and Wright counters traditional understandings of policy as a linear, mechanistic and hierarchical processes that fail to recognize the way policy is enacted in the socio-material assemblages that take place in schools.

Analysing policy enactments with ANT

ANT focuses on the heterogeneous nature of networks as nodes or links of messy negotiations, conflicts and contestations through which stability and order seem to emerge (Fenwick, 2010; Nespor, 2004). That is, in networks, certain kinds of materials and people are assembled and translated to become aligned. By "assembled" we mean put together in heterogeneous networks of human and non-human entities and by "translated" we mean the process that happens when things connect, changing one another and forming links (Latour, 1986). While diffusion is used in many institutional theories to explain the movement of an object through space and time, the notion of translation "emphasizes the changes that occur in meanings and interpretations as a physical or social object moves through a network" (Lawrence & Suddaby, 2006, p. 67).

According to Law (1992), translation is the process "which generates ordering effects, such as devices, agents, institutions, or organizations" (p. 366). Law (2009) also indicated that the research focus of ANT is to "explore and characterize the webs and the practices that carry them ... [describing] the enactment of materially and discursively heterogeneous relations that produce and reshuffle all kinds of actors" (Law, 2009, p. 141). For example, Hamilton (2011) drew upon ANT to explore how a standardized individual learning plan (ILP) that was intended as a formative assessment tool was translated into an administrative instrument for measurement and quality assurance. Teachers and administrators acted to incorporate the tool into their practices but the introduction of different formats to track the initiative, and the additional paperwork to synchronize the adoption of the tool among teachers, translated the ILP into a set of accountability practices that diverged from the initial goal of the policy, which was to provide a literacy self-assessment tool for individuals.

Similarly, Nespor (2004) investigated how tests of student achievement as policy artifacts participated in shaping educational practices in schools. Teaching and learning processes were translated into test categories that allowed for certain types of measurement that triggered the emergence of particular social and material arrangements in the school. That is, teaching and learning spaces were ordered in ways that facilitated the enactment of the testing regime. New hierarchies, roles and identities appeared as a result of the material re-ordering of the school. Simultaneously, these arrangements validated specific forms of knowledge in detriment of other forms of knowledge. Indeed, policies on high-stakes testing "mobilize a whole series of events and people to align with its forms: administrators force curricula to conform to the test's demands, teachers drill classes in test preparation, remedial classes are arranged to improve students' test achievements" (Fenwick, 2010, p. 123). Networks of human and non-human actors assemble to respond to the policy. This explains why policy enactment differs form school to school.

Analysing policy enactments with ANT requires the adoption of an *ontological* strategy as opposed to an *epistemological* strategy. Law and Singleton (2005) distinguished between these strategies to study objects. The epistemological strategy requires seeing objects through a particular perspective. Multiple perspectives imply multiple descriptions of a single object, descriptions that can conflict or contradict each other. The ontological strategy moves from "thinking about multiple interpretations of objects ... to think about multiple objects themselves" (p. 334). Law and Singleton noted that realities are "enacted into being" (p. 334) through the actors' practices. They suggested that the differences between objects must be understood ontologically, in their socio-material relations, highlighting how entities come into being, and not just epistemologically, that is, how objects are represented or interpreted by subjects in their consciousness. An entity is enacted as a reality through the intricate interactions of other entities and practices. One implication of this is that objects are brought to presence in multiple ways: different sets of practices and material relations may enact an object in multiple ways.

Mol (1999) argued that objects are enacted into existence as relational effects of networks constituted by other objects, practices and people. Cordella and Shaikh (2006) argued that ANT "introduces a new way of conceptualizing the understanding of reality" (Cordella & Shaikh, 2006, p. 14), in that a relational ontology theorizes a *becoming* of entities through relations, through interactions between actors. Looking at the relationality of entities suggests we are not just considering the connections between things that already exist but rather seeking to understand how relationality "*actually configures ontologies*" (Fenwick, 2010, p. 119). *Reality,* according to Mol (1999), is not stable, given, or universal. She characterized reality as "historically, culturally and materially located" (p. 75) and argued that "' the real' is implicated by the 'political' and vice versa" (p. 74). This mutual implication suggests that reality is enacted and performed by actors and objects interacting in complex assemblages. That is, reality is multiple and its multiplicity stems from the various networks of actors and objects that enact multiple and sometimes contradictory contexts of practice.

A stark example of how networked assemblages of human and non-human entities enact objects into reality was presented in Law and Singleton's (2005) study of the treatment of Alcoholic Liver Disease (ALD). They found that the actual object of the disease, the damage of the liver, was enacted differently in the hospital, the substance abuse center, and the general practitioner's office:

> In the hospital, it is a lethal condition that implies abstinence. In the substance abuse centre, it is a problem that implies regulation and control. In the GP's surgery, it is a reality that is better than hard drugs. (2005, p. 347)

Additional to these different understandings of what is the object of ALD, the diagnosis, the treatment, and the treatment effects were different in the community treatment center, the hospital and the physician's office. This incongruence is particularly dramatic because modern evidence-based treatments in medicine operate under the assumption that a disease is a "singular, distinct and identifiable object" (Fenwick, 2010).

Mol (1999) offered an example of ontological multiplicity relative to practices in the case of anemia. She identified at least three ways in which anemia is performed. First, there is a clinical performance, in the doctor's office, in which the doctor examines the patient for visible symptoms (e.g. white eyelids, dizziness). Second, there is a statistical performance, where a blood sample taken from the patient is tested for hemoglobin levels and the levels are contrasted against statistical data. If the sample's levels are lower than the standard levels, then the patient is diagnosed with anemia. Third, there is a pathophysiological performance, in which the patient's blood is tested to find if, in that particular patient, the hemoglobin levels are enough to transport oxygen through the body. If the levels are low then the patient is diagnosed with anemia (Mol, 1999). Mol noted that in practice these three different performances coexist although they may contradict each other. Indeed, sometimes people do not get dizzy or have white eyelids, but nevertheless their hemoglobin levels fall below the statistical average. Or their hemoglobin levels drop, but not enough to be deviant relative to the statistics, and so on. Cases like anemia show how different realities coexist to enact particular effects. In some contexts where doctors do not have access to laboratory analysis, the clinical performance of anemia prevails and subsequent practices ensue, such as particular treatments based on the diagnosis.

What Mol is offering here is a relational ontology, one in which entities are emerging realities enacted in networked interactions. However, multiplicity does not always imply incompatibility: "what multiplicity entails instead is that, while realities may clash at some points, elsewhere the various performances of an object may *collaborate* and even *depend on* one another" (Mol, 1999, p. 83). That is, she asserted that if realities exist as relational effects, then the multiple versions of something that exists in the world must also be relational. These realities are not plural perspectives that stand apart from each other. Rather, as Mol reminded us, realities are multiple, relational and situated. In her words, realities:

> may follow the other, stand in for the other, and, the most surprising image, one may include the other. This means what is "other" is also within. Alternative realities don't simply co-exist side by side, but are also found inside one another. (Mol, 1999, p. 85)

Mol's purpose in focusing on the notion of multiple ontologies is to suggest an ontological politics at play, namely, the idea that:

> reality does not precede the mundane practices in which we interact with it, but is rather shaped within these practices. So, the term *politics* works to underline this active mode, this process of shaping, and the fact that its character is both open ended and contested. (1999, p. 75. Italics in original)

She argued that the postulation of multiple realities suggests that "there is, or should be a choice between them" (p. 79). An exploration of ontological politics offers insights into the way a particular reality is chosen over multiple options. In exploring how a particular reality is selected, Mol suggested to investigate *where* are the options situated and *what* is at stake when the decision is made. In addition, we need to investigate to what extent there *are* really options and *how* should the decision be made. These questions are central in an investigation of the enactment of school realities. We consider Mol's conceptualization useful to our investigation into the realities of teacher learning. In our analysis of the interviews and observational data, we asked whether teacher learning was configured in ways that articulated multiple and coexisting realities. We were interested in the practices that emerged as a result of the enactment of particular policies on teacher learning.

In the following section, we engage in a conceptual argument that looks at the ways in which teacher professional learning is brought into practice by briefly illustrating scenarios that emerged from a study that examined teachers' understandings of professional learning policies (Viczko, 2009). While we have detailed the specifics of the research project elsewhere (Riveros & Viczko, 2012), the scenarios of professional learning elaborated here capture a moment of insight to advance our purposes in this paper related to questioning the ontological manifestations of teacher professional learning in its heterogeneity. Importantly, we do not aim to make claims about the nature of professional learning based on these scenarios, but rather we offer them as examples of the multiplicity in the performances of professional learning.

The examples that we analyse are based on a qualitative study (Viczko, 2009) that examined teachers' understandings of professional learning in a rural school in Alberta, Canada. To provide some background information about that qualitative study, the data were collected over a two-month period involving interviews, focus groups, and researcher journaling. That study adopted a qualitative methodology that allowed for an in-depth exploration of the narratives of the participants as well as a detailed analysis of the observations registered in a field-notes journal. While some studies using ANT focus solely on observational data, our purposes here in this article are to use the insights offered by ANT to reflect on that interview data and researcher journaling to consider "what things and people do" (Fenwick & Edwards, 2010, p. 151). As Latour reminds us, "actors know what they do" (1999, p. 20) and so we have used the data collected in that study as a point of departure to consider policy enactments. In the next section, we want to highlight aspects of professional learning that emerged for us as we considered the ways in which the teachers enacted their professional learning reflected in both way they talked about their professional learning and the observations of their teaching.

Classroom practice and professional development meetings: the performed realities of teacher learning

One aspect of professional learning we want to illuminate is the performative configuration of "spaces" of professional learning. When we talk about spaces, we are not referring to an inert, passive and transparent background for objects. We understand space as "constituted through the social, with interactions creating social space. Space is then performed or enacted as a recursive relationship between the spatial and the social as relations of power" (McGregor, 2004, p. 351). Conceiving space as performed brings to the fore a whole new set of understandings about the constitution of reality as fluid, dynamic and always becoming, an assemblage of the social and the material. In considering how teachers understood their professional learning, we found that particular performances of space were constituted through workshops and professional development meetings. These performances constituted formal or "sanctioned" scenarios of professional learning. In these prescribed spaces, organizational resources were mobilized to enroll different human and non-human actors in the enactment of the policy. The mobilization of resources, such as the rearrangement of timetables and rescheduling, were possible as an effect of the administration's capacity to exercise some degree of influence in the social and material arrangements of the school, the effect of which were particular configurations of professional learning. In other words, the administration of the school expanded its capacity to influence teacher learning by playing a role on the way resources were reorganized and learning was enacted.

The enactment of these administrative influences was elaborated in the ways that teachers talked about marked divisions between what they did in prescribed learning spaces and what they did in their teaching practices. For example, one teacher expressed how she would engage in formalized learning events staged by the central school division office during official days that were scheduled. She expressed that she attended these events out of a sense of duty, in the role of being a teacher, to the goals and strategic plans of the school division office or the Ministry of Education. However, once in her classroom, she would actively return to her personal efforts to improve her practice. Importantly, in her description of the ways she enacted her professional learning was the idea that there are formalized structures, though they did not influence her practice in a way that was meaningful to her. Rather, these formalized administrative social and material arrangements were problematic, in that she felt they were disconnected from her practice. Rather, she preferred opportunities for learning that involved thinking about how to improve her practice of teaching rather than having to "throw out all the stuff I did before."

In addition to the formal spaces, different types of professional learning spaces were constituted through some classroom practices. In these spaces, teacher learning was not necessarily circumscribed to the areas prioritized in the meetings and workshops. In the classroom, professional learning emerged at the margins of the administration's sphere of influence. Sometimes enacting forms of professional learning did not reflect the priorities set during the professional development meetings. The teachers, when talking about the ways they learned about their teaching, revealed the existence of these alternative scenarios of professional learning. In conversation, many participants indicated that their teaching priorities were predominantly situated in their particular contexts of practice. Many complained that the goals set by the administration's reading of the policy on professional development did not reflect their instructional needs and aspirations. Teachers described these administrative attempts at professional learning to be "overwhelming," as there were "too many things" with unrealistic amount of changes "that were difficult to put into action," according to one teacher. These revelations were later corroborated by observing how the classroom practices enacted forms of teacher learning that prioritized the local context in detriment of the goals set by the administration.

An example of how professional learning was enacted in idiosyncratic ways that privileged the local could be seen in the introduction of artifacts that contributed to the consolidation of classroom practices. For instance, the introduction of a poster as a new instructional tool mobilized specific literacy practices and enrolled different actors together. One of the teachers introduced the poster as a component of an instructional initiative that she found to be *realistic* in the sense that it could be incorporated with concrete effects in her classroom practices. Professional learning, as a performance, was transformed when the poster entered the classroom.

Another teacher described learning how to use new technological tools in the classroom, such as a computer program to support geography lessons, as a meaningful way to impact his practice. Specifically, he reflected that by taking the time to use this tool in his teaching he began to think differently about how students learned the topic at hand. He talked about how his own learning through his teaching impacted his practice: "it doesn't have to be something big, but it can be just something that just changes the way you might be doing something a little bit and makes you think." This teacher described how the new tool was enrolled into the classroom learning as it reoriented how he engaged with his students in the geography lessons. The translation of the technological tool into an interactive teaching lesson was meaningful learning for this teacher.

As a result of these new configurations, new classroom practices emerged and new learning took place. In this case, learning is understood as a practical and embodied engagement in the world, an effect of the re-accommodation of human and non-human assemblages that offers new possibilities, new ways of being (Fenwick & Edwards, 2010; Law, 2009; Sørensen, 2009). In the following section we offer more details on how these multiple realities of teacher learning were performed into existence.

Enacting teacher learning in socio-material assemblages: ontological politics

By focusing on the enactment of professional learning policies, we suggest that the heterogeneous nature of teacher learning is brought to the fore. The focus shifts from the teacher as the sole agential actor, so that we begin to notice other actors at play. For instance, by paying attention to artifacts and describing how their presence in the classroom contribute to the emergence of idiosyncratic performances of teacher learning, we recognize that particular enactments of learning take place in the socio-material assemblages that are constituted as humans and non-humans are mobilized and put together in networked interconnections. Taking the stance that teacher learning is enacted suggests that we must pay attention to what is performed in practice. So, learning does not sit passively waiting to be activated. Rather, it is enacted in the socio-material engagements that constitute the practice of teaching.

Another important insight offered by the study of the enactment of professional learning relates to the particular form of learning that ends up being privileged. Mol (1999) argued that the existence of multiple realities implies the possibility to select between those realities. Furthermore, the selection of one reality over the others suggests the existence of an "ontological politics" at play. We want to suggest that the capacity to influence the selection of a particular performance of learning is an effect of diverse configurations of power. Performances of teacher learning do not emerge in a vacuum: they are effects of wider entanglements of human and non-human actors. As we noted above, in this school, professional learning was enacted in different spaces: some spaces were formal and prescribed, such as the professional development meetings and workshops, and some other spaces were local and specific to the classroom situation. These performances mutate and actualize as teachers navigate the complexities of their daily lives in the school. For example, in this school, the prescribed performances of professional learning were generally circumscribed to confined spaces and scheduled events, and in many cases, they were not translated into classroom practices. For instance, some teachers pointed out that the school hosted a number of events that were conceived as events for professional learning, but failed to bring about a meaningful contribution to her teaching practices.

These occurrences of teacher learning, influenced by the administration's goals, are as real as the occurrences of learning that take place between the teachers, the students, and the artifacts in the classroom. Indeed, some teachers established a clear distinction between the professional learning that takes place in these formal spaces and the professional learning that occurs, informally, in the classroom practice, outside the prescribed spaces. In the classroom performance, learning takes place as an effect of the configuration and reconfiguration of teaching practices. This performance of professional learning does not necessarily reflect the policy goals of the school, district or province, but reflects specific needs and interests situated in the classroom. We are not suggesting a simple duality of performances here. These performances interact and connect in many cases. Some teachers moved in a fluid back and forth between the prescribed performance and the classroom performance configuring overarching practices that, in some cases, merged these two realities of professional learning. One teacher who participated in workshops organized by the administration explained to us how she experienced this fluid mobility between performances of professional learning. We found one of her comments particularly revealing. We believe it is worth the long quote:

> I know that we probably don't know off by heart what the division goals are for PD and the provincial goals are for teachers, but I know we've been told them. I know that of course legally we are working within them, but really we're being spoon fed that stuff. Today we're going to work on this because that's part of the division goal, right, so you just do it. And then the next week you go back to your poster. (Teacher)

In the workshop, professional learning was oriented to articulate the provincial literacy goals. Participating in these activities gave the teachers a conceptual repertoire to understand the policy documents and discourses coming from the province and the administration. However, many teachers intimated that these newly articulated understandings were not necessarily translated into classroom practices. In the case of the teacher quoted above, her selection of a poster as a key component in the teaching of literacy, at the expense of other components of the same program, resulted in the emergence of idiosyncratic practices that emerged thanks to the presence of this particular artifact in the classroom. In this classroom, professional learning was configured as an effect of local circumstances, such as the teacher's assessment of the students' needs, the already established instructional practices and the available resources. The introduction of a poster as a key literacy tool did not necessarily reflect all the goals of the literacy policy, but reflected the particular way in which the actors in the classroom converged to enact the provincial goals on literacy. This is an example of how actors in this school became mobile and inhabited different realities of professional learning that were performed simultaneously.

Following Mol's (1999) insights, the notion of multiple realities implies an ontological politics in which realities become options that can be enacted. The actors in our study were able to participate in the enactment of these different realities; they shifted between performances of professional learning. While there may be numerous motivations for these shifts to occur, we believe these shifts are facilitated or constrained by issues of power and legitimacy within the school. The prescribed enactments of professional learning carry out organizational legitimacy as they are sanctioned by the administration and organized as formal events of professional learning. The capacity to shift away from the prescribed performance and explore different enactments of professional learning could be related to the capacity of the teachers to leverage the risks of stepping out of the norm and incorporate new practices into their classroom performance. A key difference between these two performances of professional learning is that in the annual report to the school board the prescribed performance becomes visible and legitimate, whereas the classroom performance becomes invisible and disappears.

A study of the multiple enactments of professional learning in schools provides valuable insights into the ways school actors configure spaces of resistance and transformation. This is true of other instances of educational reform, for example, Fenwick and Edwards (2010) noted that in the case of curriculum standards, teachers reconfigure policies in contextualizing practices that challenge the idea that reforms are always imposed on school actors:

> Standards exist in multiple ontological forms that are performed simultaneously and that, as networks themselves, are continually changing shape. Educators, like other practitioners, are quite used to juggling these shape-shifting forms and their tensions of simultaneity within the high voltage dynamic of everyday commotion. In these ways, ANT highlights the limitations of conventional accounts of standards as globally formed ideals troubled by imperfect local implementation, or as cases of domination and subjugation that require local resistance to top-down exercises of power. (2010, pp. 97–98)

This is an area that requires further interrogation in understanding the multiplicity of ways in which professional learning policies are enacted into different school realities. This avenue of research provides a situated way to understand the various forms of teacher learning that emerge in schools everyday. Our analysis aims to portray teachers, among other human and non-human school actors, as performers that participate in the enactment of school policies in networked associations with other actors and objects.

The materiality of policy and teacher learning

In our analysis, we were interested in tracing the material manifestations of the policy and in particular, in identifying how the assemblages between human and non-human actors constituted enactments of policies on professional learning. In this regard, Waltz (2006) argued that artifacts in schools are not mere tools that represent human intentions: "In treating non-humans as representatives of human ends, their particular contributions are obscured – as are the complex ways in which they interact with humans in the constitution of social events" (p. 56). In ANT terms, humans and non-humans participate in networked associations with one another, there is no categorical difference between them, and thus no special privilege is granted to humans in the constitution of social reality.

Our findings suggest that these networked associations between humans and non-humans were constitutive of particular enactments of teacher learning. One case that caught our attention during our analysis included the use of a "teacher growth plan" and the introduction of a poster that displayed grade-level literacy goals in an elementary classroom. The poster was introduced as part of a literacy-based program that took place in one of the formal spaces of professional learning that we previously described, more specifically, the program included monthly workshops organized by the school district. Although the program comprised other elements and strategies, in this particular classroom, the poster became a significant protagonist in the enactment of the literacy program. Once the poster was incorporated into the classroom, a new range of practices were brought to the fore. For instance, the poster became a central focus of the teacher's professional growth plan. In this school, teachers were required to create and follow a professional development plan that outlined a number of learning goals to be accomplished throughout the school year. The growth plan, which emerges in our analysis as another networked participant in this assemblage, was important in that it provided a sense of direction and contributed to articulate classroom practices that aligned with the goals outlined in the plan.

For the teacher, writing down the goal on her professional growth plan was significant. Namely, the learning goal became something visible: a tangible reminder that she will be evaluated by the administration at the end of the school year. As an artifact that intersects professional learning opportunities and school performance evaluation policy, the current enrolment of personal and individual learning could serve to mask the complexity of activities happening in the school. Furthermore, she commented that "writing it down" was a way to indicate what was important to her, as opposed to it being "an unwritten goal that I've had for a quite a few years." The use of the poster as a goal in the teacher's professional growth plan, allows us to appreciate how professional learning emerges as an effect of socio-material relations that converge to create a particular reality. Learning, in this case, was constituted by the encounter of several actors, humans and non-humans. The particular arrangement that included the teacher, the poster and the growth plan could be traced back to the administration's capacity to influence the way resources circulate in the school.

However, this example also shows how enactments of professional learning are local, reflecting particular idiosyncrasies inhabiting the classroom. This could be noticed in the selection of the goals and the inclusion of the poster in detriment of other strategies and goals available to the teacher. In this case, it is possible to see how the two performed spaces of teacher leaning, the workshops and the classroom, interacted in a continuous back and forth that ultimately informed multiple realities of practice. In conversation, the teacher intimated that the poster used in this specific literacy program better connected her to the curriculum, stating that the program "… is so fabulous for me for teaching. The poster outcomes are so fabulous for me to revisit my curriculum often" (interviewed teacher). Here we can see a concrete manifestation of the policy initiative integrated in the network of materials and people that enact a particular policy on professional development. The poster, as a concrete manifestation of the policy, is not just a tool that entered the classroom, it actively contributed to shape the actions and practices of the people around it. The teacher acknowledged the poster's influence in her practices and furthermore declared that due to the possibilities of action afforded by the poster, this particular professional learning initiative was more "*realistic*" than other initiatives that could not achieve a material manifestation in the classroom.

The introduction of a new object into the classroom context initiates a series of transformations or *translations* in which actors transform their own practices as they interact with the new artifact. The realities that are performed in the classroom are thereby transformed by the new socio-material arrangements brought about by the new artifact and the other actors' interactions with the object, and thus, educational policy becomes enacted in the practices of the school actors.

Conclusion

In this paper we have offered an exploration of the ontological dimensions of professional learning in schools. Based on examples taken from a study that explored the enactment of policies on professional learning in a rural school in Canada (Viczko, 2009), we have suggested that teacher learning not just a cognitive, individualistic process, but a set of complex and performed assemblages that include a multiplicity of networked actors. Furthermore, we argued that these assemblages constitute idiosyncratic spaces of professional learning that produce multiple social realities. Following Mol (1999, 2003), we suggested that professional learning is performed in multiple ways, pointing to the existence of multiple realities of professional learning inhabiting the school. In our analysis, we identified emerging spaces of professional learning where the policies on professional learning are enacted. These enactments of policies on professional learning provide an example of how school actors, human and non-human, bring policy abstractions to concrete realities through networked assemblages. This presents a challenge to the traditional assumption that policy is a production of authoritative individuals that is transferred down the institutional hierarchy only to be "implemented" by school actors (Colebatch, Hoppe, & Noordegraaf, 2011). In these instrumentalist narratives, when the implementation does not match the intentions of the policy designers, the resultant practices are casted as errors or resistance. We have shown that the notion of policy enactment (Ball, Maguire, & Braun, 2012) offers a situated and context-sensitive way to talk about the transformations and adaptations of educational policy that overcomes the limitations of the instrumentalist models in policy analysis.

We have highlighted the notion of ontological politics (Mol, 1999) and argued that the ontological dimension of professional learning intersects with its political dimension. This was evidenced in the capacity of the different actors to shift, influence and bridge different performances through practices. Our analysis aimed to shed light on the enactment of policies on professional learning. ANT analyses of educational policy enactments show that the complex networks of people and objects that enact educational policies are situated in specific social, cultural and historical contexts. Our aim in bringing this analysis to the professional learning field is to show that when the notion of enactment is invoked, there is a depth to the quality of professional learning that better considers the complexity within which the practice of teaching is configured in schools (Riveros &

Viczko, 2012). We believe that these intricacies must be reflected upon when considering and developing strategies aimed at transform teacher learning.

References

Bacchi, C. (1999). *Women, policy and politics: The construction of policy problems*. London: SAGE.

Ball, S., Maguire, M., & Braun, A. (2012). *How schools do policy: Policy enactments in secondary schools*. London: Routledge.

Benner, P. (1984). *From novice to expert: Excellence and power in clinical nursing practice*. San Francisco, CA: Addison-Wesley.

Borko, H. (2004). Professional development and teacher learning: Mapping the terrain. *Educational Researcher, 33*(8), 3–15. doi:10.3102/0013189X033008003

Colebatch, H. K., Hoppe, R., & Noordegraaf, M. (2011). *Working for policy*. Amsterdam: Amsterdam University Press.

Cordella, A., & Shaikh, M. (2006). *From epistemology to ontology: Challenging the constructed 'truth' of ANT* (Working Paper Series, No. 143). London: London School of Economics and Political Science. Retrieved from http://is2.lse.ac.uk/wp/pdf/WP143.PDF

Dall'Alba, G. (2009). Learning professional ways of being: Ambiguities of becoming. *Educational Philosophy and Theory, 41*(1), 34–45.

Dall'Alba, G., & Sandberg, J. (2006). Unveiling professional development: A critical review of stage models. *Review of Educational Research, 76*, 383–412.

Dreyfus, H. L., & Dreyfus, S. E. (1986). *Mind over machine: The power of human intuition and expertise in the era of the computer*. New York, NY: Free Press.

Fenwick, T. (2010). Un(Doing) standards in education with actor-network theory. *Journal of Education Policy, 25*(2), 117–133. doi:10.1080/02680930903314277

Fenwick, T., & Edwards, R. (2010). *Actor-network theory in education*. London: Routledge.

Hamilton, M. (2011). Unruly practice: What a sociology of translation can offer to educational policy analysis. *Educational Philosophy and Theory, 43*(1), 55–75. doi:10.1111/j.1469-5812.2009.00622.x

Hodkinson, H., & Hodkinson, P. (2005). Improving school teachers' workplace learning. *Research Papers in Education, 20*(2), 109–131. doi:10.1080/02671520500077921

Latour, B. (1986). The powers of association. In J. Law (Ed.), *Power, action and belief: A new sociology of knowledge?* (pp. 264–280). London: Routledge.

Latour, B. (1999). On recalling ANT. In J. Law & J. Hassard (Eds.), *Actor network and after* (pp. 15–25). Oxford: Blackwell.

Latour, B. (2005). *Reassembling the social: An introduction to actor-network theory*. Oxford: Oxford University Press.

Law, J. (1992). Notes on the theory of the actor-network: Ordering, strategy, and heterogeneity. *Systems Practice, 5*, 379–393. doi:10.1007/BF01059830

Law, J. (2009). Actor network theory and material semiotics. In B. S. Turner (Ed.), *The new Blackwell companion to social theory* (3rd ed., pp. 141–158). Chichester: Blackwell.

Law, J., & Singleton, V. (2005). Object lessons. *Organization, 12*, 331–355. doi:10.1177/1350508405051270

Lawrence, T., & Suddaby, R. (2006). Institutions and institutional work. In S. Clegg, C. Hardy, W. R. Nord, & T. Lawrence (Eds.), *Handbook of organization studies* (pp. 215–254). London: SAGE.

Maguire, M., Braun, A., & Ball, S. (2014). Where you stand depends on where you sit': The social construction of policy enactments in the (English) secondary school. *Discourse: Studies in the Cultural Politics of Education Advance online publication*. doi:10.1080/01596306.2014.977022.

McGregor, J. (2004). Spatiality and the place of the material in schools. *Pedagogy, Culture and Society, 12*, 347–372. doi:10.1080/14681360400200207

Mol, A. (1999). Ontological politics. In J. Law & J. Hassard (Eds.), *Actor network theory and after* (pp. 74–89). Oxford: Blackwell.

Mol, A. (2003). *The body multiple: Ontology in medical practice*. Durham, NC: Duke University Press.

Nespor, J. (2004). Educational scale-making. *Pedagogy, Culture and Society, 12*, 309–326. doi:10.1080/14681360400200205

Nicoll, K., & Edwards, R. (2012). Positioning adult educators in discourses of professional development. *Studies in Continuing Education*, *34*, 233–249. doi:10.1080/0158037X.2011.646980

Nielsen, G. B. (2011). Peopling policy: On conflicting subjectivities of fee-paying students. In C. Shore, S. Wright, & D. Pero (Eds.), *Policy Worlds: Anthropology and the Analysis of Contemporary Power* (pp. 68–85). New York, NY: Berghahn.

Popkewitz, T. S. (1994). Professionalization in teaching and teacher education: Some notes on its history, ideology, and potential. *Teaching and Teacher Education*, *10*(1), 1–14. doi:10.1016/0742-051X(94)90036-1

Riveros, A. (2012). Beyond collaboration: Embodied teacher learning and the discourse of collaboration in school reform. *Studies in Philosophy and Education*, *31*, 603–612. doi:10.1007/s11217-012-9323-6

Riveros, A., Newton, P., & Burgess, D. (2012). A situated account of teacher agency and learning: Critical reflections on professional learning communities. *Canadian Journal of Education*, *35*, 202–216.

Riveros, A., & Viczko, M. (2012). Professional knowledge 'from the field': Enacting professional learning in the contexts of practice. *McGill Journal of Education*, *47*(1), 37–52. doi:10.7202/1011665ar

Rizvi, F., & Lingard, B. (2010). *Globalizing policy field*. London: Routledge.

Shore, C., & Wright, S. (2011). Conceptualising policy: Technologies of governance and the politics of visibility. In C. Shore, S. Wright, & D. Pero (Eds.), *Policy worlds: Anthropology and the analysis of contemporary power* (pp. 1–26). New York, NY: Berghahn.

Sørensen, E. (2009). *The materiality of learning: Technology and knowledge in educational practice*. Cambridge: Cambridge University Press.

Stronach, I., Corbin, B., McNamara, O., Stark, S., & Warne, T. (2002). Towards an uncertain politics of professionalism: Teacher and nurse identities in flux. *Journal of Education Policy*, *17*(1), 109–138. doi:10.1080/02680930110100081

Viczko, M. (2009). *A comparative case study of teacher professional learning in England and Alberta* (Unpublished master's thesis). University of Alberta, Edmonton.

Wagner, P. (2007). Public policy, social sciences and the state: A historical perspective. In F. Fischer, G. J. Miller, & S. Sidney (Eds.), *Handbook of public policy analysis: Theory, politics and methods* (pp. 63–78). Boca Raton, FL: CRC Press.

Waltz, S. (2006). Nonhumans unbound: Actor-network theory and the reconsideration of 'things' in educational foundations. *Educational Foundations*, *20*(3–4), 51–68.

Wilson, S. M., & Berne, J. (1999). Teacher learning and the acquisition of professional knowledge: An examination of research on contemporary professional development. *Review of Research in Education*, *24*, 173–209.

When things come undone: the promise of dissembling education policy

Jill Koyama

Educational Policy Studies and Practice, University of Arizona, Tucson, AZ, USA

This article focuses on the enactment of No Child Left Behind (NCLB), the USA's broad sweeping federal education policy, in a persistently low-achieving school in which the majority of students are refugees and immigrants. Drawing on a 26-month ethnography, I reveal the ways in which a NCLB-guided school turnaround plan is enacted variably, especially for refugees. I utilize *assemblage,* a term often associated with actor network perspectives, to study how people, their material objects, and their discursive practices are brought together to implement the plan. Assemblage analysis reveals the struggles and contestations between various entities as they aim to establish the authority and legitimacy of ideas and practices of schooling refugees – most of whom speak languages other than English and have had several prolonged interruptions in their formal education. I trace how certain ideas come to cohere as a more-or-less durable curriculum assemblage, and how they are mobilized, defended, and challenged. The findings reveal that even under the constraints of assessments and sanctions, the assemblage is disrupted and comes apart as new actors, including refugee parents and community leaders, bring unexpected elements into play, introducing emotion, challenging expertise, questioning motives, and resisting the practices produced by the authorized policy actors.

Introduction

Education policy in the USA has increasingly become technical, rational, comparative, and quantified; 'an "evidence-based" approach to policy and a focus on "what works" has come to be seen as efficient and necessary practice, as well as a practical morality' (Gorur & Koyama, 2013, p. 639). Contrastingly, the multiplicities of policy, the programs they mandate, and the practices they aim to influence lend themselves to being examined as nonlinear, somewhat arbitrary, contested, and complex social processes. One emerging and promising shift in the study of policy is understanding policy as assemblages, fluid networks, or entanglements (Fenwick & Edwards, 2010; Heimans, 2012; Nespor, 2002).

Assemblage, a term often associated with actor-network (AN) perspectives, becomes a useful method and analytic for examining how people, their material objects, and their discursive practices are brought together to enact policy in productive ways. Assemblage thinking captures policy as an enactment that draws together an immense collection of people and things that, together, produce subpolicies, devise plans, generate materials, initiate practices, assess performances, criticize processes, and imagine alternative policies. Assemblages – emergent and fluid networks of material objects, discourses, practices, and people – are embedded with the aims, resources, and histories of human actors brought together under the contingent nature of policy, as well as influenced by people and things that are not explicitly linked. The human actors, with the enlistment of texts and discourses, variably interpret, negotiate, and selectively appropriate policy. At times, they challenge, disrupt, reconstitute, and undo policy.

Assemblage thinking is particularly apt, as noted by Gorur (2013) for studying controversies:

> Controversies, or disorderly situations, are exciting places teeming with actors and action. In controversies, no single view or practice has become dominant enough to silence others. A variety of proposals are in play and many possibilities are open. (2013, p. 215)

Here, I apply the notion of assemblage to controversies revealed in a 26-month ethnographic analysis of one school's turnaround plan under the US federal education policy, No Child Left Behind (NCLB).

NCLB mandates that states implement accountability systems that assess students annually and, based on those assessments, determine whether schools and districts are making adequate yearly progress. Each state sets annual performance goals for individual schools and for up to 40 demographic subgroups, including English language learners (ELLs), within each school. These subgroups are assigned performance targets on high-stakes tests. Schools that fail to reach any single subgroup target for two or more consecutive years are considered to be 'in need of improvement' and are required to take actions to improve achievement. Schools that do not improve over time are considered persistently low achieving (PLA) and face a series of sanctions, the most severe of which includes closure. Since 2009, increased funding under NLB has been provided to PLA schools, including the one in this study, which submit state-approved turnaround plans aimed at increasing academic achievement.

In this article, I examine the controversies that emerge as entities aim to establish the authority and legitimacy of ideas and practices for educating the majority of the school's student population, refugees – most of whom speak languages other than English and have had prolonged interruptions in their formal education. I consider how certain ideas come to cohere as a more-or-less durable curriculum assemblage; I trace how people, the material objects they create, and the discourses that inform their actions are mobilized, defended, and challenged. I draw attention to 'productive policy play,' which Koyama & Varenne (2012) describe as the selective maneuvering or appropriation of policy 'as policy directives move from administrative centers to diverse local contexts of implementation' (p. 158). Even under the statutes of the turnaround plan, the curriculum assemblage explored in this piece is disrupted and comes apart as new actors, including refugee parents, teachers, and community leaders (as well as their material products, ideas, and objectives), bring unexpected elements into play, introducing emotion, demanding answers, challenging expertise, questioning motives, and resisting the practices produced by authorized policy actors.

This article draws on data I collected between January 2011 and March 2013 in a mid-sized city in upstate New York during an ethnographic study of immigrants and refugee networks. That larger project traced the connections between social services accessed by refugees and their educational decisions/experiences. As part of that research, I conducted a case study of the public school featured in this piece to better understand the ways in which adult refugees were, or were not, involved in making educational decisions about their children's schooling.

Policy assemblages, meshworks, and entanglements

Actor-network theory (ANT), which was initially developed (and then challenged and reworked) by Latour (1988, 2005), Callon (1986), and Law (1986) as a theoretical framework of science studies and technology, insists on following the ongoing processes 'made up of uncertain, fragile, controversial, and ever-shifting ties' (Latour, 2005, p. 28). It does not attempt to fit the actors and their activities into pre-determined bounded categories, geographical sites, or groups of analysis. Rather than a single, coherent theory, Law (1986, p. 2) suggests that ANT is 'a sensibility to the messy practices of relationality and materiality of the world'; for these reasons, I prefer to use assemblages or AN perspectives, rather than ANT.

Three particular features of assemblage make it ideal to trace the ways in which social actors enlist and join with material objects and socially constructed discourses. First, there is a focus on material objects, in addition to human actors. Objects with subjective investments mediate resettlement practices and 'shape intentions, meanings, relationships, routines' (Fenwick & Edwards, 2010, p. 6). Assemblage thinking shifts attention from what these nonhuman actors are to what they can do. For example, a refugee student's test score on an English test can align the placement of refugees in classes, determine their readiness (or nonreadiness) for learning content subjects, redistribute resources across the school, and redefine the role of English as Second Language (ESL) teachers. More broadly, a designation by the state as a school in need of improvement can alter multiple aspects of curricula, pedagogy, and organization.

The second salient feature of assemblage is the process through which each entity in an emerging assemblage works upon others to get things done. The network develops, expands, and contracts through what Latour calls 'translation' – a process in which different actors come together, influence and change one another, and create linkages that eventually form a network of action and material: 'when translation has succeeded, the actor–network is mobilised to assume a particular role and perform knowledge in a particular way' (Fenwick & Edwards, 2010, p. 10). As articulated by Gorur (2013), the idea of translation 'explores how entities relate to each other' (p. 216). In this article, a district administrator aims to convince a veteran teacher to adopt the standard curriculum of the turnaround plan. A parent organization challenges the turnaround plan implemented by the district through online media, convincing several ESL teachers to partially abandon the curriculum of the turnaround plan. Such negotiations between these sorts of actors are examined, as they 'persuade, coerce, seduce, resist and compromise each other' (Fenwick & Edwards, 2010, p. 4), as well as negotiate their positions.

Finally, AN perspectives contest *a priori* or bounded contexts, such as schools. This is particularly salient for the study of education policy and its effects on refugee youth, who cannot be dislodged from the complex material, social, and ideological conditions of resettlement. Of the nearly three million refugees who have been resettled in the USA since 1975, 25% are school-aged children between 5 and 18 years of age. Most are identified as students with interrupted formal education (SIFE), and also designated as ELLs, two categories that under NCLB are held to particular accountabilities, and are often recognized as the lowest-achieving student subgroups. These youth are constructed and embedded in the materially heterogeneous relations of school activities, such as ESL classes and extended learning time. As the refugees' path to schooling is often not linear and spans multiple countries, numerous actors become invested in their education. These include local, national, and international law, refugee resettlement agencies, and ESL curriculum, among many others, that challenge the global–local dichotomy.

Assemblage-inspired ethnographies of education are unruly as 'what can be observed locally are the ways in which "out there" is produced in the patterning of relations between actors or entities in a network' (Clarke, 2002, p. 112). The work of several scholars (Hamilton, 2010; Fenwick & Edwards, 2010) who put ANT or assemblage to work in studying education notes that what the framework brings to ethnographic methodological approaches is a careful tracing of the

> micro-movements through which little humdrum bits, human and non-human, negotiate their joinings (or their un-joinings) to assemble the messy things we often try to ignore [,take for granted,] or explain away in our everyday words (Fenwick & Edwards, 2010, p. 146)

Reflective of assemblage framing, their scholarship focuses on how education policy is materialized as it is enacted.

The best articulation of what I consider an AN approach has been recently offered by Heimans (2012). His work on policy entanglements, which is informed by multiple perspectives, including ANT, offers important insights into the study of policy. Drawing on his research of policy processes in one Australian vocational and training institute, he centers his inquiry on the entangled elements, where entanglements refer to material and discursive relations in a differentiating world. He argues, as do those using ANT, for the study of 'what is human and what is not, be researched in "process" so that the ways in which people, policy and materiality "emerge" in particular ways' are revealed (p. 315). Rather than utilizing 'network,' he offers, as did Ingold (2007), the concept 'meshwork' to better describe the policy practices involved in policy enactment. This, Heimans suggests, more accurately reflects that 'practice is both always discursive and material [and] reimpose[s] the messiness of bodies into accounts of practice' (2012, p. 318). His study highlights the ways in which entities, or in Heimans' words, 'bodies,' emerge and become linked in policy.

Policy enactment, in Heimans' framing, attends to some of the criticisms made of ANT – namely the assertion that ANT, in viewing human and nonhuman entities with general symmetry, fails to address issues of power and differentials of agency. By postulating how three axes of policy enactment are inextricably bound, Heimans explains how power and agency can be, and are, addressed. He aptly summarizes three possible axes of education policy enactment as a continuum of intra-action. In the first, a provenance axis, 'that which is pre-determined (statutory) enactment to that in which the (statutory) force of policy is able to be unmade through particulars of, for example pedagogic practice' (p. 319). The second axis centers on the material-discursive elements of practice:

> [I]t provides a way in which to think about policy in terms of the ongoing entanglements of knowledge and power and matter, the bodily (human and other) knowledge power matrix through and into which policy ideas mix and have effects. (2012, p. 320)

The third axis 'captures the multiple temporal and spatial scales that are at work in the policy process' (p. 321), to highlight how policy is materialized.

Assembling and disassembling a turnaround plan

NCLB mandates the annual measuring, comparing, categorizing, and evaluating of student test scores across America's public schools. The school in this study, which failed to meet NCLB accountabilities, was labeled as a 'persistently low-achieving school'. It was, during the study, mandated to implement a turnaround plan, which included a new curriculum, extended afterschool and weekend learning time for the lowest-achieving students, a newly hired principal and assistant principal, and a turnover of 20% of the teachers. In this piece, I focus on one aspect of the turnaround plan, the mandated curriculum, the assemblage of which required the enrollment of all the material elements of the plan, the ideologies and discourses undergirding the plan, and the newly placed administration and teachers, as well as human actors already working in and with the school. I pay particular attention to the entanglements of the material and discursive processes in the appropriation of the curriculum for refugee students, who are greater than one half of the student population and who account for nearly all of the 412 students who are identified as 'English language learners'.

Turnaround curriculum: there's numbers, and there are numbers

> You tell me how one curriculum fits all our students – refugees, newcomers, SIFE [Students with interrupted formal education], ELLs, and every mix. That's the only numbers that matter to them [policy authorities]. The number of refugees changes things here and that's not even close to, that doesn't factor into, the numbers they used to make us PLA. It's all test scores this and test scores that. ... There's numbers and there *are* numbers. (Interview, kindergarten ESL teacher, 7 November 2012)

> It's a numbers game these days. You've got to get enough students passing tests. This turnaround curriculum should do just that, get the necessary number of students passing ... [I] don't mean to sound crass, but numbers matter. ... Enough students need to get high enough scores on tests. (Interview, New York State Department of Education official, 23 August 2012)

According to these two accounts, numbers matter, although which numbers matter, or should matter, was controversial. The curriculum, which was based on accountability, aimed to increase test scores and did not take into account the diverse demographics of the students. According to the turnaround plan, the curriculum was to increase students' test performance by targeting instruction to the content to be tested. The curriculum was embedded with the government's efforts to impose order and standardization in education, a set of practices that is complexified by the inter-related, the local, the specific, and the idiosyncratic. Meanings and intentions were 'solidified through the movement of ideas from spoken fora to written policy texts (which both use and produce bureaucratic practices [and textual products]' (Heimans, 2012, p. 320). What came to matter under NCLB, and also in the school's turnaround plan, was how many students passed the tests. Increasing test scores through new curricular materials exemplified the pre-determined, political-statutory (authority) provenance on the first axis of Heimans' model.

However, the resulting pedagogical practice was uneven, and mostly not in step with the plan. The (statutory) force of the policy was, as Heimans' model predicts, unmade through practice. Insufficient curricular materials, especially texts, existed at each grade level, and teachers were often photocopying portions of curricula for their students. Some

ESL classes had no curricular materials. When asked about this, teachers and the principal explained that the publisher was not able to keep up with demand since the curriculum had been adopted as part of several turnaround plans across the state. Even when teachers had the curricular material, many found it overly scripted and refused to use it. According to a veteran ESL teacher, the 'scripts are basically meaningless for ELLs because there's only teacher-directed instruction' (Interview, 11 October 2012). Several other teachers complained that the turnaround curriculum was useless for refugees and other newcomers because it did not have a variation of instructional methods, characteristic of the SIOP (Sheltered Instructional Observational Protocol) Model they had been using.

The SIOP Model, which was developed in a national research center funded by the US Department of Education, is an instructional model aimed at addressing the academic needs of ELLs. Teachers trained in SIOP integrate eight inter-related components – lesson preparation, building background, comprehensible input, strategies, interaction, practice/application, lesson delivery, and review and assessment – into their teaching. SIOP has become known as an instructional model that uses English to extend time for language support while still providing subject content.

Since its adoption, SIOP had been constructed at the school as the 'most effective' model. Through the production, or the joining of selected discourse and design, SIOP emerged, and was distributed across classrooms, study halls, and tutoring spaces, as *the* curriculum prior to the turnaround plan. The new mandated curriculum confronted the teachers' interpretations of SIOP and their pedagogical practices. One ESL teacher described the controversy as follows:

> We've gone from using collaborative approaches and visuals and targeted vocab. exercises [all features of SIOP] to lecturing from a script and teaching to the test ... this just smashes up against what we know works. (Personal communication, 2 November 2012)

Others concurred and admitted that they were still infusing their teaching with SIOP elements.

What arose through the pedagogical practices was a curriculum assemblage that included SIOP materials, lesson plans from the new texts, some teacher-created lessons, and a combination of discourses expounding 'best practices' for teaching newcomers. An assemblage of changing materiality (or that which is appropriated in teaching practice), competence (or what teachers need to know or should know), and pedagogy (or day-to-day practices) emerged. Through the practice, material and discursive elements of the assemblage were distributed across the school (and later across the district), making them 'available for interpretation' (Heimans, 2012, p. 321) and evaluation, as well as open to opposition.

The controversy over integrating SIOP for newcomers aiming to learn English with the standardized turnaround curriculum brewed not only within the school, but also in the central offices of the school district. There, 'the newly established views and practices become enmeshed with other established views and practices' (Gorur, 2013, p. 215), threatening the implementation of the turnaround plan supported by the district. There was not consensus. Even two district administrators responsible for choosing the turnaround curriculum expressed uncertainty; one of them admitted that he was not now sure that it was the best option for ELLs.

Yet the authoritative power of official policy was always in play, and according to 7 of the 10 district administrators I interviewed, the turnaround model would persist in spite of schools like the one in this study that might not necessarily follow it. One district administrator explained, pointing to graphs of increased achievement, comparative tables of test scores, and results of complex 'success' algorithms strewn across her desk:

> Look. All these numbers don't lie. The state's not backing down. This plan can turnaround the PLAs. It is what it is. Principals and teachers need to get onboard with this. ... The student demographics don't matter and that's the beauty of the plans. They work for everyone if done exactly as made. (Interview, 10 January 2012)

By 'scientising' the turnaround plan with graphs and tables, the administrator rendered particular schools, and the people and materials within them, inconsequential. With respect to space and time – or Heimans' third, spatiotemporal, axis – the discursive-material enactment of the turnaround curriculum in *a* school was ephemeral, but the ideas and discourses supporting the turnaround model both materialized, and were embedded in, spatial and temporal relations and settings throughout New York and the country.

Turnaround expertise: there's knowledge and there's knowledge

> I didn't get a good education. But that's why I'm getting my daughter the best ... I learned English in the Kenya, in the [refugee resettlement] camp so that I could teach her English ... I go to school and talk to that teacher and sometimes I take my case worker. I know things they don't. I know my daughter and our home. I know more children, families in the community. (Interview, Somalian refugee and parent of child in the school, 3 June 2011)

> We've got to be clear here. I'm not putting down what teachers and parents and families know, even though we know that parents are not involved in schools here and most of them don't speak English yet. Some can, but not many. They just don't know how to, what it takes to, turnaround a school. ... They think in terms of individuals, my students, my children, my class. We think in terms of schools and districts – whole schools and whole districts. That kind of scale is different. (Interview, New York State education official, 15 September 2011)

As seen in the juxtaposition of these two perspectives, the informal interpretation and assessment of knowledge, or more accurately, knowledges, are elements of policy assemblages. They exemplify elements of the ongoing entanglements of knowledge, power, and matter articulated in Heimans' model. Examining the various ways in which actors perceive, exercise, and codify their knowledge is useful in demonstrating how relying on and reifying quantitative accounts in a one-size-fits-all turnaround plan is not as objective as it first appears. Local knowledge – and here, I include the accumulated knowledge of all interested and involved human actors – which is temporarily challenged and displaced by policy directives, can disrupt and disassemble the policy-directed turnaround plan.

Several ESL teachers spoke at length about how the new curriculum narrowed subject content by requiring them to teach what will be tested. A fifth grade ESL teacher explained:

> We use the gen ed. curriculum not ESL ... we're never supposed to go off this script and nothing else, but we slip in some SIOP when we can, and when no one's looking. ... They think the scores will go up with repetitive instruction and they probably will, but not enough

and that's not really getting kids proficient. (Interview, first grade ESL teacher, 18 March 2013)

The school's ESL coordinator stated that it was even worse than that; she argued that 'language learning for our students is left to chance with this curriculum', and it is only because teachers are willing to risk their jobs that anything at all good is being done (Fieldnotes, 21 October 2013). Through their pedagogic practices, some ESL teachers enacted their emerging roles in the turnaround plan by precisely identifying what was unable to be enacted – the standardized curriculum.

The ESL teachers further challenged the authority of the statutory enactment of the turnaround plan, diverging from expected teacher practices by making their concerns public. Four of them joined with literacy volunteers, case workers from local refugee resettlement agencies, and members of a parent action group to file a petition with the city's department of education – an event that was covered by a local television station. Over 10 months, various configurations of this loosely coupled group, the members of which had been enrolled and mobilized in the curriculum assemblage, wrote opinion pieces in local publications with small distributions (material objects), held ill-attended rallies at school board meetings, and started social media sites (discourse) alerting the public to the dearth of attention given to refugees and newcomers in the turnaround plan. They articulated objects and discourse through their public actions.

As emerging entities in the curriculum assemblage, the teachers were flexible, resourceful, and expansive in their practices. In Heimans' (2012) words:

> These bodies appear to have no time to slow down and the practices, which produce and include them, tend towards disaggregation; that is, the breaking up of processes, so that there are breakdowns in responsibilities through discontinuity. The result is that none of the bodies displays [the pre-determined policy] outcomes. ... (p. 324)

They began modifying the plan's mandated curriculum. On my observations of ESL classes after the meeting, I saw several teachers – the four who joined the group taking actions about their concerns and three others – utilizing ESL strategies that were not a part of the turnaround curriculum. One actually created her own curriculum, complete with texts, online resources, and student materials that she made available for free online.

The discursive material practices of the teachers altered their connections to the principal, who had been hired as part of the turnaround plan, and who had become aware of the teachers' modifications and substitutions of curricular materials. As they negotiated their positions, the entities (or bodies) in the assemblage emerged and reemerged in relation to the others. They were mutually constituted through their 'intra-actions,' which Heimans (2012) following Barad (2007) distinguishes from 'interactions,' that draw attention to recognizable and distinct individuals at the sacrifice of the emergent interplay and coproduction of agencies.

At the beginning of the 2012–2013 academic year, the principal held a meeting to discuss the controversy over the turnaround curriculum's relevance to ELLs. Sitting around a larger table in one of the school's makeshift conference rooms, a group of ESL teachers, several lead English language arts (ELA) teachers, the principal, two literacy coaches, and members of the district's school turnaround department pored over the documents scattered across the table. Math and ELA progress was represented on multicolored bar and line graphs. Five years' worth of The New York State Report Card

Accountability and Overview Reports were in a pile. Grade-specific assessments and assessment scorecards were in the lid of a box.

For three hours, various human actors, using the material objects as support, gave their support or opposition to the curriculum. The ESL teachers, although afraid of their own teaching evaluations, were unanimous in arguing that the turnaround curriculum did not address issues for the refugees and other newcomers. The district members pointed to the importance of standardizing the curriculum for all students. There was contestation and 'much lobbying and confusion' (Gorur, 2013, p. 215). The meeting, but not the controversy, ended with compromise. The ESL teachers could integrate some of their SIOP strategies into the curriculum, but only with prior approval of the principal and district.

Yet, even after the compromise, members of a vocal district parents' organization and several community agencies that worked directly with refugees were not satisfied. Using social media venues, they encouraged parents to move their students to a newly started charter school only blocks from the school in this study. The parent organization held information meetings at the local community action center. There, those with varying, usually oppositional, views explained their perspectives on the turnaround plans in general, and the curriculum specifically. Several of those who attended and spoke told me that they were 'walking a fine line' between their own values and their responsibilities as educators, administrators, and refugee resettlement workers. A law student who worked as a refugee case worker and also an afterschool tutor at the school felt torn. She summarized the tension well:

> We all want these kids to do well. We need to use SIOP and way more appropriate lessons if they are going to learn English and succeed, but then they need a school, too.... If the school doesn't work this turnaround plan, it can be shut down and then these kids will be bussed all over the city to schools that have no clue. You tell me, what's worse? (Interview, 29 November 2012)

As the case worker noted, there was no one obvious solution. In emergent controversies, there are not. Actors are jostling for influence, aiming to enroll other actors in their cause as outcomes are still uncertain.

In fall 2012, 20 refugee students transferred to the newly opened charter school. The parents' organization claimed that these transfers were the result of their opposition to the turnaround plan. This assertion was supported by the records of two resettlement case workers who had assisted the refugee families with the transfers. Later that year, a series of SIOP training was offered by a community organization to educators and the public at a location just a few blocks from the school. According to the training sign-in sheets, 34 teachers from the school in this study attended the trainings, even though they were mandated to teach the turnaround curriculum.

In assemblage, standards, and standardized procedures – in this case, curricula and lessons – become a nonlinear series of negotiations that lead to multiple translations, interpretations, and practices. They were entanglements. As such, there is possibility that a standard way of doing something toward a set goal may be challenged, undone, and even reconfigured through practice. Turnaround curriculum can be, for instance, infused with SIOP and newly created lesson materials. Even though the technical and standardized accounts of the school turnaround plan were adopted as the school's last chance for increasing achievement, 'spaces of uncertainty' (Callon, Lascoumes, &

Barthe, 2009) emerged in the curriculum assemblage as diverse entities, such as ESL teachers and community activists brought new ideas, aims, and concerns into the policy arena. The challenges, contestations, conflict, and tensions across difference invited, as noted by Kostogriz (2002), additional material and discursive resources for 'cultural reinvention, transformation and change' (Janks, 2005, p. 31). The spaces of uncertainty, of difference, or of marginality reflect sociomaterial scales in which students needing language support were discursively reframed.

Studying policy and policy-guided practices with assemblage

The school turnaround curriculum became, what Latour (2005) refers to as a 'matter of concern' – which distinguishable from a 'matter of fact' – is replete with politics. Matters of concern are, in Latour's words: 'much more interesting, variegated, uncertain, complicated, for reaching, heterogeneous, risky, historical, local, material and networky' (p. 19) than matters of fact. The curriculum was thus an object that had become a 'thing,' a matter of fact that had given rise to complicated entanglements (p. 41). It was an assemblage – a network of people, things, and discourse – that once emerged in history became temporarily a thing. It became an actor, a cultural mediator rather than a passive artifact that required actors to respond to it with particular responses. It mobilized human actors – teachers, administrators, parents, community members, and so on – to reshape their daily activities and practices in ways that were, at times, incongruent with their stated beliefs and responsibilities.

The turnaround curriculum could not be ignored without consequences, and so this article began with the responses of human actors, who enrolled other actors in their enactment of the plan, gathered additional material objects to mediate future action, and worked back on the plan, troubling and changing it. The curriculum served as my point of analytic entry in this paper, but I might also have chosen to begin tracing the turnaround assemblage through the plan's extended afterschool program. The key is to trace or follow the movement, the interactions, the linkages as they are made, remade, and unmade. It is to take up or follow the actors' everyday work to reveal how the everyday routines hold together, even if temporarily, how they disconnect, and how they reform in other configurations. As Gorur (2013) demonstrates in her study of the marketization of Australian education, assemblage thinking delves into 'how socio-material devices ... and practices they configure and routinize – coordinate and operationalise' (p. 228) education policy.

In assemblages, a plethora of participants are drawn together to accomplish ever-shifting objectives. There are assemblages within assemblages, linked to assemblages, and so on, and at any one time, some are expanding as new actors are enrolled, some are changing their focus as actors as mobilized, and some are being disrupted and disassembled. Most actors are simultaneously participating in several assemblages. The turnaround curriculum is an entity in multiple education evaluation and publishing networks. The ESL teachers in the emerging turnaround curriculum assemblage described in this paper belong to networks of teachers organized by their union, and assemblages of ESL educators in the school, the district, the state, and the nation. Their exact location can be somewhat unclear, and at any one time, they may be more or less involved in any of these assemblages. Most of us could, however, identify them as part of schooling. It is more difficult to discern the position of those not necessarily recognized as elements of schooling, such as community organization and refugee resettlement agencies – and yet, as we see in this piece, they, too, are linked.

Interestingly, it is often these more 'difficult to associate' actors in a policy assemblage that are involved in challenging and aiming to change the policy. In fact, contestations and controversies that arise during or as a result of policy enactment become spaces of 'conflict and negotiation among actors that would others happily ignore each other' (Venturini, 2010, p. 261). And it is precisely these spaces in which actors find themselves drawn to unclear and uncertain positions in education policy, drawing on and generating material objects that once they ignored, to influence others, make changes, and legitimize their work. These are important spaces at which to point our research lenses if we are serious about studying education policy as enactments and social processes. As noted by Koyama and Varenne (2012), as researchers of education policy, we need to painstakingly discover who is involved, in what ways, for what purposes, and for what consequences in policy processes. And then we need to examine how they link together, the nature of those links, and the constraints, contexts, and situations under which those linkages stimulate action. Heimans' (2012) model of entanglements provides us with a useful analytic with which to describe and understand such enactment of education policy. Finally, more attention given to how policy things come together, and also how they come undone, will likely provide insights into the totality of policy enactment, and the productivity of such processes.

References

Barad, K. (2007). *Meeting the universe halfway: Quantum physics and the entanglement of matter and meaning*. Durham: Duke University Press.
Callon, M. (1986). Some elements of sociology of translation: The domestication of the scallops and the fishermen of St Brieuc Bay. In J. Law (Ed.), *Power, action and belief: A new sociology of knowledge?* (pp. 196–223). London: Routledge & Kegan Paul.
Callon, M., Lascoumes, P., & Barthe, Y. (2009). *Acting in an uncertain world. An essay on technical democracy*. Cambridge: MIT Press.
Clarke, J. (2002). A new kind of symmetry: Actor-network theories and the new literacy studies. *Studies in the Education of Adults*, *34*(2), 107–122.
Fenwick, T., & Edwards, R. (2010). *Actor-network theory in education*. New York, NY: Routledge.
Gorur, R. (2013). My school, my market. *Discourse: Studies in the Cultural Politics of Education*, *34*, 214–230. doi:10.1080/01596306.2013.770248
Gorur, R., & Koyama, J. P. (2013). The struggle to technicise in education policy. *The Australian Educational Researcher*, *40*, 633–648. doi:10.1007/s13384-013-0125-9
Hamilton, M. (2010). Privileged literacies: Policy, institutional process and the life of the IALS. *Language and Education*, *15*, 178–196.
Heimans, S. (2012). Coming to matter in practice: Enacting education policy. *Discourse: Studies in the Cultural Politics of Education*, *33*, 313–326. doi:10.1080/01596306.2012.666083
Ingold, T. (2007). *Lines. A brief history*. London and New York, NY: Routledge.
Janks, H. (2005). Deconstruction and reconstruction: Diversity as a productive resource. *Discourse: Studies in the Cultural Politics of Education*, *26*(1), 31–43. doi:10.1080/01596300500040078
Koyama, J. P., & Varenne, H. (2012). Assembling and dissembling: Policy as productive play. *Educational Researcher*, *41*, 157–162. doi:10.3102/0013189X12442799
Kostogriz, A. (2002). *Rethinking ESL literacy education in multicultural conditions* (Unpublished doctoral thesis). Armidale: University of New England.
Latour, B. (1988). *The pasteurization of France*. Cambridge: Harvard University Press.
Latour, B. (2005). *Reassembling the social: An introduction to Actor-Network Theory*. Oxford: Oxford University Press.

Law, J. (1986). *Power, action and belief: A new sociology of knowledge?* London: Routledge & Kegan Paul.

Nespor, J. (2002). Networks and contexts of reform. *Journal of Educational Change, 3*, 365–382. doi:10.1023/A:1021281913741

Venturini, T. (2010). Diving in magma: How to explore controversies with Actor-Network Theory. *Public Understanding of Science, 19*, 258–273. doi:10.1177/0963662509102694

Teaching without faculty: policy interactions and their effects on the network of teaching in German higher education

Alexander Mitterle, Carsten Würmann and Roland Bloch

Institute for Higher Education Research, Martin-Luther-University Halle-Wittenberg, Wittenberg, Germany

> The impact of higher education reforms on teaching at faculty level in Germany has seldom been explored. Research on teaching at university so far centres on how to teach. Yet, before any (best) practice can take place, teaching requires a specific site where a specific teacher meets a specific number of students. To bring about teaching, teaching loads have to be matched with student numbers, which to a large degree depends on how existing policies interact. Drawing on actor-network theory, we show that due to a peculiar entanglement of the products of present as well as past policies – staff planning charts, curricular norm values, student numbers, block grants, etc. – in several cases administration defines teaching loads higher than the actual teaching staff at faculty level can provide. In order to close this gap, faculties have to accommodate a teaching load that is true to administrative calculations but fictional in reality. Paradoxically, the only way to do so within the given policy entanglement is to use academics for teaching on the premise that they explicitly do not count as teachers: they have to remain disconnected from the teaching faculty.

Introduction

Teaching is a complex task in German higher education as well as elsewhere. In fact, judging from the wide-ranging literature on quality, support instruments and training centres, teaching appears to pose a massive challenge. In nearly all of the cases this problem involves a teacher[1] who should find a way of engaging mostly everybody in his/her class. So while a lot of questions are raised to address the various best ways of doing so, almost no one seems to be astonished by the rather unique fact that a person actually made it in front of a number of students at a specific time in a specific room somewhere in the university buildings. In fact, this specific arrangement and its conditions seem to play a rather marginal role in the discussion about good teaching, at least in the German discussion.

Although questions of higher education funding, legal regulations (notably capacity law), academic work loads and proper management are important issues in research on higher education, they are seldom discussed as interrelated and in relation to actual teaching. In a similar fashion, several reform policies during the last decade aimed at changing specific conditions within one field while leaving others untouched (e.g. new public management-oriented reforms). The overall impact of these reforms on the practice and the conditions of teaching in German higher education has not been explored yet. One of the reasons is that these conditions are complex and a lot of information can only be acquired within the mess of policy entanglement at the faculty/departmental level. Additionally, academics and deans are very often only partial experts on these entanglements. They seldom see the whole picture and rather work with reforms and new classifications as they come along. Furthermore, teaching regulations and reforms differ between the German states (*Länder*) as these are legally (and financially) responsible for higher education.

In the following, we will describe some of the administrative ordering and policy interactions that bring teachers and students together at one middle-sized university in one German state by taking a perspective informed by 'after actor network theory' (Law & Hassard, 1999). Rather than concentrating on individual teachers and how they obey, ignore and resist administration, we will focus on figures normally left in the dark: instruments related to the calculation of teaching capacity within the German capacity law, such as staff planning charts, teaching load measures and standardised faculty/student ratios, and how these instruments interact with policy reforms that change the funding scheme of teaching. This list could be expanded in various directions. However, we will unroll the network of teaching in German higher education from one of its effects at the local level, namely teaching without faculty. Due to the specific interaction of all the aforementioned figures in German higher education, sustaining or even improving teaching conditions is only possible if some teachers are explicitly not seen as teaching. In abstracting from the particular German case, our aim is to discuss the performative effects of non-human actors evolving around students and teachers, how they interact with each other and how teaching becomes the result of contingent relations between various usually separated areas of higher education research. Therefore, we seek to describe the stabilising as well as the destabilising elements of this network and to show how it is constantly changing its shape as it has to accommodate ever new policy interactions.

Methodological remarks

We began our research on the structure of teaching in German higher education by determining the actual teaching load of eight universities on the basis of all courses taught during one semester. The source of our data was the course catalogues of these universities that were in a second step connected with employment data of the teaching personnel at these universities. Some findings were easy to account for on a structural level, such as compensating for a low share of professors in teaching with a higher proportion of adjunct faculty (cf. Bloch, Franz, & Würmann, 2010). However, some findings were rather puzzling: although having the same official teaching load across all disciplines, professors in some natural sciences degree programmes appeared to teach more than they ought to according to their employment contract. It was unclear why this happened, especially as teaching at German universities is often seen as a time-consuming burden that hampers research (Schimank, 1995). Why should a German professor over-perform in teaching?

In a follow-up study, we conducted 15 semi-structured interviews with teachers from various disciplines and hierarchies (including over-performing professors in the natural sciences) as well as five semi-structured in-depth interviews with the deaneries[2] of five faculties at one German middle-sized university. We hoped to gain a better understanding of how teaching is organised on the individual as well as on the faculty level, and to account for open questions such as the over-performing professors in the natural sciences. We came back with a lot of strange figures – weekly semester hours, curricular norm values, staff planning charts, block grants, study places, etc. – and various descriptions of what caused problems in teaching and why it did so. While the problems were similar, the explanations varied. The experts of the field seemed to be themselves entangled in a net of 'something' that they only partly understood and they could only engage with in certain ways. Apart from some studies on higher education law and planning (Braun, 1993; Leszczensky, 2007; Löwer, 2010; Oehler, 2000; Winter, 2013), there is not much research on these figures. In fact, a lot of it is scattered in administrative documents, grey literature and remains as expert but common knowledge to those working with it. On the basis of policy documents issued by the university, the state and the federal state, laws and decrees that seemed to have an effect, power point presentations and calculations as well as by discussing our findings with colleagues and administrators ('There is a guy in the cellar who does all the calculation', 'the magician', etc., were phrases we encountered), we tried to trace back the genealogy of some of the figures in the literature of the last decades. In relating the various sources with the expert knowledge of the interviews, a network of contingent human-figure interactions evolved that formed various socio-material practices that were not necessarily aligned.

At this point, our work started to inscribe itself into the broad research field around what Law calls 'after actor network theory' (after ANT) (Law, 1999). After[3] ANT takes the symmetry of human and non-human actors as a common denominator and prefers relations to essential objects as ontologically constitutive (Harman, 2009).[4] To insist on 'radical relationality' means to regard actors as 'effect[s] produced through a set of relations that is constantly in motion' (Fenwick, 2010a, p. 118). This means our various figures are neither just classifications and standards nor are they simple ordering devices. They themselves have histories and are the result of reform policies and naming practices. They vary in meaning depending on whom and what they interact with and they likewise perform the meaning of those they engage with or in whose name they engage with others (cf. Fenwick, 2010b). Take for example the professor. For a dean, the professor is a stack of teaching loads; for the accountant, it is a deficit position; for the flight assistant, she is an upgrade option; for the scholarly article, he is a reference point; for herself, she is a moral obligation to perform both teaching and research and so on. Without being a non-gendered deficit in the accountant's sheets, there would be no reason for that woman to stand in a seminar somewhere in a mouldy building or fly business class to a conference in Brisbane, where that guy in the first row realises that N. Surname is more than five papers in ornithology and vice versa.

From this perspective, classifications not only perform simplified representations of the 'real world' for some remote administration but also 'saturate' (Bowker & Star, 1998, p. 234) the 'real world's' daily practice (cf. Bowker & Star, 2000). Classifications, however, can become seen as 'simple' classifications if they force a role on something *it* is not. Take, for example, the above professor whose teaching load is distributed by the dean but who is not a deficit position in the accountant's tables. In none of the two relations is he necessarily fictitious, but there is a translation problem. In that case, the whole relational network is under threat (cf. Latour, Harman, & Erdélyi, 2011): either it collapses because no professor shows up to teach the distributed loads or it somehow finds a way of re-aligning the dean's professor to the accountant's professor. The fracture has to be *translated* into something that changes the relations and thereby re-stabilises the network (cf. Czarniawska, 2009; Latour, 1999, p. 311;). In order to analyse this network, we will have to 'stay with the trouble' (Law & Singleton, 2013, p. 489) and explain the actors involved bit by bit.

We will, therefore, stick to prominent actors and introduce new ones as far as they seem appropriate. Here, standards turn into what Latour (1987) called 'immutable mobiles' that seem to maintain their form as they move through space/time. Fenwick (2010) rightly points out that standards and classifications, just like other actors, change their relationships constantly and hence cannot be fully understood as 'immutable'. However, by concentrating on specific classification trajectories, this article *produces* a certain stability in order to make relational changes traceable. Accounting for the network of teaching, hence, is heavily based on decisions about which actors are allowed to develop and which actors remain rather undescribed. Thus, the realities of teaching are not only shaped by the interactions we describe, but also through our way of describing those interactions (Bacchi, 2012; Latour, 2004; Law, 2009).

Calculating teaching capacity

The overwhelming majority of German higher education institutions are funded by the state. There are no tuition fees in the public sector. Rather, there is a complex process of allocating state resources that is described in this section by introducing the main actors involved.

Since the turn from elite to mass higher education, German universities have faced ever-increasing student numbers (Neave, 2010). However, public funding has been stagnating since the mid-1970s, in contrast to higher education policy's strong objective to widen access to higher education. As ever more high school students obtained the highest secondary degree (*Abitur)*, entitling them to study, universities demanded entrance barriers to compensate for the stagnating funding. This demand was strongly opposed by the federal government who feared that the universities wanted to counteract the politically desired ongoing expansion (cf. Bloch, 2009, p. 53–55). Furthermore, the universities' demand created a legal problem. As the German constitution guarantees the free choice of occupation, any attempt to bar persons entitled to study (by the *Abitur*) from entering university is considered as an intrusion to basic constitutional rights. Nevertheless, the federal government agreed that there was a limit to the number of students a university could take, especially as it was constraining funding. The compromise was to allow for taking the *Abitur* grade as entrance barrier[5] if the teaching capacity of a study programme was exhausted, i.e. utilised to 100%. This figure was already regarded as a temporary overload quota (cf. Mattonet, 1982). As students could contest these barriers based on the degree of capacity utilisation in court, a law was needed to regulate the calculation of teaching capacity – the capacity law (*Kapazitätsverordnung*) which is in use to date.

For calculating the teaching capacity, the capacity law assembles at its core three actors: (1) staff planning charts which are meant to provide the input into teaching in terms of teaching personnel; (2) weekly semester hours (SWS) to measure the teaching load of the teaching personnel; and (3) curricular norm values (CNW) that define discipline-specific faculty/student ratios.

Staff planning charts have long been around in the German university and served different purposes. Until recently they have always been connected to funding from the state's decision-making centre. In the seventeenth century, they represented the positions dukes and kings were prepared to fund, while in the twentieth century they were funded and approved by state parliaments and ministries (cf. Bornhak, 1900, p. 107–112; Ferber, 1956, p. 18). With the introduction of capacity law, staff planning charts additionally became a device for determining the supply side of teaching in numbers of teaching personnel.

However, not all personnel teach the same amount. Different personnel categories – professors, lecturers, research associates, etc. – are aligned to different teaching loads. To measure the teaching load, the SWS was introduced. It summarises all the 'spatially dispersed tasks of various duration' (Nespor, 2006, p. 25) associated with teaching – preparation, organisation, in-class teaching, supervision, examination, etc. – in one single administrative category, and thereby achieves 'ordering of a practice at a distance' (Fenwick & Edwards, 2010, p. 85). The SWS in fact is both a timeframe that represents teaching loads and an ordering device for teaching: it not only summarises the 'mess' of teaching work (Malcolm & Zukas, 2009) but also transforms and reduces it to visible time-categories (cf. Mitterle, Bloch, & Würmann, 2014). For the administration, every single SWS represents a certain amount of contact hours: for seminars and lectures one SWS equals 45 minutes, while different forms of practical courses vary from state to state and one SWS may count for 45–135 minutes. Shared or team-teaching divides the number of SWS by the number of teachers involved. Every other teaching-related task 'falls out of the picture' (Nespor, 2006, pp. 43–44). Depending on the state, full professors at universities usually have to teach 8–10 SWS, permanent research associates 4–8 SWS, non-permanent research associates 4 SWS and lecturers up to 25 SWS.[6] Therefore, from the viewpoint of capacity law it is irrelevant how a teacher actually enacts his or her teaching, rather, it operates with SWS containers whose sum defines the teaching load of a unit.

However, staff numbers and teaching loads vary in practice. While the category of the non-permanent research associate indeed has to teach 4 SWS per semester, the individual academic may not. Positions in staff planning charts can be split up upon several individuals who then occupy a third, a half or three quarters of the position which in turn decreases the individual teaching load.[7] Every faculty has a certain number of professors, research associates, lecturers and adjuncts listed in the staff planning charts. They make up the core faculty and translate into a specific amount of funding the faculty receives from the university's budget. Again, the capacity law is not concerned with specific local conditions. Rather, it follows an abstract position principle (*abstraktes Stellenprinzip*) in taking the number of positions listed in the staff planning charts and its associated teaching load for calculating the teaching capacity, regardless of whether positions are split or even occupied at all.

Yet, in another step, capacity law has to translate the calculated teaching capacity (on the basis of staff planning charts and teaching loads in SWS) into a fixed number of students who are allowed to enter a specific study programme. Here, the basic unit is so-called 'study places', *Studienplätze* (WRK, 1989). A 'study place' occupies space in two distinct ways. First, it takes up a physical space in the university, represented in square footage guide values, e.g. 4–4.5 m^2 for one student in the humanities; 15–18 m^2 for one student in the natural sciences (cf. Braun, 1991). Second, it takes up a certain amount of the faculty's overall teaching load in SWS for an average duration of the degree programme.[8] While the first concept of physical space was especially used for the constructional expansion of higher education (buildings etc.), it lost its relevance as the second concept of teaching loads was ruled decisive for the calculation of a degree programme's intake capacity (cf. Oehler, 2000). Nevertheless, disciplinary differences in the teaching capacity deemed necessary for a 'study place' prevailed. Similar to the square footage guide values, a formula that connected student numbers to course types was introduced to account for disciplinary differences in teaching intensity. Broadly speaking, curricula with less teacher-intensive courses and a high share of lectures (mostly humanities and social sciences programmes) require a lower share of the overall teaching load than those with small laboratory courses (mostly natural and life sciences programmes). As a result, the former can supply more 'study places' than the latter. This discipline-specific teaching intensity is codified in so-called curricular norm values [*Curricularnormwert* (CNW)].[9]

The CNW is probably one of the most prominent black boxes in German higher education. Even though it highly influences the faculty/student ratio in highly frequented study programmes, it may not be known at all on the local level. As one interviewee commented, 'Curricular norm value? I am sorry, I have never heard that word before!' (transl.; vice-dean for teaching, deanery humanities). One reason for this neglect is that in most German states CNW are fixed in state decrees and very difficult to change. Therefore, the difference between knowing and not knowing does not impact much on local teaching conditions. In the eyes of the faculty, a pre-defined (but rather stable) number of students has to be accommodated without being able to influence this number. Academics live with the CNW and the student numbers they define. CNW are also black boxes in another sense, as it is rather obscure where they come from (Löwer, 2010). To this day, the CNW of most German states originate in calculations derived from early 1970s curricula rather than contemporary degree programmes. They represent a combination of lectures, seminars and practical courses deemed necessary by whoever made up the curriculum at the time (in most cases faculty and students). Discussions by political administrators, politicians, stakeholder input as well as financial and rough sensibility calculations based on aggregated degree programmes (DUZ, 1978) finally led to a list that contained fixed CNWs for specific degree programmes (cf. Mattonet, 1982). Since then, CNWs have been re-published on a regular basis in curricular norm decrees with only slight alterations and an ever-growing number of listed degree programmes (cf. Winter, 2013).

As a result, the interaction of these three actors – staff planning charts, teaching loads in SWS and CNW – creates performative relations. Its effects are not limited to the production of 'cryptical calculations' (transl.; deanery, natural sciences) that result in figures such as 104 'study places' for one-degree programme. It also functions as a blue print for degree programmes in general. Because in the 1970s a specific combination of courses was fixed by decree, today's degree programmes still approximate this specific combination as the only legal way to control student numbers. Furthermore, over the years the specific combination was altered in ministerial rooms due to other factors (especially financial constraints), which led to a reduction of CNW in most cases. Contemporary degree programmes therefore represent an idealised 1970s curriculum, albeit with a higher maximum capacity (a lower CNW) than originally deemed appropriate (WRK, 1989). In other words, the type of course (lecture, seminar and practical course) a teacher can choose from and the number of students she/he is confronted with while entering the classroom depends on the network around a simple figure, the CNW, that proves to be as stable and very often as old as the building she/he teaches in.

Changing teaching by funding: block grants as part of new public management reforms

Although the calculation of teaching capacity has remained stable until today, other actors have appeared and related to it. One of them is the new funding scheme for universities that has been established under the auspices of new public management (NPM) reforms in the last decade. Prior to these reforms, only those degree programmes were in trouble where the demand exceeded the available study places because funding was not related to student enrolment. As long as funding was mainly built on staff planning charts, a low or high number of students in a degree programme did not have implications on anything other than study conditions (see Figure 1; depiction of old funding model).

This changed when the cameralistic funding scheme of the university (single-entry book-keeping) was replaced by block grant budgets in the wake of NPM reform projects. The cameralistic funding scheme basically consists of several different but rigid funding streams that can only be spent on specific assets during a one-year period (cf. Waltenberger, 2006, pp. 6–11). The introduction of block grant budgets in the state where the analysed university is located altered this scheme: the number of financial assets was reduced and they became to a large degree interchangeable. Consequently, fixed staff planning charts as one of the main funding streams disappeared, as universities were given a (supposedly) greater autonomy in spending their resources. Funding streams were disentangled and replaced by simple categories. In accordance with competitive funding approaches, university funding started to rely heavily on student enrolment numbers. Depending on the degree programme, every enrolled student is worth a fixed cluster price that in sum makes up for the largest part of the university's budget. In other words, in addition to their original conceptualisation, study places have become an income stream. Taking physical space and its costs (laboratory, chemicals, etc.) and teaching intensity into account, the difference between natural sciences students and social sciences/ humanities students translates into money flows. The former yield a price three to four times higher than the latter (cf. Seitter, 2014).

While managerialism claims to order and simplify organisational practice in the university through competition, it often 'makes [new] mess' (Law & Singleton, 2005, p. 341). Efficiency is envisioned as a result of market-like relations through which goods (such as 'study places') can move freely without obstacles. However, neither do the prices vary – a cluster price is fixed and paid for by the state – nor does the replacing of one funding scheme through another make a clean sweep. The staff planning charts had not disappeared but remained within the university. First, they stick to budgets. Having been entangled with the quasi non-dismissible employee status of public service, it basically does not matter how universities accumulate their budgets: a large amount goes into fixed personnel expenses that remain aligned to the staff planning charts (cf. Jansen, 2010, p. 43). Moreover, any chair is endowed with one or more research associate positions. These endowments are set in appointment negotiations with newly hired professors. Hence, while block grants were expected to dispose of staff planning charts the latter were translated into a severe obstacle to institutional autonomy in terms of resource control and especially flexibility.

Second, staff planning charts maintained their prominent position in the network of capacity law. Even though they have lost their visibility in the new funding scheme, they resist their extinction in multiple ways. Students who are rejected to enter a highly frequented degree programme[10] because of their grade can appeal the decision in court by

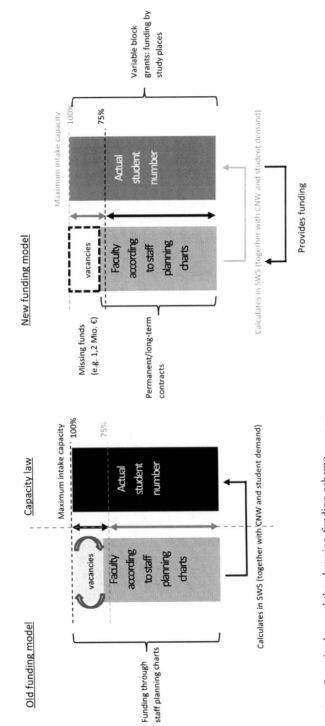

Figure 1. Capacity law and the changing funding scheme.

questioning whether the degree programme has utilised its maximum teaching capacity. The court then re-calculates the teaching capacity in question. It does this on the grounds of the capacity law that remained untouched by any funding reform effort. Again, staff planning charts, teaching loads and CNW are assembled to calculate the teaching capacity. Even if the university claims that staff planning charts have been dissolved by the new funding schemes, the court will draw on the last ones available, no matter how old they may be (administrative court: VG Frankfurt, 2006).

Figure 1 displays the relationship between the old and the new funding scheme and capacity law. Both schemes calculate the student intake number on the basis of staff planning charts, teaching loads and CNW. Both apply the abstract position principle to this calculation. However, in the old scheme funding was tied to the staff planning charts. The number of study places was the result of calculations based on these charts, irrespective of how these study places were funded. In the new funding scheme the study places take on a double role. On the one hand, they are the calculative result of the planning charts; on the other hand, they are the main funding basis for the teaching faculty. The 'mess' becomes visible. By changing the funding scheme the various actors from the different policy worlds (funding and capacity) have become even more entangled and interrelated. In disconnecting the staff planning chart from funding, the 'cryptical calculations' now impact on the funding of faculties directly.

Staff planning charts have remained *within* the university, too, and turn up as part of target agreements between the faculty and the university leadership. While the staff planning charts' overall role within target agreements is not fully clear,[11] they are still used by the university administration as the current basis for calculating the student intake numbers. Being disconnected from the new funding scheme the staff planning charts, however, do not equate the staff appropriations the faculty receives:

> Unfortunately not all our positions [in the staff planning charts] are fully funded. Our central administration calculates [the capacity] as if all positions were fully funded. On this basis the students are assigned to us. But the money we receive is approximately 1.2 million [euro] less. (transl.; deanery, natural sciences I)

Like capacity law, the university administration applies the abstract position principle for calculating the teaching capacity respectively the student intake numbers. As long as funding equalled these abstract positions it was essentially[12] assured – no matter whether the actual teaching staff was in constant flux or student demand was changing. That a professor's teaching load remained in the capacity calculation even if he had left or retired was an institutionalised measure to push for a prompt reappointment of the position (Zimmerling & Brehm, 2003). The new funding scheme turns this picture around: money (block grants) follows student enrolment. Funding is only assured for those positions with legally binding permanent or long-term contracts.[13] While faculties have to take in students in accordance with their staff planning charts, whether the funding for these 'study places' is used to provide an adequate number of teaching staff for the taken in students is up to the distribution of the funds through the university leadership.[14] It may be so that the actual teaching faculty is below the number of the staff planning chart. The non-funded positions in the staff planning chart turn into actors that may have to teach students while they receive no direct payment. Given the situation that the full capacity is exhausted, teaching is due to happen without actual teaching faculty.

Generally speaking, by integrating the staff planning charts into target agreements a more flexible adjustment to the actual student numbers as the main funding source would be possible. This would mean turning staff planning charts from contingently produced actors into long-term representations of student flows. Such an adjustment however creates tensions between the faculty and the university leadership:

> We are in constant discussion with the university leadership concerning our staff planning chart ... This is because the communication within the university is not so easy when it comes to how the staff planning chart should really look like. To some extent the faculty administration has a different opinion than the university leadership. (transl.; deanery, social sciences and humanities)

The resistance to the university leadership is connected with the old staff planning charts. While the new funding scheme aims at making faculties more responsive to student numbers, faculties are historically bound to the staff planning charts, not to student demand:

> Well, and then we have the historically given condition that in one subject lecturers have permanent positions ... they are there and it doesn't matter how much this subject actually is frequented by students ... you can't get rid of them, even if you say 'well, you just have three students in your course' ... one does not intend to do so and in any way this is not possible due to contractual reasons. (Transl.; deanery, humanities)

Because in the old funding scheme staff positions did not originate from student numbers the relation between staff positions and student numbers varies widely between the faculties. Some reach or even exceed their limit in intake capacity and thus would be able to secure sufficient funding for their staff through the new funding scheme. Others with non-utilised capacity turn from good study conditions into deficits, as they lack the student numbers needed for funding their personnel in the new scheme. The strong entanglement of capacity law and funding creates the strange situation that study places become Janus-headed depending on whether they refer to teaching or funding. A lower number of students leads to better study conditions but jeopardises funding whereas an overloaded degree programme provides the necessary funding but worsens study conditions.

Rather than 'unleashing' leading potential under the new funding premises as proponents of NPM suggest (Müller-Böling, 2000), the university leadership is more concerned with mediating between deficient and overloaded faculties. In fact, it not only serves as a mediator between faculties but also between actors from different policy worlds: staff planning charts, courts, diversity and research on the one side; cluster prices, target agreements and block grants on the other side. Mediation mainly works through tactical adjustments while engaging with the faculties. Faculties that offer degree programmes with a high student demand have to be prevented from decreasing their staff planning charts to the actual teaching staff as mentioned above. The difference between funding by students and actually employed faculty increases the university's flexibility for allocating resources – these can be channelled into faculties 'in deficit' with their student numbers. To some extent the occupied study places become disconnected from the staff planning chart they were aligned to in the capacity calculations. In the university administration's tables 16 economics students may fund an anthropology teacher with four students, while the economics faculty lacks someone to teach these

16 students. Flexible resource allocation can be further enhanced by delaying the appointment of new professors or by temporarily blocking the position. In the meantime, vacant positions can be filled by cheaper personnel such as interim professors or associate lecturers, thereby increasing funds at university leadership's disposal. Such delaying practices can hit both faculties with high and with low student demand and these practices are less connected to the actual teaching conditions on faculty level than to professors retiring or leaving. Finally, the decision to introduce entrance barriers on degree programmes with high demand rests with the university itself:

> With 100% … we will not be allowed [to introduce barriers], they will rely on us to get out all that we possibly can, that will bring us in huge trouble … [the university leadership] made it perfectly clear that nothing will happen before we reach 110% capacity. (Transl.; deanery, natural sciences I)

From a legal point of view, a 100% degree of capacity utilisation sets the limit for taking in students. In the 1970s, this was seen as the maximum student number to uphold an appropriate education under overload conditions. However, for the university leadership, not introducing barriers allows to enrol student numbers above the highest intake capacity. It thereby increases the leadership's flexibility in resource allocation.

Strategically, a university could readjust its degree programme portfolio by channelling those programmes with low student numbers into one single degree. For example, a new programme of 'Asian language studies' could combine Sanskrit lecturers, Korean specialists and Chinese professors and in the long run make it possible to either reduce staff funding or increase student numbers.

However, in total, increasing the university's flexible funds further burdens those faculties that have a sufficient student demand. Indeed, the pressure on faculties 'in deficit' rises but the permanent staff, the research profile, and the university's ongoing commitment to a diverse degree programme portfolio run counter to a quick adjustment to student numbers. This translates directly into the individual's teaching conditions. Changing funding schemes, resistant staff planning charts, blocked positions, etc. all translate into a higher number of students that teachers are confronted with when they enter a classroom or a lecture hall. The room may be too small for all the students or workplace security issues in a laboratory may arise that may make it necessary to split the course. If there is no spare faculty available the same teacher may be responsible for teaching now two courses which may lead to either cutting both courses to half the originally estimated time for teaching it or working (unpaid) extra hours.

Teaching without faculty

How is it that degree programmes still enrol a sufficient number of teachers if administrative fictions (derived from the abstract position principle) are obliged to teach students whose number may be above the limit? This question points to further actors that are involved to help maintain the networks' stability at all ends. In the following, we will concentrate on additional short-term funding schemes and the enrolment of actors as teachers that can be only partially recognised through administrative lenses.

Some funding programmes on federal and state level allow the hiring of additional personnel without impacting on student intake capacity. These programmes are said to be neutral to capacity calculations, i.e. they do not count for respective calculations.

Such funds may be distributed to faculties by the university leadership on the premise of decreasing student overload:

> There is a model, which says that starting from a certain capacity ... one receives a [certain sum] per nose ... I think that was [75%],[15] [and with] [95%] one receives additional money for each student ... and if one is above such and such percent then there's even more. And that leads to the fact that some faculties which were hopelessly overloaded, with an overall budget of perhaps three million [euro], had one million [extra] per year. (transl.; deanery, natural sciences I)

While the funding itself is 'capacity-neutral', the funds are allocated based on the degree of capacity utilisation. As a consequence, some faculties profit from this special funding, others do not, and only the former can spend relevant funding on extra teaching personnel or teaching-related infrastructure:

> The money has been spent to increase the capacity. Well, not the student intake capacity but the teaching capacity. All those funds don't count in capacity calculations and that obviously had an effect on reducing the course size. A simple example: seminar before the introduction [of the special teaching funds]: 120 people. After introduction: 40 people. Because the seminar was offered three times. (Transl.; deanery, social sciences and humanities)

The use of this additional short-time funding scheme results in the strange fact that teachers are employed specifically for teaching without counting into the calculated teaching capacity.[16] They can be funded only because they are not teachers in the eyes of capacity law.

Another form of funding concerns research. In the natural sciences, third-party funding for research happens on a larger scale than in the humanities and social sciences. Obviously, being hired for research purposes third-party funded personnel is neither obliged to teach nor does it count for the capacity law. Nevertheless, it may be part of a non-codified enrolment of teachers. At the two faculties of natural sciences in our sample, the analysis of their course catalogues revealed that some professors teach considerably more than they ought to according to their SWS teaching obligations.[17] In terms of capacity, this is a short-term engagement that neither shows up in the staff planning charts nor changes the official teaching capacity. However, the motivation of professors to work extra hours on such a scale remained a puzzle to us. When showing these charts of over-performing professors to the respective deaneries it became clear that it was not a human professor actually teaching this load as it was displayed in the course catalogue. Rather, beyond the professor's name, teaching load was delegated to doctoral researchers – for each of the two faculties there were around 100 doctoral researchers teaching. Half of these belong to the chair endowments of professors and are therefore also displayed in the staff planning charts.[18] The other half, however, is financed exclusively through research funds. This personnel is employed for research only, is paid for research only and should therefore strictly speaking spend its working time on research, not teaching. Hence, the false translation serves as hiding the association of large numbers of researchers to the teaching faculty:

> They don't show up. They are used in the same manner as those on the staff planning chart. This is not fully legal, but we do it tacitly because it [teaching] wouldn't work otherwise. (transl.; deanery, natural sciences II)

Bowker and Star (1998) call this the 'deliberate non-representation in the informational infrastructure' (p. 242). Actors are deliberately disconnected in order to assure the functioning of a network. Yet, there are further reasons for this disconnection. Research staff is not only hidden due to funding reasons but also to avoid being exposed to capacity calculations. It is treated as if it were additional capacity-neutral personnel similar to those financed by short-term teaching funds. When rejected students can go to court and challenge the 100% capacity utilisation of a degree programme, they test all the introduced actors in order to enter the teaching network. To challenge entrance barriers in court, students (or their lawyers) have to prove the staff planning charts wrong and to show that the teaching capacity is actually higher than calculated (Zimmerling & Brehm, 2003). Faculties then have all the more reason to hide their actual teaching personnel. They may even alter information displayed in course catalogues to obliterate their intake capacity.[19] Nevertheless, this does not mean that third party-funded teachers play a role in capacity calculations at any point. In fact, several court decisions have affirmed that such personnel usually do not count as additional to the personnel in the staff planning charts (e.g. state administrative court decisions: Bayerischer VGH, 2012; Hessisches VGH, 2009). However, if they are displayed visibly, the possibilities for legal cases on that premise increase. Therefore, other than the explicitly invisible special teaching funds, these forms of teaching are not visibly codified. Apart from some internal administrative accounting, there is no contract and no evidence that the research staff's teaching actually takes places. But it does.

Figure 2 depicts the matching of teaching staff with staff planning charts. It shows that using hidden teaching faculty or capacity-neutral funds can compensate for an understaffed faculty. However, as funding is connected with the university leadership's aim to exceed the highest intake capacity calculated by capacity law, teaching without faculty becomes instrumental to accommodate an ever-higher number of students without adjusting the staff planning charts. Nevertheless, it becomes clear that to uphold the teaching network, certain actors have to work in such a way that an explicit connection between research and teaching has to be constantly disconnected. Only if teaching

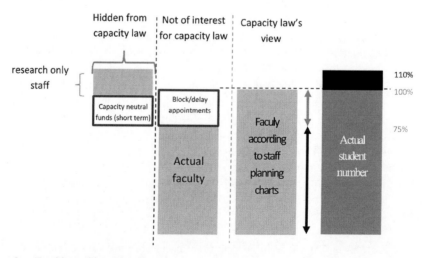

Figure 2. Teaching without faculty.

happens partly without formal faculty, teaching at the investigated German university can be maintained.

Conclusion

The network of teaching conditions at German universities is, as we have elaborated, a complex entanglement that involves various actors with their own history and their own way of engaging with teaching: staff planning charts, teaching loads measured in SWS, course structures of the 1970s, faculty/student ratios informed by CNW, study places, courts, block grants, target agreements, faculties 'in deficit', etc. They are related in such a way that the policies of capacity and of funding can be aligned only if capacity-neutral extra funds and hidden teachers stabilise the network relations. Rather than just taking up one issue, as many studies do, we have concentrated on the interrelations between supposedly separated areas of teaching in German higher education and how they perform on faculty level.

In doing so, we have shown how initial instruments have been strengthened, altered, reframed or contradicted by reformatory actors and how in due course several teaching worlds have come to play that are not fully commensurable to each other. On the one hand, there is the perspective of administration that makes teaching visible through administrative termini that claim to order and represent the teaching conditions. While their allocation scheme provides truth to administration, the administrative termini differ considerably from the messy everyday practice of teaching. What actually happens at the local level 'falls out of the picture'; students, teachers, actual teaching time and funding disappear. What remains are administratively visible courses, taught by teachers that are not associated with the teaching faculty. Here indeed, teaching takes place without faculty.

On the other hand, faculties are able to accommodate instruments even when they are altered: third party-funded research personnel teach but are hidden, faculty teach more than they ought to, courses are split up, access barriers are erected, degree programmes are constantly revised, etc. All these actors are mobilised to sustain teaching *in spite of* the capacity law, its calculations and its enforcement. However, the network of teaching conditions appears to be rather stable, functioning precisely because it is being modified within the faculty, and has been based on administrative modifications of teaching conditions all along.

We were able to account only for a small number of actors and their relations in the network of teaching conditions in this paper. In fact, a new emphasis on quality in teaching that has been enforced through the introduction of the two-tier degree structure (bachelor/master) and its connection to quality assurance measures through accreditation does play a relevant role for this network. However, it surprisingly does not alter the described network considerably but works alongside it, leaving faculty/student relations so far untouched. It is never possible to assemble all the actors involved in a network, not least because the boundaries of networks are not clear. Some actors may be discharged but re-engage in a different way with the network, such as staff planning charts that were supposedly driven away by new approaches but still remain in the university today. There is neither a starting point to teaching in a university nor is there an endpoint. After all, teaching without faculty is a very unique response to a very unique formation of actors constantly altering each other, black boxing certain realms of teaching so that some actors work simultaneously for the network while being visibly disconnected. The network of teaching in German higher education awaits the next policy interaction, be it with faculty teaching loads that are disconnected from any staff planning charts and lack any reference to the actual teaching faculty[20] or through the launching of federal programmes that supply capacity-neutral extra funds on a large scale.[21] In any case, a stable network is constantly being destabilised (and presumably re-stabilised), as new actors gain in prominence and existing actors are hidden or move to a different position.

Acknowledgements

This work originates from the research project 'STRUKAKALE – Wer lehrt was unter welchen Bedingungen? Untersuchung der Struktur akademischer Lehre an deutschen Hochschulen' [Who teaches what under which conditions? Analysis of the structure of academic teaching at German higher education institutions] funded by the German Ministry of Education and Research [BMBF].

Notes

1. Knowing that the notion of a 'teacher' in higher education can sound rather disturbing because it blinds out research activities, we use the term to underline the focus on teaching in this article. However, this does neither favour teaching nor exclude research. While we struggle to actually find a clear distinction of two separable categories some evidence in this paper shows that especially the teaching we are concerned with is not possible without research (funding).
2. These include deans, vice-deans and faculty administration.
3. The 'after' in 'after actor network theory' is a methodological opening point – a fixed time event *after* which ANT evolves in new ways, integrates earlier works and leaves specific premises that lead into the direction of theoretical rigorousness (Law, 1999, 2009). It recognises and includes the multiplicity of studies that encircle this approach without them needing to be absolutely commensurable (cf. Fenwick & Edwards, 2010; Latour, 1999).
4. Harman raises important obstacles to such a view and he may be right (Harman, 2009; Latour et al., 2011). Yet, we follow Latour in pointing out that the focus is more on chasing the 'prey' – here: over-performing professors – than to thoroughly answer philosophers on every aspect of a coherent ontological foundation. The latter is only in so far necessary as to point out that actor-network theory is indeed aware of touching ontological questions while not being willing to sacrifice the "follow the actors"-approach through a re-foundation on thorough ontological pillars (cf. for STS research in general, Lynch, 2013).
5. These barriers are highly volatile: they can come and go from year to year and in most cases create relationships with higher secondary degree grades and waiting semesters. In short: the better the grade compared to other applicants, the earlier a student is allowed to study the degree of his choice. Admission in these terms does not signal exclusivity but overload: the faculty/student ratio in courses with grade barriers is probably higher than in similar courses without barriers.
6. Meanwhile, the teaching load has been differentiated further. For example, all states have introduced teaching professorships with a teaching load between 10 and 16 SWS. Furthermore, in some states the teaching loads of research associate can range from 4 to 20 SWS. So far, these new categories are not used commonly. Another distinction prevails between institutional types: at universities of applied sciences, the teaching loads are significantly higher.
7. In the humanities, it is a common practice to assign only half positions to doctoral researchers. (Ph.D. students are commonly employed as research associates at German universities.) In contrast, in the natural sciences they often get full positions as these face a stronger competition with the non-university labour market (industrial research and extramural research institutes; cf. Bloch & Würmann, 2013).
8. This means the teaching load of one semester is fixed and projected into the future for the regular duration of a degree programme for an individual student (e.g. 6 semesters × 72 SWS). This regular duration does not oblige the student to graduate in this time period. Rather, it is an actor that is both relevant for capacity law and for the individual curriculum trajectory by constantly pointing to a fictive endpoint of studying.
9. For example, the teaching load of an economics faculty amounts to 72 SWS per semester. It offers one bachelor degree programme of a regular duration of six semesters. 72 SWS multiplied by the regular duration of six semesters leads to an overall teaching load of 432 SWS. This then is divided by the CNW for bachelor programmes in economics, e.g.

2.5 (SWS). 173 study places are calculated as the intake capacity of this programme. In contrast, a degree programme in medicine with a CNW of 8,2 (SWS) could take in approximately 53 students. This is the basic idea. As degree programmes export and import courses and have student dropouts throughout the semesters these calculations become more complicated.
10. This is most common in medical degree programmes and psychology. However with the implementation of the bachelor/master degree structures and the decentralisation of admission procedures applicants to various degree programmes (e.g. Japan studies and business administration) take place as well.
11. Inner-university target agreements are neither published nor accessible.
12. Even before the cameralistic funding scheme was abolished staff planning charts were not necessarily fully funded. The responsibility, however, lay with the ministry and not, as it is now, with the university.
13. Any serious resource allocation by student enrolment must then strive to get rid of these positions as they may not meet their intake targets, especially in marginal subjects studied only by few students.
14. We 'black-box' the university leadership and university's central administration as one entity.
15. For anonymity reasons these figures had to be slightly altered. Their relationship has been maintained.
16. The reason that courts seem to tolerate this has to do with the temporality of these funds. They do not build up capacity but only provide additional funds for a certain time period.
17. Data from course catalogue of other universities and inquiries on departmental level provide some evidence that this is a rather common phenomenon.
18. Their capacity indeed counts, even if it is not represented in the course catalogue.
19. During our research we found one-degree programme at a different university whose course catalogue is not publicly accessible in order to prevent lawsuits of rejected students.
20. This has been proposed by the German Science Council (Wissenschaftsrat, 2008) in order to allow for a flexible use of professors' teaching loads. Basically, it is then up to the faculty with which personnel to supply its teaching load.
21. Such as the latest pact for quality in higher education teaching (*Qualitätspakt Lehre*) for which the federal government and the states supply extra funds of €2 billion until 2020 and which allows to hire extra teaching personnel only on the premise that it does *not* count for calculating the intake capacity.

References

Bacchi, C. (2012). Strategic interventions and ontological politics: Research as political practice. In B. Angelique & C. Beasley (Eds.), *Engaging with Carol Bacchi: Strategic interventions and exchanges* (pp. 141–156). Adelaide: University of Adelaide Press.

Bayerischer VGH (2012). *Beschluss vom 17 April 2012* [Bavarian administrative court: Court order 17 April 2012]. No. 7 CE 13.10003.

Bloch, R. (2009). *Flexible Studierende? Studienreform und studentische Praxis* [Flexible students? Study reform and student practice]. Leipzig: Akademische Verlagsanstalt.

Bloch, R., Franz, A., & Würmann, C. (2010). Wer lehrt was unter welchen Bedingungen? Zur Struktur akademischer Lehre an deutschen Hochschulen [Who teaches what under which conditions? On the structure of academic teaching at German universities]. *Hochschulmanagement, 5*(3), 72–77.

Bloch, R., & Würmann, C. (2013). Alles oder nichts? Zur Reproduktion von Ungleichheit in der Personalstruktur des deutschen Wissenschaftssystems [All or nothing? On the reproduction of inequality in the personnel structure of the German higher education system]. In F. Gützkow & G. Quaisser (Eds.), *Jahrbuch Hochschule gestalten* [Yearbook shaping higher education] (pp. 65–73). Bielefeld: Webler.

Bornhak, C. (1900). *Geschichte der preussischen Universitätsverwaltung bis 1810* [History of the Prussian university administration until 1810]. Berlin: Georg Reimer.

Bowker, G. C., & Star, S. L. (1998). Building information infrastructures for social worlds—The role of classifications and standards. In T. Ishida (Ed.), *Lecture notes in computer science* (Vol. 1519, pp. 231–248). Berlin: Springer.

Bowker, G. C., & Star, S. L. (2000). *Sorting things out: Classification and its consequences. Inside technology.* Cambridge: MIT Press.

Braun, H. (1991). Ökonomie der Hochschule – Steuerungsinstrumentarium des Staates [Economy of the higher education institution – the steering instrument of the state]. In U. Backes-Gellner & C. Helberger (Eds.), *Schriften des Vereins für Socialpolitik, Gesellschaft für Wirtschafts- und Sozialwissenschaften: N.F., 181,2. Ökonomie der Hochschule* [Annals of the Verein für Socialpolitik, Society for Economical and Social Sciences: N.F. 181,2. Economy of the higher education institution] (pp. 39–52). Berlin: Duncker & Humblot.

Braun, H. (1993). Die Entwicklung und Bedeutung hochschulstatistischer Kennzahlen [The development and significance of statistical classification figures in higher education]. In A. Neusel, U. Teichler, & H. Winkler (Eds.), *Hochschule-Staat-Politik: Christoph Oehler zum 65. Geburtstag* [Higher education – state – politics: for Christoph Oehler's 65. birthday] (pp. 11–28). Frankfurt, NY: Campus.

Czarniawska, B. (2009). Emerging institutions: Pyramids or anthills? *Organization Studies, 30*(4), 423–441. doi:10.1177/0170840609102282

Deutsche Universitätszeitung. [DUZ] (1978). Erläuterungen zur Kapazitätsberechnung mit Curricularrichtwerten [Annotation to capacity calculations with curricula guiding values]. *Deutsche Universitätszeitung, 33*(1), 38–40.

Fenwick, T. J. (2010a). Reading Educational Reform with Actor Network Theory: Fluid spaces, otherings, and ambivalences. *Educational Philosophy and Theory, 43*(Suppl. 1), 114–134. doi:10.1111/j.1469-5812.2009.00609.x

Fenwick, T. J. (2010b). (Un)Doing standards in education with actor-network theory. *Journal of Education Policy, 25*(2), 117–133. doi:10.1080/02680930903314277

Fenwick, T. J., & Edwards, R. (2010). *Actor-network theory in education.* New York, NY: Routledge.

Ferber, C. (1956). *Die Entwicklung des Lehrkörpers der deutschen Universitäten und Hochschulen 1864–1954. Untersuchungen zur Lage der deutschen Hochschullehrer* [The development of the teaching faculty at German universities and higher education institutions 1864–1954. Studies on the situation of teachers in German higher education] (Vol. 3). Göttingen: Vandenhoeck & Ruprecht.

Harman, G. (2009). *Prince of networks: Bruno Latour and metaphysics.* Prahran, VIC: Re.press.

Hessisches VGH. (2009). *Beschluss vom 24 September 2009* [Hessian administrative court: Court order 24 September 2009]. No. 10 B 1142/09.MM.W8.

Jansen, D. (2010). Von der Steuerung zur Governance: Wandel der Staatlichkeit? [From steering to governance: A change in statehood?] In D. Simon, A. Knie, & S. Hornbostel (Eds.), *Handbuch Wissenschaftspolitik* [Handbook science politics] (pp. 39–50). Wiesbaden: VS Verlag für Sozialwissenschaften.

Latour, B. (1999). *Pandora's hope: Essays on the reality of science studies.* Cambridge, MA: Harvard University Press.

Latour, B. (2004). On using ANT for studying information systems: A (somewhat) Socratic dialogue. In C. Avgerou, C. Ciborra, & F. Land (Eds.), *The social study of information and communication technology. Innovation, actors and contexts* (pp. 62–76). New York, NY: Oxford University Press.

Latour, B., Harman, G., & Erdélyi, P. (2011). *The prince and the wolf: Latour and Harman at the LSE.* Washington, DC: Zero Books.

Law, J. (1999). After ANT: Complexity, naming and topology. In J. Law, & J. Hassard (Eds.), *Actor network theory and after* (pp. 1–14). Malden, MA: Blackwell/Sociological Review.

Law, J. (2009). Actor network theory and material semiotics. In B. S. Turner (Ed.), *The new Blackwell companion to social theory* (pp. 141–158). Chichester: Wiley-Blackwell.

Law, J., & Hassard, J. (Eds.). (1999). *Actor network theory and after.* Malden, MA: Blackwell/Sociological Review.

Law, J., & Singleton, V. (2005). Object lessons. *Organization, 12*(3), 331–355. doi:10.1177/1350508405051270

Law, J., & Singleton, V. (2013). ANT and politics: Working in and on the World. *Qualitative Sociology, 36*, 485–502. doi:10.1007/s11133-013-9263-7

Leszczensky, M. (2007). Hochschulreform und Kapazitätsverordnung—Umfeldänderungen [Higher education reform and the capacity decree—changes in the environment]. *Wissenschaftsrecht, Supplement, 18*, 38–59.

Löwer, W. (2010). Rechtsfragen der Einführung eines Curricularwertes [Legal questions concerning the introduction of curricular values]. *Wissenschaftsrecht, Supplement 20*.

Lynch, M. (2013). Ontography: Investigating the production of things, deflating ontology. *Social Studies of Science, 43*, 444–462. doi:10.1177/0306312713475925

Malcolm, J., & Zukas, M. (2009). Making a mess of academic work: Experience, purpose and identity. *Teaching in Higher Education, 14*, 495–506. doi:10.1080/13562510903186659

Mattonet, H. (1982). Kapazitätsermittlung [Capacity calculation]. In C. Flämig & V. Grellert (Eds.), *Handbuch des Wissenschaftsrechts* [Handbook of laws pertaining to higher education] (pp. 742–767). Berlin: Springer.

Mitterle, A., Bloch, R., & Würmann, C. (2014). Time to teach: Revisiting teaching time in German Higher Education. In W. Matiaske, S. Fietze, G. Grözinger, & D. Holtmann (Eds.), *Labour time–Life time, special issue, Management Revue*. Manuscript submitted for publication.

Müller-Böling, D. (2000). *Die entfesselte Hochschule* [The unleashed university]. Gütersloh: Bertelsmann-Stiftung.

Neave, G. (2010). Grundlagen (Basics). In W. Rüegg (Ed.), *Geschichte der Universität in Europa. Band IV. Vom Zweiten Weltkrieg bis zum Ende des 20 Jahrhunderts* [History of the university in Europe. From the Second World War until the end of the 20th century] (Vol. 4, pp. 47–75). Munich: Pension Beck.

Nespor, J. (2006). *Technology and the politics of instruction*. London: Lawrence Erlbaum.

Oehler, C. (2000). *Staatliche Hochschulplanung in Deutschland: Rationalität und Steuerung in der Hochschulpolitik* [State planning of higher education in Germany: Rationality and steering in higher education policy]. Bielefeld: Webler.

Schimank, U. (1995). *Hochschulforschung im Schatten der Lehre* [University research in the shadow of teaching]. Frankfurt, NY: Campus.

Seitter, W. (2014). Nachfrageorientierung als neuer Steuerungsmodus. Wissenschaftliche Weiterbildung als organisationale Herausforderung universitärer Studienangebotsentwicklung [Demand orientation as a new mode of steering. Academic further education as an organisational challenge for the development of university degree programmes]. In S. M. Weber, M. Göhlich, A. Schröer, & J. Schwarz (Eds.), *Organisation und Pädagogik. Organisation und das Neue* [Organization and pedagogy. Organisation and the new] (pp. 141–150). Wiesbaden: Springer.

VG Frankfurt (2006). *Beschluss vom 14 März 2006* [Frankfurt administrative court: Court order 14 March 2006]. No. 3 FM 2887/05.W (1) u. a.

Waltenberger, M. (2006). *Rechnungslegung Staatlicher Hochschulen: Prinzipien, Struktur und Gestaltungsprobleme* [Accounting at public higher education institutions: Principles, structure and configuration problems]. Munich: Bayrisches Staatsinstitut für Hochschulforschung und Hochschulplanung.

Westdeutsche Rektorenkonferenz. [WRK]. (1989). *Ausbildungskapazität und Ausbildungsqualität: Abschlußbericht über das WRK-Projekt zur Neufestsetzung der Curricularnormwerte* [Educational capacity and educational quality: Final report for the Western German Rectors' Conference on the refixation of the curricula norm values]. (No. Band 1: Hochschulen mit Promotionsrecht). Bonn: Author.

Winter, M. (2013). Studienplatzvergabe und Kapazitätsermittlung—Berechnungs- und Verteilungslogiken sowie föderale Unterschiede im Kontext der Studienstrukturreform [Study place allocation and capacity calculation—logics of calculation and distribution as well as federal differences in the context of the curricula reform]. *Wissenschaftsrecht, 46*, 241–273. doi:10.1628/094802113X13841770055498

Wissenschaftsrat. (2008). *Empfehlungen zur Qualitätsverbesserung von Lehre und Studium* [Science Council: Recommendations for improving the quality of teaching and studying]. Köln: WR, Geschäftsstelle. Retrieved from http://www.exzellente-lehre.de/pdf/empfehlungen_zur_qualitaetsverbesserung_von_lehre_und_studium_2008.pdf

Zimmerling, W., & Brehm, R. (2003). *Hochschulkapazitätsrecht: verfassungsrechtliche Grundlagen; Kapazitätsverordnung; Kapazitätsprozess* [Higher education capacity law: Constitutional foundations; capacity decree; capacity process]. Cologne: Carl Heymanns.

Producing calculable worlds: education at a glance

Radhika Gorur

The Victoria Institute, Victoria University, Melbourne, VIC, Australia

> The OECD's international education indicators have become very influential in contemporary education policies. Although these indicators are now routinely, annually published in the form of *Education at a Glance*, the calculability upon which the indicators depend was an achievement that involved the mobilisation of a huge machinery of expertise, trust, pragmatism and other resources. This paper traces the ways in which varied constraints were addressed, interests translated, categories defined, classifications negotiated, frameworks agreed upon, choices made, methodologies established and protocols developed, as the indicators exercise moved from being nearly impossible to becoming routinely produced. Using resources from Science and Technology Studies (STS), it demonstrates that the work of making such assemblages is both instrumentalist and performative, and argues for an undertaking of critique as a moral enterprise.

In recent years, the Organisation for Economic Co-operation and Development (OECD) has become a key producer of education indicators that participate in policy enactments in many countries. These indicators seek to describe education systems not only precisely but also *comparatively* and *predictively*, with details about a host of parameters, such as the proportion of students expected to complete tertiary education; the differences in the career aspirations of boys and girls; spending on education; labour market outcomes; rates of transition from school to work; teaching time; and class size. The triennial Programme for International Student Assessment (PISA) surveys and their international rankings of student performance generates greater media attention; however, another publication, the now annual *Education at a Glance* (EAG), is a far more comprehensive document, and is deeply influential in policy circles:

> The use of [EAG] indicators for comparisons and strategic mobilization is now a regular part of educational politics. For example, after comparing unfavorably among the 1996 EAG indicators of teacher salaries with their Belgian and German neighbors, Dutch teachers used these indicators to lobby for increases in their salaries. Similarly, in the United States, comparisons of nations across a statistical indicator of dropouts were used to highlight comparatively low high school completion rates in 2000. In an extreme, but illustrative, case, one nation's incumbent political party requested that the publication of EAG be delayed until after parliamentary elections because of the potentially damaging news about how its education system compared to other OECD nations. (Smith & Baker, 2001, p. 142)

In part, EAG's influence derives from the vast amount of information it carries. Despite its name, EAG is anything but 'at a glance' – it is a long and serious gaze that 'examines the quality of learning outcomes, the policy levers and contextual factors that shape these outcomes, and the broader private and social returns that accrue to investments in education' (OECD, 2011, p. 3). As one OECD official involved in the publication of EAG at the OECD explained:

> It's 30 indicators, it's 230 tables, 140 charts and more than 100,000 figures. ... It's 'at a glance' but we have 500 pages, 550 in English. ... And this is one of the flagships of the OECD. PISA is more famous because it concerns more countries and also all students pass the same exam, but in EAG you have very useful indicators on how the educational system all over the world works, and ... we have the outcome, we have the finance, we have the input as well as the output. (OECD official, interview transcript)

EAG is a remarkable document indeed, with comparable data for the 34 OECD member nations as well as several non-member nations. The OECD presents EAG as 'the authoritative source for accurate and relevant information on the state of education around the world' (OECD, 2012, back cover), and, further, that EAG's indicators address:

> the needs of a range of users, from governments seeking to learn policy lessons to academics requiring data for further analysis to the general public wanting to monitor how its country's schools are progressing in producing world-class students. The publication examines the quality of learning outcomes, the policy levers and contextual factors that shape these outcomes, and the broader private and social returns that accrue to investments in education. (OECD, 2012, p. 3)

The insouciance and confidence with which the OECD routinely, annually, produces such a range of indicators to inform and influence governments, academics and the general public belies the decades of hesitation, experimentation, negotiation and effort that went into the development of these international education indicators. As Norberto Bottani, who headed the OECD's international education indicators project for several years from its inception, reflected:

> When in 1988 the Organization for Economic Co-operation and Development (OECD) launched a project aiming to produce a set of international education indicators, only a minority of experts, statisticians, decision-makers, scholars and, last but not least, OECD colleagues believed that it would be possible to produce a reliable, robust and policy-relevant set of international education indicators. Six years later the OECD education indicators are internationally recognised as essential statistics, frequently quoted by the international press, widely used in debates on education policy in national parliaments and carefully scrutinised by civil servants within ministries. (Bottani, 1994, p. 333)

It is this transition from being a nearly impossible project to becoming 'essential statistics ... widely used in debates on education policy in national parliaments' that is the focus of this paper. Tracing how these indicators come to cohere and gain traction, I describe how varied constraints were addressed, interests translated, categories defined, classifications negotiated, frameworks agreed upon, choices made, methodologies established and protocols developed. It is a story of policy assemblage at a transnational, transdisciplinary scale, involving their increasing acceptance as neutral and scientific representations; as artefacts of method, from which traces of the decisions and actions of the many actors involved have gradually been erased (Derksen, 2000).

This story is itself an assemblage, pieced together mainly from publications by Norberto Bottani, who was associated with the OECD from 1976 onwards in various capacities. With a Master's degree in Education from the Faculty of Philosophy, University of Fribourg, Bottani's initial work at the OECD was in early childhood education. From 1983 to 1987, he headed the Education, Cultural and Linguistic Pluralism project at the OECD. He was Head of the OECD Unit for Education Statistics and Indicators between 1994 and 1987, and Head of the Project for International Indicators of Education Systems (INES), the unit that was responsible for developing the international education indicators system which this paper is about, from its inception in 1988 through to 1997, which was just around the time that PISA was being conceptualised and developed. Throughout this time, Bottani published prolifically in OECD publications. Publications between 1992 and 1998, with titles such as *The OECD Education Indicators: Purposes, Limits and Production Processes* and (with OECD colleague Walberg) *Introduction: What are the International Education Indicators For?*, were optimistic about the advantages of having such indicators, but also careful to highlight their limitations. The general thrust was that, in the hands of those who understood their limitations, international indicators could provide valuable information. In 2008, by which time Bottani was no longer at the OECD and after EAG had become well established and routinely used, Bottani published *The oil level, the engine and the car; the stakes involved in assessing the quality of education on the basis of indicators* as one of the framing background papers for a conference on international comparisons in France in November 2008. That paper reflected his disillusionment with the indicators, and even more so with how they are being misunderstood and misused.

Other important sources of information have been the publications of Claude Sauvageot, who was the Vice-Chair of the INES Advisory Group between 2008 and 2011. He was the French representative to OECD's Centre for Research and Innovation in Education (CERI – INES grew out of CERI) from 2004 to 2011, and a member on the Standing Group for Indicators and Benchmarks of the European Commission. Two key publications by Sauvageot have informed this paper: *Indicators for Educational Planning: A Practical Guide*, published in 1977 by UNESCO, and a 2008 paper on the International Standard Classification of Education (ISCED) published in the special edition of Education & Formations to provide background to a conference on international indicators. The *Guide* was a result of his work in indicator development in a number of African nations, and provides advice to governments and indicator developers on what makes a good indicator and how to develop indicators. Other firsthand accounts that informed this paper were those of John Smyth, who was associated with UNESCO from 1972–2000, and of Stephen Heyneman who was with the World Bank from 1977 to 1998. Both Smyth and Heyneman wrote about the International Classification of Education (ISCED) which underpin the OECD international education indicators.

The paper is set out as follows: a brief introduction to Science and Technology Studies (STS) and 'sociology of measurement', which explains the theoretical approach used in this study is followed by an explanation of indicators and how they are different to statistics. After that, I tell the story of the OECD indicator development project. The section that follows analyses the changing roles of scientists – statisticians, education and assessment experts, social scientists and psychometricians – as the project progressed. Further discussion follows about how 'calculable worlds' are produced. The paper concludes with an argument for the moral imperative of recognising and critiquing the performativity of contemporary policy enactments.

STS and 'sociology of measurement'

The methodological and analytical approach in this paper is informed by STS (sometimes known as 'Science Studies' or 'Science, Technology and Society'). From its origins in the early 1960s, STS has drawn together historians and philosophers of science, sociologists, anthropologists, economists and scholars in political and legal sciences. Seeing science not only as a human endeavour, but also as a social system, STS scholars reject dichotomies such as nature and science, and society and culture. The central concern of STS is to understand how knowledge is produced, mobilised and validated, how it circulates and how it comes to be challenged. This provides a very useful way to study governance modes such as 'evidence-based' policy making, since science and the state are seen as co-produced (Jasanoff, 2004). STS provides the tools by which we might:

> explore how knowledge-making is incorporated into practices of state-making, or of governance more broadly, and, in reverse, how practices of governance influence the making and use of knowledge. States, we may say, are made of knowledge, just as knowledge is constituted by states. ... Knowledge, in particular, is seen as crystallising in certain ontological states – organiszational, material, embodied – that become objects of study in their own right. (Jasanoff, 2004, p. 3)

The study of the interplay between the state and statistics has been the focus of some STS scholars, who have elaborated the how statistics became an invaluable and necessary means of governing large and complex provinces. Tracing the history of statistics, Desrosières (1998) explored 'the politics of large numbers', and described how the practices of scientists and the meanings attached to sciences change over time, and how these changes influenced, and were influenced by, the needs of state-making. Porter (1995) described how it is that numbers have come to be trusted and how 'objectivity' has come to be attached to numbers. Scott (1998) described how order and measurement make governance possible, and how the very act of ordering and measuring the world also changes the world. STS thus offers useful concepts with which to study the imbroglio of knowledge-making and state-making that has made the world of education calculable and comparable.

Latour's work on tracing the practices of 'science in action' (Latour, 1987, 1999; Latour & Woolgar, 1979) guides my methodological approach in this study; I regard the development of international education indicators as *science in the making*, much as Latour approached the studies of scientists in laboratories. My focus is on the practices by which OECD's international education indicators, once thought to be nearly impossible to produce, cohered as a viable assemblage and are now routinely and annually produced and widely used.

Woolgar's 'sociology of measurement technologies' (Derksen, 2000; Gorur, 2014; Woolgar, 1991b) has been particularly useful to this study of the practices of *measurement*. Regarding measurement as a 'technology', Woolgar draws attention to the 'instrumentalism' of measurement practices (the ways in which things are 'made to work' in a pragmatic sense) and the use of instruments (in this case, surveys, methodologies, calculations and models). Another crucial aspect of such a sociology is understanding measurements as not merely *descriptive*, but *productive* (Knorr Cetina, 1999) or *performative* (Law, 2009a; Pickering, 1995) i.e., they are 'world making' processes. As soon as the measurement exercise begins, it acts upon the world, changing priorities and influencing behaviours, policies and practices. In telling this abbreviated history of the OECD indicators, I focus on their *instrumentalism* as well as their *performativity*.

Indicators – more than mere 'statistics'

Quantification and statistical mapping have been features in education since the 1850s, when education came to be recognised as a field of statistical inquiry. For many decades, the data collected included the numbers of schools, students enrolled and teachers employed. Sauvageot (1997) suggested that such statistical information was not very useful, because data were often not accurate, let alone timely or consistent, and there were too many details. Crucially, they did not include any *analysis*. What a busy policy maker needed, Sauvageot argued, were *indicators*:

> A decision maker needs more analytical and relevant information, which is presented in a user-friendly way. The development of an *indicator system*, which is updated regularly, is essential if information is to be used properly. (Sauvageot, 1997, p. 3, my emphasis)

Indicators are different to mere statistics in significant ways. They are *selected statistics* specifically *designed to inform policy makers* about the state of the education system (Blank, 1993). They anticipate policy questions and provide information for policy decisions. They often combine data from multiple sources, including data specifically collected within certain regulated, purpose-built frameworks to facilitate comparison:

> Uniquely different from the usual policy-related statistical analysis, statistical indicators are derived measures, often combining multiple data sources and several 'statistics' that are uniformly developed across nations, are repeated regularly over time, and have come to be accepted as summarizing the condition of an underlying complex process. (Smith & Baker, 2001, p. 141)

Indicators are thus *purposefully processed* according to assumptions about how education systems function, using mathematical models that inscribe the assumed relationships. They are not self-explanatory; rather, their meanings are connected with the situations within which the measures are constructed (Jaeger, 1978). They can be constructed to map and represent 'the combined effect of several variables, including exogenous factors' (Mainguet & Baye, 2006, p. 154). Indicators thus wrap up complex relations into a simple shorthand (Cullather, 2007).

The function of indicators is not to identify or assess problems, but to alert policy makers to them, and to help identify and measure the seriousness of the problem, rather like a warning signal on a dashboard. As Sauvageot (1997, p. 17) explained, 'When the light goes on, a specialist has to find out why, and then find the solution to the problem'. Good indicators, according to Sauvageot, are constructed around the most important policy phenomena and policy objectives of an education system, and should describe education systems simply and precisely; provide a general overview; provide points of comparison and other analysis, including trends over time; and report on diversities or disparities.

The making of the OECD education indicators

Established as an organisation focused on economics, there was initially no explicit mention of education as an area of concern for the OECD. However, an awareness of the relationship between social and economic factors, and the idea that education could contribute to economic growth, led to its involvement in education in the 1960s. In 1968, it set up the Centre for Educational Research and Innovation (CERI). In the 1970s and 1980s, CERI research focused on early childhood (Bottani headed the Early Childhood Project) and the transition of young people into the life of work. In the 1990s, amid growing discourses and practices of globalisation, CERI began to actively facilitate an exchange of views and information on education between countries.

The OECD's early efforts to develop international education indicators in the 1970s were daunted by the challenges of comparability and the lack of data, but interest in setting up international indicators emerged again strongly in the 1980s. In 1988, the International System of Education Indicators (INES) grew out of CERI to explore more vigorously the feasibility of developing a set of rigorous international education indicators for its member nations. Norberto Bottani, who headed the INES project from its inception for nearly a decade, reports that the purpose of the project was to 'gather, process, improve, and report statistics and indicators on education and related fields' (Bottani, 1996, p. 279). The project came to be seen as urgent following the sense of crisis in education that ensued after the publication of the influential *A Nation at Risk* (National Commission on Excellence in Education, 1983) in the USA. The type and quality of data available at the time were considered inadequate for comparing systems and improving performance (Bottani, 1996).

As member nations' desire for robust international indicators gathered force, a conference was organised by the US Department of Education and the OECD Secretariat in 1987 in Washington, DC, attended by representatives from 22 member nations, along with invited experts and observers from OECD nations (Bottani & Walberg, 1992). Two important points emerged from this conference: international benchmarks and comparisons had become 'an integral component of the improvement of the quality of education'; and there was a broad understanding that schooling needed to be improved, and data were needed to do that (Bottani & Walberg, 1992, p. 7).

Another conference soon followed at Poitiers, where 'the need for better and more comprehensive information about the outcomes of education' (Bottani & Walberg, 1992, p. 8) was emphasised. This meant going beyond the types of data (enrolment, number of teachers etc.) that were required for 'management' in an era of massive expansion of education provision, and towards a focus on data on the *quality* and the *outcomes* of education.

The main challenges facing INES were the lack of good statistical data, and the weak degree of comparability of the data that were available (Bottani, 1994, p. 334). In addition to these technical issues, INES had to grapple with a complex array of ambitions, priorities, fears and pressures:

> [T]here were many sources of pressure aiming to stifle or modify the project right from the start. In the coalition of opponents, we find the following: education statisticians with

scientific claims condemning the indicators' imprecision and the biased view of education they convey; representatives of teacher associations with political arguments contesting the existence of the education quality crisis, particularly in the public sector; a wide range of teachers or specialists in the education sciences engaged in pedagogical innovations and progressive educational movements, invoking ethical arguments condemning the governments' intent to introduce new forms of education standards based on new public administration techniques, public sector governance and administration performance management. (Bottani, 2008, p. 16)

Early on, one of the big debates was which indicators to include, and how many indicators should be published. A wide range of indicators would address issues important to a number of countries. However, having too many indicators would make them difficult to navigate and more likely to be ignored. Not all countries produced the data that were needed for important indicators, and would need to invest funds to collect them for the purpose of developing new indicators. All this required negotiation between the users and the providers of data.

The recognition that the project could never be perfect was key to its feasibility. It was also clear that this enormous and challenging task could only be accomplished with a great deal of cooperation and goodwill. Several voluntary networks sprang up to assume different tasks in what has been described as 'one of the largest educational research efforts ever carried out':

By the completion of the exploratory and development phases of the indicators in 1991, several hundred policy makers, senior government staff and leading scholars had been involved. Measured by such involvement, the scope of the variables and the hundreds of millions of educational staff and students counted and surveyed, the OECD indicators project is undoubtedly one of the largest educational research efforts ever carried out (Walberg & Zhang, 1998, pp. 55–56)

As a result of this massive effort, a report was produced in 1991, and was discussed in a meeting in Lugano between the producers of the indicators and policy makers who would used the indicators. This meeting generated a great deal of debate, particularly around the inclusion of student attainment data. Given its uneven quality, statisticians were unwilling to include attainment data, but given their assumed importance, policy makers were keen to include them. Another challenge was deciding how many and which indicators to include and which ones to abandon.

The following year, the report was modified and published as the first EAG 1992, with some student attainment indicators included. EAG 1993 and 1995 followed. From then on, EAG has been published annually, and over time has grown to include a number of new indicators, as well as reporting on more education systems. No longer 'at a glance', the report produces indicators under following headings (OECD, 2012):

A. The output of educational institutions and the impact of learning
B. Financial and human resources invested in education
C. Access to education, participation and progression
D. The learning environment and the organisation of schools

The move from the initial tentativeness to the confident annual publication of EAG is a story of 'science in the making', involving many processes of 'ordering' (Berg & Timmermans, 2000; Bowker & Star, 2000; Law, 1994) to standardise a diverse world. In the next section, I elaborate a small part of the fascinating story of how the OECD made the world calculable. The focus is on the changing fates of science and scientists – the measurement experts, the statisticians and the assessment experts – in the move from the early attempts at developing indicators in the 1970s, to the current routine, annual publication of EAG.

Science serving policy: sacrificing precision and purity

The theoretical and scientific challenges of the task of developing international indicators were well known to the OECD experts long before INES was set-up. The OECD had first begun developing education indicators in the 1970s. In 1973, it published *A System of Education Indicators to Guide Public Policy Decisions,* which attempted to measure the influence of education on social well-being (Bottani, 2008). With this very first attempt, the experts on the working group came up against a significant conceptual conundrum. In determining the facts that affected education and social well-being, 'internal factors' (relating to individuals) and 'external factors' (relating to macro or societal issues) were inextricably linked together and could not be meaningfully extricated for analysis. The dual role of these factors as both inputs and outputs confounded measurement – were they 'parameters' or 'variables'? The response from the working group to these conundrums was to abandon the search for a workable theoretical model, and instead build the indicators around the notion of *usability*:

> The group of experts responsible for drawing up this first OECD report on education indicators concluded by deciding to adopt a methodological approach which was unusual in scientific circles of the time, abandoning as it did the idea of developing a theoretical model of the education system. (Bottani, 2008, p. 14)

Several rationalisations were used to justify the adoption of this 'unusual' methodological approach such as constraints of time and 'great political pressure on the group of experts to deliver an *operational* set of indicators':

> The group realised that it could not initiate lengthy preliminary discussions on a universal model of education system because an agreement would probably never be reached and so it opted for an empirical approach based on the study of national education-policy objectives. This led to developing a set of 46 indicators but these were never calculated, given that *the project's fundamental scientific ambition was inconsistent with the available means and the interests of the government authorities which would have had to fund the initiative.* And so the social science specialists were unable to see their project through to its conclusion. It was a failure. (Bottani, 2008, p. 14, my emphasis)

The publication of *A Nation at Risk* in 1983 generated a panic about the quality of education systems, prompting renewed efforts to generate international indicators.

One of the challenges to developing a sound conceptual framework to underpin the choice of indicators is that a large number of factors influence educational outcomes (Bottani, 1998). Moreover, their impact depends on the presence of a host of other factors. Because it is not possible to measure all the factors that affect student attainment, it would be reasonable to include those factors which are considered relevant by most nations. But agreement on relevant factors was not easy to obtain. Therefore, the working groups had to choose which indicators would be most useful, and '[t]hese choices are neither simple nor neutral' (Bottani, 1998, p. 62).

The OECD adopted a very simple input/output conceptual framework with a view to producing broad information about education systems which, whilst not suitable for detailed analysis of relationships between resource investment and results, would nevertheless serve to 'raise certain relevant questions at the macro-economic level' (Bottani, 1998, p. 63).

So from the beginning, INES regarded this project as one where science was in the service of policy. Rather than fuss about precision and purity of methodology, a pragmatic approach was taken, using the rationale that imperfect data were better than no data at all. Indeed, an insistence on 'statistical purity' was seen as obstructionist:

> The lack of truly comparative data has been used as a block to the development of indicators and to question their validity and reliability. ... In developing a set of education indicators, it is ... *important to refrain from applying an overly rigorous test for the validity of the indicators,* and rejecting provisional measures or organising schemes because they do not account for all of the complexities of education and society. *The point is that indicators are not primarily designed for scientific research.* They can be useful in a more limited and practical way, even if they do not account fully for these complexities. (Bottani, 1994, p. 335, my emphasis)

Thus distinctions were made between a 'scientific research' enterprise on the one hand, and a 'practical' policy enterprise on another. At this point, not taking a 'research-oriented' approach was seen as sufficient, since the project was not intended to be used to make causal inferences or any detailed evaluations:

> In order to produce policy-relevant variables that can be clearly and succinctly summarized, presented and considered, it was not necessary to adopt a complex and research-oriented model ... *The indicators were deliberately not organized according to a 'model'. A model would imply a sophisticated, causal connection among indicators; it is not reasonable to assume that the variables represented by these indicators function in these ways.* From the very beginning of the INES project there was consensus about the fact that the organization and the selection of the data was not compatible with a causal model. (Bottani, 1998, p. 63, my emphasis)

Taking a less scientifically rigorous approach was seen as a way to prevent too much from being made of the indicators. This policy-orientation meant that the scientists were prepared not to apply the same criteria of validity and soundness as they would, had it been a 'research project'.

Which indicators to include?

Another major challenge was how to contain the number of indicators. Realities always appear to exceed the capacity of the metrics that describe them. Given the range of factors that influence student attainment, the scientists were faced with the tension between being adequately descriptive and adequately usable:

> At the first INES General Assembly held in Semmering (Austria) in 1989, an initial list of some 160 indicators was established, but not discussed, everybody being aware that a set of 160 indicators was unmanageable and moreover unacceptable for policy makers. At the second General Assembly in Lugano (Switzerland) in 1991, this figure was reduced to an

'ideal' list of some 50 indicators, derived from a conceptual framework which provided guiding principles for the development of a set of international indicators. It took three editions of EAG [Education at a Glance] to come close to the ideal number of indicators. (Bottani, 1996, pp. 280–281)

These challenges encouraged the adoption of a 'flexible organising framework' 'using both *conceptual* and *pragmatic* bases and incorporating policy concerns' (Bottani, 1994, p. 335, his emphasis). Bottani went on to elaborate:

> An approach of this nature seems to be the most appropriate way to organise comparative international data on education for a number of reasons. First, these indicators will be used less for narrow, immediate management purposes and more for global analysis of general trends and differences among countries. Second, the issues important to various countries will vary somewhat, so these cannot be used as an organising principle. Thirdly, this approach encompasses the different intellectual traditions of OECD member countries and draws strength from the synergy of the combined approaches. Finally a systematic conceptual view of education has emerged that seems to have general acceptance and validity. (Bottani, 1994, p. 335)

The hope that the indicators would be used 'less for narrow, immediate management purposes and more for global analysis of general trends and differences' appears naïve in hindsight. Once the indicators enter the world and begin to circulate, it becomes very difficult to control how they will be used. Footnotes, cautionary prefaces and technical manuals are quite ineffective in stopping causal inferences from being made. As Latour (1987) has warned, the fate of facts is in the hands of the user.

Scientists lose ground

As a consequence of panic with regard to the quality of education and the quality of data to support policies, following *A Nation at Risk*, 'the players' involved in the decisions about education indicators were increasingly policy makers rather than the scientists and researchers:

> In the third phase, the players change; they are no longer the specialists in social or education sciences but the policy-makers themselves, those with the responsibility of management and change in education systems. Their appearance on the indicator scene takes place between 1987 and 1992 following the crisis and uncertainty surrounding the quality of teaching and education systems. (Bottani, 2008, p. 16)

The chaotic jumble of priorities and passions of the 1970s and 1980s resolved into a situation where policy makers became the dominant stakeholders, being the prime users – *and funders* – of the indicators. So the report with the new indicators, developed by INES and presented at the 'international meeting of indicator creators and decision-makers' (Bottani, 2008, p. 16) in Lugano for discussion, was presented to a meeting where policy makers had a dominant role. Here, after a heated debate, it was decided to include education attainment data into the report, and to publish it as the first EAG (1992):

> It was following an intense discussion [between] opposing policy-makers and scientists during the Lugano plenary sessions that the member countries mandated OECD with revising the prototype set of indicators to include a section on student attainment, using the very patchy data available on the international scene at that time. (Bottani, 2008, p. 16)

The Lugano meeting can be seen as a watershed moment in the relations between the scientists and the policy makers. It marked the occasion when scientists started to lose their grip even on the 'production' side of the indicators, let alone their 'use' side. At the beginning, measurement experts, education experts and social science experts – the scientists – sought input from policy makers to understand what type of data might be useful to them. They translated this into measurement practices as best they could. In devising these indicators, they refrained from insisting on precision and did not quibble too much about validity. But they still had control over how much was compromised. With the 1991 meeting and the forced agreement to include student attainment data, the control appears to have been wrested from the statisticians and social scientists and assessment experts, and placed in the hands of the government officials, with psychometricians as allies. As Bottani elaborates in an article in the *International Journal of Educational Research*:

> It is evident that OECD did not find appropriate data for producing a stable set of achievement indicators which provide information expected by the public, users of education systems and policy makers (OECD, 1995). In EAG 3, OECD was obliged to use, for the second time, data from the 1991 IRA Reading Literacy Survey (Elley, 1992). In EAG 2, reading literacy data had been used for calculating three standard indicators on student achievement: multiple comparisons, student score distributions, and within and between school variances. In the third edition, the same data were used for calculating an indicator on the progress in reading between the ages of 9 and 14. The survey's background questionnaires were used for calculating a second indicator on the amount of reading, based upon the frequency of reading as reported by 14-year-olds. (Bottani, 1996, pp. 283–284)

This use of the same data to make multiple inferences, and using data to provide information for which it is not designed, was anathema to science. This could be discussed in a research journal, but with policy makers playing a more dominant role within the OECD, the scientists were forced to include some very uncertain attainment results. So disgruntled was Bottani with this use of scientifically unacceptable data, that he notes: 'one can get the impression that these indicators have been invented to avoid leaving empty cells in the subgroup of student achievement' (Bottani, 1996, p. 284).

The obsession with performance indicators

In the years that followed, the focus on student attainment did not diminish in any way. In the 2000s, which Bottani (2008) describes as a decade of 'obsession with performance indicators and the triumph of comparative psychometry', a number of changes were made, including improvements in the quality of data, a modification of the theoretical framework underpinning the indicators, and, perhaps the most significant of all, the launch of PISA, reflecting the rising importance of student attainment indicators.

> The most striking result of this phase is the increased importance given to performance indicators. There were 9 of them in the 2001 edition where a distinction was still made between a section dealing with 'performance at individual and social levels, and on the labour market' (5 indicators) and student attainment (4); in the 2002 edition, they increased to 14; 15 in 2003; and 12 in 2004. With the 2002 edition, the section concerning the set of 'performance' indicators which was the last item in the Education at a Glance index for some ten years, was moved up to take position as the first item. (Bottani, 2008, p. 17)

ASSEMBLAGE, ENACTMENT, AND AGENCY

What started out as a project to provide broad indicators as a useful basis for 'global analysis of general trends' rather than 'narrow, immediate management purposes' changed dramatically as the outcomes indicators became more and more important and occupied pride of place in EAG. The focus on student assessment brought to the fore another community of experts – psychometricians – who appeared to gain traction with policy makers. The focus on outcome data dramatically changed EAG:

> the conceptual framework and organisation of education indicators was changed in 2002, without any truly democratic debate on the subject. All of a sudden, a decade after the publication of the first set of international education indicators which, after much hesitation and precaution, included five performance indicators labelled 'experimental and temporary', at the heart of the most renowned set of education indicators in the world, we find performance indicators based on data collected during a mass assessment programme designed to serve the cause and processed using specific psychometric methodologies imposed by an influential scientific community. (Bottani, 2008, p. 18)

The issue for Bottani with the kind of inferences encouraged by the inclusion of such performance data in EAG is that the OECD confuses 'indicators' with 'assessment'. Indicators were intended to merely alert policy makers to potential problems, signalling the need for further assessment of the system and the search for possible remedies. But EAG had now come to present itself as an *assessment of education systems*, combining in a single framework a host of diverse entities from shifts in systems to indicators on education provision to assessment of individual attainment and system efficiency.

The curse of success

The move from the first hesitant steps amidst scepticism about the feasibility of the project, to its confident and strident assertions about all manner of information about education systems was now complete. The first EAG (1992), a bilingual document in French and English, was 150 pages long. The second, 1993, had already doubled in size to 300 pages. By 1995, the French and English versions were published separately and each was 370 pages long (Bottani, 2008). Today it stands at 550 pages, as more and more entities have come within the fold of these OECD indicators.

The obsession with performance data is now closely coupled with a tendency to make a range of causal inferences. The early cautions about using the indicators only as broad-brush descriptions rather than evaluations have been long forgotten. The OECD indicators have now become institutionalised and deeply entrenched in policy making processes in many countries (Smith & Baker, 2001).

The 'numbers people' within the OECD continue to be challenged with several aspects of EAG. One of their frustrations relates to how the data are misunderstood, because policy and media people go by numbers without an appreciation of all that lies beneath those numbers. The highly technical nature of EAG serves sometimes to misguide rather than to illuminate, as one OECD official described evocatively:

> I think we were numbers people, and we should become policy people. We should change a little bit because EAG was and still is quite a technical publication and now it is no more sufficient to keep this technical part. The technical part is very important for us; you will see if you go through the publication, sometimes the sentence is quite complex because for us … [the] ways we use these terms is quite complex. [Take] graduation rate – do you know what is 'graduation rate'? It is very complex, because behind this graduation rate there is a lot of

calculation. The calculation is very complex. People will mix attainment, graduation rate, completion ... they will mix [these things] all the time. For me, [these are] completely different. They come from different sources, there are different definitions behind them, etc. So in this publication you have different concepts which are very technical and very well explained. ... But when it is used for media, it will be '[x%]of Australians have a tertiary degree'. (OECD official, interview transcript)

The EAG continues to see itself as a document in the service of policy makers. It anticipates policy questions and attempts to provide the answers to those questions. While it does not explicitly provide policy advice, it is conscious of its ability to shape the thinking of policy makers and the public through its engagement with them:

We have been asked to answer the questions policy makers might have. We don't give advice, but we are here to use our data for the questions of policy makers. Earlier it was more technical – when we talk of graduation rate, when we compare, when we talk about the finance we compare the finance, but now we should not stay with this type of information ... we should give some figure to the policy maker and give them some direction – to compare countries together to give some direction. (OECD official, interview transcript)

The complexity of the technical is such that the message sometimes needs to be simplified until it is no longer even accurate, in order to be understood:

We have changed our work also. And sometimes we have to forget all the technical issue, because it won't be understood by media, so we know that we have to say some sentences to media that are not correct, because we are statisticians and [we know] what is behind [the numbers], but we should have stories that [are] understandable to everybody. (OECD official, interview transcript)

These changes have gone hand in hand with the growing influence of the OECD on the economic and education policies globally. Their reach has gone far beyond the OECD member nations, as PISA has gained popularity – non-OECD member nations outnumber the members in PISA. OECD data are now widely accepted in a number of spheres, and education has become an important aspect of its work.

The story of EAG provides an opportunity to study closely the tug of war between science and politics, between knowledge and governance and between different types of expertise. But it also demonstrates how the two projects – the scientific project and the governance project – are impossible to keep apart. The politics of science might be different – but it requires the same negotiations and translations and domestications that the arena of policy and governance need. Retaining a sense of technicality and neutrality is important not only to legitimate the indicators, but also the policies that use these indicators as their basis.

Producing calculable worlds

The INES story illustrates that description, from the outset, requires production. No description seems possible without some underlying conceptual framework or theoretical basis, however compromised. Indeed, we might argue that production precedes description – i.e., the world is changed in order to render it describable (Scott, 1998). When the 'world' involved is very diverse and complex, it must first be standardised using a variety of classificatory mechanisms, mathematical formulae, selections and deletions before any description can be attempted.

Once the measurements are in place and become powerfully routine, as with EAG, the repeated patterns of indicators create certain expectations which form a background against which things appear as expected (Thrift, 2004). The associations made in the indicators – between performance and the GDP, or between per-student expenditure and student performance – become reified as causal or otherwise related entities, even if this was not the original intention. In turn, governments use this information to change their policies. Policy convergence owes much to these comparative tables and charts, which promote associations that might not have been made otherwise. At the same time, what gets left out of these calculations would arguably lose importance and currency in the minds of the public and of policy makers.

For any progress in measurement to be made at all, the first thing that needed to be forged – 'invented', to use Bottani's term – was 'a new style of co-operation' between various actors:

> Considering the hostility of many educationalists and key decision makers towards the development of education indicators when the activity was started in 1988, it was necessary to invent a new style of co-operation between member countries, able to generate mutual trust and consensus among all participants. (Bottani, 1998, p. 71)

The complexity of education systems, the requirements of large amounts of data from a variety of sources, and the lack of an agreed model or framework meant that agreements had to be constantly negotiated. INES depended on the data produced at national levels to do its international calculations. The idiosyncrasies of national systems meant that data producers also needed to agree to new ways of collecting data or provide ways to translate their data into formats that articulated with INES requirements:

> The development of a set of indicators at the international level is a complex, multi-stage operation. Many actors are involved, having various degrees of accountability. Moreover, data gathering in education is not easy: some information is rather simple, some consumes a lot of resources, some may be considered ethically indefensible. It is therefore essential to reach an agreement between the data producers and data providers. (Bottani, 1998, p. 71)

Bottani reports that this emphasis on collaboration and a *participative and democratic approach* was vital to the development of the indicators. But the cooperation came at a cost:

> The Networks resemble clubs – a set of people who meet regularly and acquire a 'group identity' find it easier to work together than strangers. This makes them more effective, but also potentially leads to decisions taken in the interests of the club that take insufficient account of wider interests and priorities. (Bottani, 1998, p. 73)

The INES 'General Assemblies' where the networks came together, along with a range of other stakeholders, provided the forum for debate and discussion. The heated debates of 1991 which resulted in the inclusion of student attainment indicators in the first EAG is an example. However, after 1992, these Assemblies became much tamer affairs, particularly as the participation by policy and government representatives increased:

> Between 1989 and 1995, the INES (International Indicators of Education Systems) project organised three General Assemblies with the participation of practically all those concerned worldwide by the production of a set of international education indicators. The last of these events was held in 1995 at Lahti (Finland). Since then there have been no more General Assemblies concerning the international education indicator project. ... OECD organised a fourth General Assembly of the INES project in Tokyo in 2000, but this meeting was a General Assembly in name only, for participation per country was reduced to limited delegations and the indicator producers no longer participated. And so it was an intergovernmental conference by OECD standards which took place in Tokyo rather than a General Assembly. (Bottani, 2008, p. 17)

Over time, the indicators have become taken for granted and routinised, produced year after year. Policy makers have become so used to these indicators that even if the EAG team suggests that some tables or indicators might be dropped, there is resistance to this move. Even when an indicator disappears from the print version, it is still preserved in the web version.

> [I]t is very difficult – it's a question mark we have each year – should we drop some of the indicators? But people are used to them, and if we drop one table, you can be sure we will receive some question about why this table has been dropped. It's like – some people say it's a bible. It's not a bible, but people are just used to working with some indicators and they don't like it if we decide to drop them. (Interview transcript, OECD Official)

The consultation with countries still occurs, with meetings twice a year:

> So for the organisation of this publication, we work with the countries. We have two meetings per year ... we meet all the countries to discuss the table of contents of EAG 2013 ... we have to decide which indicators we will keep and which we will drop and we try to have for each publication a new story ... Even if we drop a table, it will go to the web, we don't drop it [altogether], because we have the information and it could be useful for [some] people. (Interview transcript, OECD Official)

Consensus can be regarded as a form of translation (Callon, 1986; Latour, 1999) which silences or at least minimises obstruction. By incorporating the varied interests – or by domesticating countries into needing what is on offer rather than what is not – EAG can be routinised and produced with efficiency. The protracted debates have turned into agreements, which in turn have become routines – routines of data generation, applications of statistical formulae and of annual publication. Such methodological routinisation produces a 'mechanical objectivity' which is prized by policy makers (Porter, 1995).

Calculation and critique as moral projects

That measurement is a productive rather than descriptive activity, as I have demonstrated in this paper, has been argued by a number of STS scholars (Jasanoff, 2004; Knorr Cetina, 1981; Latour, 1987; Law, 2009b). There are two aspects to this productivity that are worth teasing out. The more easily argued one is that once a measurement is in place it acts upon the world by changing understandings and behaviours. The other is that investing 'a character of calculability' (Mitchell, 2002) itself changes the world. When we see measurement as not just imperfect descriptions (i.e., reductionist, inaccurate, etc.), but as *world-making processes*, critiquing them becomes not just an epistemological exercise, but a political and ontological one.

When we regard measurement as a performative or productive process that brings worlds into being, critiquing measurement becomes a form of interference (Law, 2007) which is necessarily a moral project. Jenny Oakes (1986) asserts that 'we cannot be unaware of the political pressure resulting from the mere existence of a set of indicators' (Oakes, 1986, cited in Bottani, 2008, p. 15). She explains that teachers and schools might try to influence data in their favour, or influence the choice of indicators, particularly since they often have no control over the many factors for which they could be blamed. Bottani also raises the issue of the performative aspects of the indicators:

> Can we really maintain that the use of indicators constitutes a neutral cognitive approach which does not aim to modify education systems? ... Is it not rather naive to claim that indicators are mere tools for acquiring knowledge with no incidence on the realities of education, on how the education system performs? Is the fact of producing a set of indicators, supported and encouraged by educational authorities, completely neutral? (Bottani, 2008, p. 21)

Bottani also makes the more interesting point of that there is no ontological divide between reality and its modification, since knowing involves changing:

> ... no cognitive approach leaves the subject of its observation, measurement, analysis, comparison, deciphering, completely unscathed. There is no clear ontological divide between science and techniques, between cognitive reality and its modification. It is therefore impossible to attribute a distinct ethical status to each of these two elements and consider that we have unlimited freedom when it comes to cognitive processes and a different, limited responsibility when we apply knowledge to processes or acts aiming to modify reality. Indicators produce knowledge of education systems and the moment we design, implement or produce indicators, they modify systems. (Bottani, 2008, p. 22)

This assertion from Bottani perhaps explains why some of the people most involved with the project of indicator production have felt compelled to write and speak with such frankness about the precarious and tentative nature of these indicators and why they continue to challenge and raise cautions about indicators (see, for example, Bottani, 1996, 1998, 2008; Heyneman, 1999; Oakes, 1986; Sauvageot, 2008; Smyth, 2008).

Bottani's assertion that to know is to change, and his challenge that there is no ontological divide between 'science and techniques, between cognitive reality and its modification' sums up the moral imperative of my own project of doing 'sociologies of measurement', at a time when such measurements have become deeply influential in policy. No accounts of contemporary policy enactments can be given today without an account of various forms of standardisations, classifications and quantifications and other means of translating the world into numbers (Gorur, 2011). While the role of numbers in policy is well recognised, critique is often content to either show that numbers are reductionist or to challenge their accuracy. While both of these are important, neither, I argue, is sufficient. Those critiques arise from a representationalist, rather than productive or performative, understanding of measurement (Pickering, 1995; Woolgar, 1991a). Detailed accounts of the making of numbers and their insinuation in policies are required to understand their instrumentalism and their world-making functions (Woolgar, 1991a). The former – an understanding of their instrumentalism – provides potential points of active intervention and challenge. The latter – an understanding of measurement as a productive rather than a descriptive practice, provides the moral and ethical impetus to take on such studies.

Funding

This work was supported by Victoria University under the Victoria University Researcher Development Grant Scheme and by the Collaborative Research Network (CRN).

References

Berg, M., & Timmermans, S. (2000). Orders and their others: On the constitution of universalities in medical work. *Configurations, 8*(1), 31–61. doi:10.1353/con.2000.0001
Blank, R. K. (1993). Developing a system of education indicators: Selecting, implementing, and reporting indicators. *Educational Evaluation and Policy Analysis, 15*(1), 65–80. doi:10.3102/01623737015001065
Bottani, N. (1994). The OECD international education indicators. *Assessment in Education: Principles, Policy and Practice, 1,* 333–350.
Bottani, N. (1996). OECD international education indicators. *International Journal of Educational Research, 25,* 279–288. doi:10.1016/0883-0355(96)82857-6
Bottani, N. (1998). The OECD educational indicators: Purposes, limits and production processes. *Prospects, 28*(1), 61–75. doi:10.1007/BF02737780
Bottani, N. (2008). The oil level, the engine and the car: The stakes invovled in assessing the quality of education on the basis of indicators. *Éducation et Société, 18*(2), 11–23.
Bottani, N., & Walberg, H. J. (1992). Introduction: What are the international education indicators for? In Centre for Educational Research and Innovation (Ed.), *The OECD international education indicators – A framework for analysis* (pp. 7–12). Paris: OECD.
Bowker, G. C., & Star, S. L. (2000). *Sorting things out – Classification and its consequences.* Cambridge and London: MIT Press.
Callon, M. (1986). Some elements of a sociology of translation: The domestication of the scallops and the fishermen of St Brieuc Bay. In J. Law (Ed.), *Power, action and belief: A new sociology of knowledge?* London and Boston, MA: Routledge & Kegan Paul.
Cullather, N. (2007). The foreign policy of the calorie. *The American Historical Review, 112,* 337–364. doi:10.1086/ahr.112.2.337
Derksen, L. (2000). Towards a sociology of measurement: The meaning of measurement error in the case of DNA profiling. *Social Studies of Science, 30,* 803–845. doi:10.1177/030631200030006001
Desrosières, A. (1998). *The politics of large numbers – A history of statistical reasoning* (C. Naish, Trans.). Cambridge, MA and London: Harvard University Press.
Elley, W. B. (1992). *How in the world do students read? IEA study of reading literacy.* Hamburg: International Association for the Evaluation of Educational Achievement.
Gorur, R. (2011). ANT on the PISA trail: Following the statistical pursuit of certainty. *Educational Philosophy & Theory, 43*(5–6), 76–93.
Gorur, R. (2014). Towards a sociology of measurement technologies in education policy. *European Educational Research Journal, 13*(1), 58–72. doi:10.2304/eerj.2014.13.1.58
Heyneman, S. P. (1999). The sad story of UNESCO's education statistics. *International Journal of Educational Development, 19*(1), 65–74. doi:10.1016/S0738-0593(98)00068-6
Jaeger, R. M. (1978). About educational indicators: Statistics on the conditions and trends in education. *Review of Research in Education, 6,* 276–315. doi:10.3102/0091732X006001276
Jasanoff, S. (2004). The idiom of co-production. In S. Jasanoff (Ed.), *States of knowledge: The co-production of science and the social order* (pp. 1–12). London and New York, NY: Routledge.
Knorr Cetina, K. (1981). *The manufacture of knowledge: An essay on the constructivist and contextual nature of science.* Oxford: Perammon.
Knorr Cetina, K. (1999). *Epistemic cultures: How the sciences make knowledge.* Cambridge, MA: Harvard University Press.

Latour, B. (1987). *Science in action: How to follow scientists and engineers through society.* Cambridge: Harvard University Press.
Latour, B. (1999). *Pandora's hope: Essays on the reality of science studies.* Cambridge, MA and London: Harvard University Press.
Latour, B., & Woolgar, S. (1979). *Laboratory life – The construction of scientific facts.* Princeton, NJ: Princeton University Press.
Law, J. (1994). *Organising modernity. Oxford, UK and Cambridge.* MA: Blackwell.
Law, J. (2007, May 18). *Actor network theory and material semiotics*, version of 25 April 2007. Retrieved from http://www.heterogeneities.net/publications/Law-ANTandMaterialSemiotics.pdf
Law, J. (2009a). Actor network theory and material semiotics. In B. S. Turner (Ed.), *The new Blackwell companion to social theory* (pp. 141–158). Oxford: Blackwell-Wiley.
Law, J. (2009b). Seeing like a survey. *Cultural Sociology, 3,* 239–256. doi:10.1177/1749975509105533
Mainguet, C., & Baye, A. (2006, March). *Defining a framework of indicators to measure the social outcomes of learning.* Paper presented at the Measuring the Effects of Education and Civic Engagement: Proceedings of The Copenhagen Symposium. Retrieved from http://www.oecd.org/education/innovation-education/37425733.pdf
Mitchell, T. (2002). *Rule of experts: Egypt, techo-politics, modernity.* Berkeley and Los Angeles: University of California Press.
National Commission on Excellence in Education. (1983). *A nation at risk: The imperative for educational reform.* Washington, DC: US Department of Education.
Oakes, J. (1986). *Educational indicators: A guide for policymakers* (p. 39). Santa Monica, CA: RAND Corporation.
OECD. (1995). *Measuring what students learn.* Paris: Author.
OECD. (2011). *Education at a glance 2011: OECD indicators* (p. 497). Paris: Author.
OECD. (2012). *Education at a glance 2012: OECD Indicators* (p. 567). Paris: Author.
Pickering, A. (1995). *The mangle of practice: Time, agency, and science.* Chicago, IL: University of Chicago Press.
Porter, T. (1995). *Trust in numbers – The pursuit of objectivity in science and public life.* Princeton, NY and Chichester: Princeton University Press.
Sauvageot, C. (1997). *Indicators for educational planning: A practical guide.* Paris: International Institute for Educational Planning.
Sauvageot, C. (2008). A tool for international comparison: The international standard classification of education [ISCED]. In A. Charras & C. Sauvageot (Eds.), *Education & formations: International comparisons* (pp. 211–221). Paris, France: Ministry of National Education; Ministry of Higher Education and Research Evaluation, Forecasting and Performance Directorate.
Scott, J. C. (1998). *Seeing like a state: How some schemes to improve the human condition have failed.* Binghampton, NY: Vail-Ballou Press.
Smith, T. M., & Baker, D. P. (2001). Worldwide growth and institutionalization of statistical indicators for education policy-making. *Peabody Journal of Education, 76*(3–4), 141–152.
Smyth, J. A. (2008). The origins of the international standard classification of education. *Peabody Journal of Education, 83,* 5–40.
Thrift, N. (2004). Remembering the technological unconscious by foregrounding knowledges of position. *Environment and Planning D: Society and Space, 22,* 175–190. doi:10.1068/d321t
Walberg, H. J., & Zhang, G. (1998). Analyzing the OECD indicators model. *Comparative Education, 34*(1), 55–70. doi:10.1080/03050069828342
Woolgar, S. (1991a). Beyond the citation debate: Towards a sociology of measurement technologies and their use in science policy. *Science and Public Policy, 18,* 319–326.
Woolgar, S. (1991b). Configuring the user: The case of usability trials. In J. Law (Ed.), *A sociology of monsters: Essays on power, technology, and domination* (pp. 57–99). London: Routledge.

The sociomateriality of education policy

Paolo Landri

Institute of Research on Population and Social Policies of the National Research Council (CNR-IRPPS), Rome, Italy

> By drawing on sociomaterial approaches to education, this paper presents a case study on the creation, development and consolidation of the education zone, a new policy space in South Italy. The topological reading of the case study reveals the complex reassemblage of humans and non-humans in the enactment of the education zones, and its multiple enactments as regions, networks and fluids.

Introduction

Notable changes in contemporary education are reshaping the spaces of education policy at the global and national level (Fenwick & Edwards, 2010; Fenwick, Edwards, & Sawchuck, 2011; Fenwick & Landri, 2012). At the local level, the policy epidemic of the 'devolved environment' translates in the fabrication of new decentralised sites of governance to coordinate schools and networks of schools. These changes have been analysed in terms of the hybridisation of many discourses (managerialism, welfarism, privatisation), and development of heterarchies, i.e. of local interconnections among horizontal and hierarchical ways of governing (Kooiman, 2000). However, the new spatial configurations remain relatively unexplored since most policy analysis displays a simplified description of the 'social' enacted in education policies where: (1) the role of decision-makers is dominant in the design, implementation and evaluation of the policies; (2) social relationships are defined in terms of human-to-human associations, and materialities (objects, technologies and artefacts) have limited effect on shaping education policies; and (3) there are clear-cut boundaries and simple negotiations between producers, users of knowledge and policy-makers. To get a complex understanding of the enactment of the new educational policy spaces, this paper will address the two following questions:

- How does this education policy-making space materialise in practice?
- Is there a single, or are there multiple instantiations of education policy-making space?

To give some replies to these questions, the paper will: (1) highlight how sociomaterial approaches to education may enrich our understanding of the enactment of education policies (Fenwick & Edwards, 2010; Fenwick & Landri, 2012; Fenwick et al., 2011); and

(2) introduce and discuss a case study on the creation, development and consolidation of new education policy space in a Provincia of South Italy (Grimaldi, 2010; Grimaldi, Serpieri, & Romano, 2011). The case study will illustrate the materialisation of the *zones for the improvement of education provision*, i.e. the setting up and dynamics of education policy spaces where representative schools, networks of schools, municipalities, central and local authorities, etc., are expected to concur to educational making processes in a more open democratic ways. The description of the case will draw attention to the assemblages between humans and non-humans in the enactment of the education zone, and its multiple instantiations as regions, networks and fluids. This article will unfold as follows: first, it will present the main characteristics of sociomaterial approaches to education policy; second, the article will describe the case study, highlighting the fabrication of an education policy space and on the negotiations between dominant, and the alternative enactments of this new emergent policy space; and finally, it will develop some conclusions about what having a sensibility to sociomateriality makes visible in terms of the analysis of education policies.

The matter of education policies

To develop a fine detailed analysis of education policy this paper investigates the enactment of education policies, by considering *sociomaterial approaches to education*. Drawing on actor-network theory (ANT) and other theoretical conceptualisations from Science and Technology Studies, feminist studies and post-structuralism, sociomaterial approaches to education challenge the humanistic assumptions of the linear model of education policy, and propose a description of the 'social' as *association*, that is as assemblages of humans and non-humans (Fenwick & Edwards, 2010; Fenwick & Landri, 2012; Fenwick et al., 2011). Societies are not exclusive human domains, and indeed may be the foci of many scientific discourses (as Tarde has already noticed, see Latour, 2010b); they are heterogeneous, and to some extent temporary associations of people, technologies and things. Sociomaterial approaches invite us, in other words, to consider 'the material presences that exert forces and are entwined with what appears to be human intention, engagement, resistance and change' (Fenwick, 2011, p. 116). In particular, they focus on how agency is empirically distributed across people, technology and things.[1] A useful conceptualisation taken from ANT for analysing the dynamics of agency in the materialisation of education policy distinguishes between *mediators* and *intermediaries* (Latour, 2005). An intermediary 'transports meaning or force without transformation … even if it internally made of many parts' (Latour, 2005, p. 39). On the other hand, 'Mediators transform, translate, distort and modify the meaning or the elements they are supposed to carry' (p. 39). In practice, there is a constant uncertainty about whether an entity (text, technology, people, etc.) may behave as *mediator*, or *intermediary*; it depends on how it comes to be associated in the assemblages of humans and non-humans. On the other hand, the particular mix of *intermediaries* and *mediators* in a growing assemblage permits to map the relative state of order/disorder. So, the unfolding of an assemblage can move from *complication* (a stabilised state no matter how many intermediaries are there) to *complexity* (a fluid state, where the drive to disorder leads to a growing number of variables not to be considered separately). The distinction brings to the forefront the situated work of the fabrication of the matter of education policy, and the effects of ordering/disordering of the reassemblages of human and non-human agencies in the education policy fields.

Sociomaterial approaches are also a way to escape from the usual vocabularies that describe the social in terms of 'containers' (micro, meso and micro contexts). They take seriously the question of the space of education policies, and develop a sensibility for sociological imagination.[2] They counter the 'containers-thinking' of the social with complex metaphors to describe the specific instantiations of education policy space, knowledge and forms of human presence (Sørensen, 2009). In so doing, they show that space is not given, and is not necessarily forced into three dimension patterns. It helps to consider educational spaces (what is next, far, beyond, etc.) as *relational formations*, which are not exclusively defined in terms of metric distance, but with regard to a multiplicity of attributes (identity, familiarity, etc.). An interesting typology, drawing on Mol and Law's work (1994), and then reconsidered by Sørensen (2009) includes: *regions* (containing well-delimited entities); *networks* (connected elements); and *fluids* (relationships that change, but maintain a recognised identity). The typology invites us to develop topological accounts of sociological practices, and to acknowledge how the materialisation of the space may have different instantiations. It recognises the multiplicity of spatialities in social fabric, and that some dominant instantiations are accompanied, and to some extent also challenged, by different performances of the social space. In that respect, educational reforms may be described as implying the development, extension and consolidation of novel actor-networks that define new sociological landscapes. This reading is particularly interesting in that it shows the difficult work of translation aimed at developing tiny networks among humans (teachers, schools, students, parents, superintendents, etc.) and non-humans (buildings, technologies, video-computers, etc.) that in turn are implicated in different spaces, and networks of assemblages. However, the formation of a new educational space does not imply the suppression, or the complete substitution of 'social spaces' already in place, and does not completely prevent the possibilities of differences, by giving room to the performance of alternative spaces (Fenwick, 2011). It directs attention, accordingly, to the multiple negotiations taking place to (re)produce an education policy space, and the ongoing struggles with forms of resistance and alternative and in-between educational spaces. In the following section I will move to a case study concerning the fabrication of a new education space in a Provincia of South Italy, in order to illustrate the dynamics of materialisation in the enactment of education policies.

Investigating the fabrication of a new education policy space

Italy is characterised by a highly state-centralistic education system with a dominant bureau-professional mode of school government (Landri, 2008, 2009). Historically, the *statist legacy* has meant limited responsibilities for territorial authorities (in Italy: 'Regione', 'Provincia' and 'Comune') in the field of education policy. Curriculum, teacher recruitment, government, funding, etc., depend basically on the state, and the local authorities are expected to play a role of support at the different level of education. At the end of 1990s, however, the reform of state redesigns the education policy space: (1) by promoting policies of de-concentration (*within the state*) through the development of autonomous schools and the shift of responsibilities to some peripheral offices of the Ministry; and (2) by trying the implementation of policies of decentralisation (*from the state to local authorities*) where Regione, Provincia and Comune had increasing and complementary roles in the field of education policy-making. This reform attributed a relevant role to 'Provincia' in the planning of local educational provision for secondary schools. This resulted in an extension of its traditional role, which consisted of being the provider of school space, furniture and facilities (benches, seats, blackboards) for schools, and in the expansion of its responsibility in educational policy-making. In particular, 'Provincia' is asked to coordinate educational provision of Comune (the Municipalities – responsible for compulsory schooling), and to design the 'right' mix of upper secondary schools with respect to educational needs. The new tasks included the preparation of an educational plan concerning the opening, closing and merging of schools at the territorial level. The plans of the Provincias (each Region has a variable number of Provincias) are then coordinated by the Region (in that case 'Regione Campania') and a final decision is then made by the Ministry of Education, University and Research (in Italian, the acronym for the Ministry is MIUR). National regulations envisage that Provincia may devise education participatory policy spaces, called literally 'functional zones for the improvement of the educational provision' (Legislative Decree 112/98 and 267/2000), to carry out these responsibilities. Some Provincias enacted not only the new tasks – including 'Provincia di Napoli' – but also others in Bologna, Milano and some local authorities in Tuscany (Grimaldi, 2010; Provincia di Napoli, Napoli, & Dipartimento di Sociologia, 2004; Serpieri, 2008), by trying to move from a bureaucratic to a democratic mode of local educational policy-making.

A long-standing research programme from 2004 to 2008 focused on the policies of school governance funded by the 'Provincia of Napoli' tried to investigate the redesign of education policy space as it happened (Grimaldi, 2010; Serpieri, 2008). The research programme involved research groups from the Department of Sociology of the University of Napoli 'Federico II', the Second University of Napoli, the University of Napoli 'Suor Orsola Benincasa', the Institute of Research on Population and Social Policies of the National Research Council (IRPPS-CNR) and Institute on the Development, Guidance, Training and Labour (ISFOL in Italian). The programme included: (1) a research project on school buildings and facilities in support of the elaboration of a new plan for the use of school buildings that envisaged a quantitative survey, some focus-groups and interviews to teachers and head teachers (with the Department of Sociology and the Second University of Napoli); (2) a research project on the enactment of the functional zones for the improvement of the educational provision (with Department of Sociology); and (3) a project on early school leaving (called SPES_GOAL) that envisaged the collaboration of Department of Sociology, IRPPS-CNR, ISFOL, University of Napoli 'Suor Orsola Benincasa', USR – Campania (The Peripheral Office of the MIUR).

I followed the research programme from the beginning as a member of the research group of the Department of Sociology leaded by Serpieri (the group here included the doctoral candidates: Grimaldi, Staibano, Napoletano and the post-doc member, Romano), and later as responsible of the research project on early school leaving carried out by the group of IRPPS-CNR. The empirical ground of this paper draws on the research project on the implementation of the education zone, and has been analysed in several publications (Grimaldi, 2010; Serpieri, 2008). Here, in particular, the set of data was collected as a joint research activity of the research group of the Department of Sociology, and as part of Grimaldi's doctoral research project. It included: (1) interviews to the staff management of the Department of Instructional Planning (10), and to the Councillor of Education of the Provincia di Napoli (2); (2) transcriptions of the Conferences of Zone[3] from 2004 to 2007 (14); (3) ethnographical notes of their everyday working practices of Department of Instructional Planning (10 days); (4) interviews to eight head teachers of two selected educational zones (a zone with and a zone without a consolidated experience of networks of school), and the notes taken ethnographically while participating at the Conferences of the selected zones as reported in Grimaldi's investigation (Grimaldi, 2010); and (5) deliberations and plans of the Provincia of Napoli concerning the activation and the decision of the Conferences of the Zones.

Methodologically, the data collection occurred while researcher/s followed the actor/s (human and non-human), and their associations over time, and tried to develop a theoretically informed understanding of what they have described, or what the actor/s said about interactions in which they have been involved. Elsewhere, the analysis of these sets of data explicitly draws on the methodology of *grounded theory* (Grimaldi, 2010; Napoletano, 2008). In what follows, however, I will propose a *socio-technical analysis* (Latour, 2010a) of the data I helped to collect, and on the interviews, and ethnographical notes published in Grimaldi's book (Grimaldi, 2010). A socio-technical analysis here leads to a *topological reading* that focuses on the 'doings' of the policy space, i.e. on what actors do, on the associations they make, on the assemblages of humans and the non-human with which they align, and on the work to hold these assemblages in line (Ceulemans, Simons, & Struyf, 2014). In this way, it directs attention to the emerging assemblages to enact an education policy space – the networking necessary to enact a 'thing' (Barad, 2003; Latour, 2005), and its multiple instantiation.

Enacting the zones as machines for deliberations

To describe the enactment of the zones for the improvement of education provision, it is relevant to consider the efforts of the staff management of the Department of Instructional Planning of Provincia of Napoli in collaboration with the Councillor of Education of the Provincia at following the tendency towards decentralisation of the governance of schooling. Until the end of the first decade of 2000 the 'Provincia of Napoli' made wide investments in school buildings, partly to recover from a critical situation where the increasing rate of enrolment in upper secondary school had created a gap between the provision of and the need for education space. The new responsibilities of local authorities in the new governance of education system meant a further extension of its area of interest, i.e. from being a bureaucratic and technical provider of school space to assuming more responsibilities in educational policy-making.

How should this passage be realised? How should the complexity of a notable number and distance of school units (almost 200 schools and 100 municipalities spread along the territory of the Provincia) be handled? How should a one-to-one bureaucratic relationship between school head teacher and the offices of the Provincia be changed into the open and many-to-many relationships of democratic educational policy-making? To face these issues, the Provincia of Napoli started to transform a complex situation by trying to shift from the chaotic, and erratic agencies of many *mediators* (teachers, head teachers, students, etc.), to the apparently more manageable complication of *intermediaries* of these agencies (texts, an information system, spokespersons for complex networks). In so doing, the group of the Provincia charted a trajectory far from being either linear or deterministic. The materialisation of the zones produced ordering and disordering effects by reshaping the local field of educational policy-making, which was revealed to be only partly predictable by the Provincia.

First, the Provincia developed *intertextual associations*: (1) the deliberation n. 415 (23 May 2002) where an association was elaborated between the Provincia of Napoli and the Regional Educational Office (the peripheral office of the Ministry); (2) the deliberation of the local government of Provincia n.146 (28 May 2003) where aligned the upcoming zones for the improvement of educational provision with the territorial zones included in the economic planning of the Provincia of Napoli, and which were elaborated in the PCTP (an acronym for economic plan of the Provincia); and (3) the deliberation n. 386 (13 May 2003) containing the agreement for developing educational governance in the Provincia. Deliberations and some guidelines – a 'fragile bridge of texts' (Latour, 2007) – represented the infrastructure of the educational zones. The next step is a deliberation that built on these associations and set up the conferences of the zone, that is the spokespersons of the zones and the loci for provincial educational policy-making (deliberation of the provincial council n. 154, 31 October 2003). The deliberation also contains the regulations for the composition of the conferences, their role, activities and competencies, and attributes to the offices of the Department of Instructional Planning the task of following, sustaining and assisting the work of the conferences.

The Provincia of Napoli visualises, then, the education zones on a map (see Figure 1). The map is a coloured display of the association between educational policy-making and economic planning in the Provincia. It locates upper secondary schools in education zones with different colours according to demographic trends, health provisions, public transport, railways, public areas, etc.

The mapping was carried out with the intention of linking educational policy-making to the general strategic planning of the Provincia (PTCP), which is focused on the available possibility of economic development. Overall, there are 10 zones: one which includes all the municipalities while the boundaries of the remaining nine were more or less drawn along the different economic sub-territories of the Provincia. The cartography

Figure 1. The map of the education zones of the Provincia di Napoli.

drew on the mobilisation of knowledge accumulated by the group in information systems on the local system of education.

The information systems were databases collecting data on schooling and on Vocational Education and Training (VET) in the Provincia of Napoli emerging from a collaboration with an in-house public company (ASUB). This data included information on school provision, statistics on the resident population, on the potential student population, the number of classes, of students enrolled, on the estimated population and student population over time (the archive was named 'Anagrafica istituti superiori', and was made with the help of a common application for database making) as well as data on school buildings (the spreadsheet was called 'Agenda degli interventi in edilizia scolastica'). The information systems supported the planning and educational policy-making by drawing on the circulation of reliable data, and on the relevant information of the socio-economic characteristics of the zones, as well as on the economic local policies and initiatives (Serpieri & Romano, 2008). The effort, here, was to support and consolidate an association between educational provision (its contents and practices) *and* the socio-economic dimension of the territories as reflected, and translated in the data, and the indicators of the information systems.

To reinforce this association, or to better fabricate it, the group also launched three projects of collaboration with the *Faculty of Sociology*, the *Faculty of Economy* and the *Faculty of Architecture* of the University of Napoli 'Federico II' (see also the section 'Investigating the fabrication of a new education policy space'). The intention was to develop a space of research for groups of sociologists, economists and architects to support the development of a devolved and participatory educational policy-making, by furnishing solutions, imagining alternative scenarios and legitimating the work of the Provincia of Napoli. During the decade, additional knowledge producers were included, i.e. other universities and public research organisations, which were contacted once specific knowledge expectations emerged from the realisation of the devolved local educational environments (for analysing this case with respect to the question of usable knowledge in educational research, see Landri, 2012). These research groups set up 'laboratories' in order to collect data, experiment and to develop knowledge on very relevant topics in the changing field of educational governance.

Eventually, to mobilise the zones, and to give them a body, each zone is inscribed in a Conference. Each zone has a Conference of Zone that is comprised of representatives of all of the schools (educational leaders) and the municipalities (mayors) in the zone; representatives of the Regional Educational Office of the Ministry and the Entrepreneurs' Union and the Centre for Employment are also members of the conference. In order to coordinate the decisions made within the local conferences, an additional 'Conference of Conferences' was created. It includes representatives elected from each 'local conference'. This complex apparatus was intended to give weight to the locally devolved environments of school governance. The map activates a regional space, i.e. containers with boundaries that include well-defined entities (schools, social services, etc.). Even the Conference of Conferences of the Zone is thought of in terms of a container of other containers.

The enactment of the education zone thus implied a complex assemblage of humans and non-humans, particularly made by: (1) the group of the Provincia of Napoli; (2) a fragile bridge of texts resulting in deliberations; (3) a map; (4) an information system; (5) the enrolment of research groups; and (6) the setting up and activation of the conferences of the education zones. A collective of agencies was put together, and in particular, an association of intermediaries and mediators was interconnected to activate the regional spaces of educational policy-making. Step-by-step, a machine for the deliberation of educational planning emerged and new spaces of education policy materialised.

Education zones: mere intermediary regions or emergent fluid spaces?

Once established, the conferences of zones are repeated regularly through the years. The call for the conferences requires preparatory work and the Provincia of Napoli group consolidated a network of practices over time. Preparatory work is quite demanding not only for the offices, particularly due to the weak links with the schools, but also, in some ways, with the many agencies in the zone. Participants were informed about the meetings through faxes, direct calls, e-mails and telegrams. Civil servants prepare materials for the meetings in order to circulate the relevant knowledge. This involves preparing folders, collecting documents and the relevant information for the conference from the existing information systems, or using new tools, usually grids, to ask for additional information about the participants and specific aspects of educational planning or educational issues. The folders are prepared with reference to the agenda meetings. The preparatory work also involves a decision to be made with regard to where the conferences will take place. Usually, the meeting takes place at the 'Provincia' Council Hall in Naples, which is laid out like a small parliament.

Additional work is needed since the conferences are recorded on tape, so that full transcriptions can be made available via the provincial website. Conference agendas depend partly on the scheduled time of the educational planning and partly on emergent issues. Usually, educational planning requires a joint decision to be made at the end of the year. However, the conferences also meet sporadically throughout the year and address issues such as guidance, transport, inclusive policies, adult education, VET, etc. The most commonly discussed issues are those relating to buildings, as in the Provincia of Naples the lack of buildings and classrooms is perceived as one of the most urgent problems. Clearly, the deliberation of educational planning is the central topic of the conferences (Figure 2).

The failure of education zones as machines for deliberation

Quite paradoxically from a linear perspective of policy analysis, the conferences of zones reveal to be a failure as machines for deliberation. Only a very small number of decisions are taken there, and most choices regarding educational planning are made elsewhere. Grimaldi's research (2010) on the experience of the conferences of zones in the Provincia of Napoli reports the notable difficulties of these sites as a place for a joint decision-making in education policy. His research particularly focuses on two zones, and on the activities of the relative conferences (respectively, Zone 1 – North Napoli, and Zone 3 – Flegreo); however, the descriptions and conclusions may be generalised to the functioning of the other conferences of zones. His analysis of the conferences from 2004 to 2008 highlights that they are not the loci for decision-making, but sites where the decisions are presented, or announced; or where critical decisions concerning 'hard' issues are removed from the table and shifted to other opportunities of choice.

The fragility of the conferences in terms of agency is seen in many ways, and was revealed particularly soon in 2005 when choices were made about: (1) an increase in

Figure 2. A photo of a conference of zone, Hall of Government.

teaching staff (limited by the state that was subject to limits for containing public spending); (2) a modification of educational provision to realise an experiment as the result of a decision taken at regional level; and (3) a call for an investment in school building at a time when the critical situation of overall school buildings led the Provincia to dedicate all its budget to solving the serious safety risks of some school sites. In these latter cases, the conferences appeared to be a group of intermediaries informed about decisions taken elsewhere.

Instead of being machines for deliberation, they appeared to be *hearings*, which were to be listened to, and where proposals could be made. They are no substitute for the usual avenues of choice (one-to-one relationships with a school, municipality, provincial offices and the Councillor) that are to some extent hidden from public accountability, and a collective discussion and deliberation. This failure is not without effect: the *illusio* paves the way to mistrust among participants of the conferences, and increases the effort required for negotiation, and in explanation of any decision presented and taken.

Moreover, the association between schools and the economic characteristics of the territory tends to include schools, municipalities and other participants in a too narrow, and fixed topological space. In particular, research on the topologies of school spaces revealed that schools are often anchored in different geographies (Provincia di Napoli et al., 2004). Schools frequently have weak relationships with other schools within the same zone, and with the secondary schools in the zone, which are seen as 'competitors'. Schools compete, generally, for the 'better students' to maintain, or increase their position in the ranking of the public prestige. While it is not appropriate to define this situation as a condition of the 'quasi-market', it nonetheless frames a visible competition among the secondary schools, which is sometimes also emphasised by the market interpretation of the policy of school autonomy. At the same time, schools display complex patterns of relationships with institutions, other schools, educational agencies and other relevant stakeholders, well beyond the limits of their zone. Therefore, there is an uneasy fit between the logic of the zone and the local space of schools.

Contrasts and conflicts are more likely to occur when the zone is enacted as a *region*, that is, as a container into which discrete entities (e.g., the representatives of diverse organisations) may be placed, clear boundaries may be defined and a hierarchy (e.g., Provincia-schools, etc.) articulated. The failure of the zone conferences as machines for deliberation then led to: (1) an indifference of some participants, who decided to abandon its meetings; (2) conflicts, contrasts and mutual distrust; and (3) an exploration of a different enactment of the education policy space.

Education zones as emergent fluid spaces

The zone and the conferences of zones may also be seen as occasions for raising awareness of the reproduction of local circuits of schools responsible for tracking schools, and a higher percentage of school dropouts, for developing collaborative forms of professional knowing aimed at creating local spaces of affinity among head teachers and groups of teachers, for producing projects, etc., and for intervening in and possibly reducing the persisting reasons for inequality. In these cases, the zone is enacted less as a hierarchical site, and more as a *fluid space* in which school boundaries are open to reflection. The definition of the 'zone' becomes problematic, and the articulation of the conference of zone is again under construction. Here, the possibility emerges of developing a space for challenging school practices and rebuilding patterns of relationships with regard to knowledge-making. In the latter case, the zone becomes a place for exchanging knowledge and generating new perspectives on school governance. This shift was also accompanied by a change in the public discourses of the conferences from the concept of 'deliberation' to the idea of 'consultation'. While in the first wave of the conferences (from the end of 2003 to the middle of 2004) the Councillor depicted them as 'the place for the collective decision'; later on, in the following rounds of the conferences (from 2005 to 2008), the difficulties of open and collective decision-making led to the development of an emphasis on educational policy-making, and to framing the conferences as places for discussing, and elaborating education policies.

Some instances of this unpredicted enactment of the zone are described in Grimaldi's research (2010). Here, the zone develops as a collective of agencies that becomes almost independent from the Provincia of Napoli. In Zone 1, for example, a group of head teachers met regularly in 2005 and 2006 to elaborate on common strategies in educational guidance, and to deal with the issue of student registration with the aim of potentially developing joint policy. The group drew on a successful pilot project in one of the municipalities of the zone, where it had been possible to establish coordination of the secondary schools and those at the primary level, and to confront data about the potential students and the educational provision of the secondary schools. The group decided to extend the project to the entire zone and to envisage possible alternative scenarios of registration. Scenarios may lead to imagined critical points (uneven distribution of students among schools, choices directed towards some schools and not to others, etc.), and to enactment of a proper strategy of guidance at the local, or at the provincial level. In

2006, the conference of zone discussed the project, and agreed to extend this policy inside the zone. The agreement became a model, and was also announced in other zone conferences as an instance of the possibility of the logic of networks of schools, that is to favour the development of collaborative networks among secondary schools to counter the risks associated with non-collaborative, or overtly competitive relationships between schools. The case also highlights the activation of forms of professional knowings that require a diverse presence amongst participation in the conference of zone. Here, the presence of school head teachers is aimed at the production of knowledge and at the refinement of their expertise in educational policy-making on a common critical issue – the 'mismatching' of student choices and school availabilities and educational provision. The recognition of a critical question leads to a collective inquiry, to the restructuring of patterns of relationships among schools and accordingly to the change of the social space they are activating. The collective inquiry sees the performance of 'reflective practitioners' developing a complex and non-linear relationship between research and policy that is a pattern of relationships that counter the approach of the group of Provincia to the involvement of the academic group of knowledge producers, following a more linear approach to research-policy. As a consequence, the zone becomes more independent, and tries to escape from the regional space initially designed by the group of the Provincia. A suggestion to sometimes convene the conference of zone in a venue inside the zone, and not at a site in the Provincia as usual emerged. The group of the Provincia, and in particular the Councillor, was not against this displacement. The Councillor declared:

> From now on the Conferences will not be organised centrally. This first wave has been centralised since we needed to be sustained by our office for the call together of the Conference. Later on, all the Conferences will be convened on the territories, we will come in the zone to reflect together on what we ought to do. (Conference of zone 1, 4 November 2004)

During the time of this research this change had not happened, and the issue was repeatedly raised in the conference agenda. A more independent zone would probably have implied a loss of control that the group of the Provincia was not prepared to deal with, or which was not completely intended. While the relevance of this instance may appear exaggerated, Grimaldi's research (2010) also suggests the development of these processes for other zones. Further, it points an unintended enactment of the policy space that implies, as the instance of Zone 1 describes, a reassemblage of humans and non-humans (head teacher, teachers, municipalities, inquiry, data, students, schools, etc.), and a materialisation of the zone not as a region with bounded elements, but as a fluid space where relationships change, and where it is possible to experiment with different patterns of relations. The zone is enacted less as a network of intermediaries, and more as a collective of mediators.

Conclusions

The description of the fabrication of a new policy space so far illustrated reveals that the partial decline of bureau-professional circuits of government opened up the possibility of experimenting with new assemblages of humans and non-humans, enacting various forms of regulation and for steering education systems, albeit without linear and deterministic trajectories. In this last section, I will reprise the initial questions of how education policy-making space materialises in practice and whether there is single or a multiple instantiations of education policy-making space to draw some conclusions and further reflections from the case study.

First of all, the case highlights that the *thingification* the zone, and more of education policies in general, is not purely 'social' in the sense that it does not solely concern associations and interactions among humans. The case illustrates how the enactment of a new education policy space implies a reassemblage of humans and non-humans. The emergence of education zones for the improvement of educational provision has meant, in particular, the fabrication and the use of texts, information systems, maps and politically shaped space (the 'parliament' enacted space of the zone conferences). The zones needed a work of *intertextuality*, i.e. work about the association between texts and documents, resulting in the production of deliberative texts. These texts establish associations between national and local regulations, introduce the regulations of the zone, and create new identities (for example, head teachers are spokespersons of schools in particular areas of provincial territory). The associations also needed to be visualised through a *map*, and some data had to be extracted from the *information systems* to clarify the type of association proposed to the school. Finally, the enactment of the zone in terms of a 'machine for deliberation' was thought of in terms of a little *parliament*, i.e. as a gathering where democratic decisions about educational policy could be finally performed. Texts, maps, information systems and the parliament site are mobilised to enact the zone, and are particularly the conditions for the performance of the conference of zones. Here, it is possible to see how the materiality may be considered as a quality to connect disparate and somewhat disparate parts (Sørensen, 2009). These materialisations do not simply reproduce the social world as it is; they help to reconfigure it by introducing and putting together elements that were not previously assembled together. This also means that materialisation(s) may fail to be a stabilising mechanism, or may have an effect that is more destabilising than stabilising. Moreover, the assemblage may not resist to the test, to the trials of strength. Thinking of and fabricating the conference of zone as a machine for deliberation turned out to be a failure, since most of the deliberations were taken elsewhere, and mostly in the usual circuit of government. In that respect, the materiality of education policy also points to the ability to resist, and for the materialities to abandon the associations in which they are involved.

Secondly, sociomaterial approaches to education policy invite us to pay attention to the *multiple enactments of the social*. The social, here, is always 'under question', and it results from a simplification of the complexities of the agencies. Faced with the multiplicity of the educational agencies, of the many mediators at work in the everyday interactions and practices, the group of the Provincia tries to fabricate a bundle of intermediaries that may transform and translate a messy situation into a more manageable, and controllable one, where the group of the Provincia may open, and make more democratic educational policy-making. This shift implies the association of many actor-networks and into tiny and fragile assemblages and new spatialities. Education policy, however, may be enacted in different ways, and be inscribed in diverse spatialities. There is not automatic equivalence between the social imagery of the decision-maker, or the starting group of policy-maker, and its materialisation in practice. Those at the 'periphery' of policy-making may create and consolidate diverse performances of the social. The usual materialisation of the social as 'container' is only one among the several possibilities. Our case illustrates that the zone may be enacted as a *region*, as a *network* or as a *fluid*. A zone may be thought of as a region, such as the bounded portion of the territory of the Provincia of Napoli, containing discrete objects and entities (schools, municipalities, etc.). Yet, zones may be performed as a network, and through the conferences of zones may be activated as *machines for deliberations*. This requires, as we have seen, a complex reassemblage of humans and non-humans, and also some expectations about the material presence of schools, head teachers, representatives of municipalities and other educational authorities inside the zone. The network therefore activates a mechanism to take decisions for a collective choice to be included in the provincial plan for educational policy-making.

Finally, the zone may be considered as a 'fluid' for rethinking about and 'from above' the possibility of developing education policy. The diverse performance of the spatialities is associated with patterns of relations between knowledge producers/policy-makers and professional identities. The materialisation of the zone as a *region* does not problematise professional identities; instead, it tends to substitute a hierarchical regime with an authoritarian one (more or less bureau-professional or democratic). This is also a reason for reproducing discrete identities and boundaries. Alternatively, the enactment of a zone as a fluid space leads to the possibility of problematising existing school boundaries and professional knowledge, or learning together how to cope with the increasingly complex apparatus of school governance. In this respect, a sociomaterial approach is also revealed to be useful to detect the complex and non-linear relationships between knowledge producers and educational policy-makers. It problematises the linear research-policy approach, by showing how knowledge producers contribute to consolidating or problematising educational policy-making, and how this emerges in the complex, and ongoing negotiations in the field. In this way it may help in showing how education policy may translate into complex sociologies of education, and in helping to think about alternative sociological imagination for educational policy-making.

Notes

1. In an interesting reflection on the social, Patrick Joyce (2002), by following ANT, noted that the social here is conceived as 'collective of different agencies'. Attention is thus on the interactions among different agencies (p. 190).
2. For some considerations on social imageries and how they may shape educational research and policy see Rizvi (2006).
3. The transcriptions of the Conferences of the Zones are available at the Provincia di Napoli website at the following link: http://www.provincia.napoli.it/Micro_Siti/Scuola/Navigazione_Sinistra/Conferenze_ambito/.

References

Barad, K. (2003). Posthumanist performativity: Toward an understanding of how matter comes to matter. *Signs: Journal of Women in Culture and Society, 28*, 801–831. doi:10.1086/345321

Ceulemans, C., Simons, M., & Struyf, E. (2014). What – If anything – Do standards do in education? Topological registrations of standardising work in teacher education. *European Educational Research Journal, 13*(1), 73–88. doi:10.2304/eerj.2014.13.1.73

Fenwick, T. (2011). Reading educational reform with actor network theory: Fluid spaces, otherings, and ambivalences. *Educational Philosophy and Theory, 43*(Suppl. 1), 114–134. doi:10.1111/j.1469-5812.2009.00609.x

Fenwick, T., & Edwards, R. (2010). *Actor-network theory and education*. London: Routledge.

Fenwick, T., Edwards, R., & Sawchuck, P. (2011). *Emerging approaches to educational research: Tracing the socio-material*. London: Routledge.

Fenwick, T., & Landri, P. (2012). Materialities, textures and pedagogies: Socio-material assemblages in education. *Pedagogy, Culture & Society, 20*(1), 1–7.

Grimaldi, E. (2010). *Discorsi e pratiche di governance della scuola.* L'esperienza della provincia di Napoli [Discourses and practices of school governance. The case of 'Provincia di Napoli']. Milano: Franco Angeli.

Grimaldi, E., Serpieri, R., & Romano, T. (2011). *Discourses of early school leaving. A policy of partnership.* Napoli: Liguori.

Joyce, P. (2002). *The social in question: New bearings in history and the social sciences.* London: Routledge.

Kooiman, J. (2000). Societal governance: Levels, modes and orders of social-political interaction. In J. Pierre (Ed.), *Debating governance* (pp. 138–163). Oxford: Oxford University Press.

Landri, P. (2008). The permanence of distinctiveness: Performances and changing schooling governance in the Southern European countries. *Mediterranean Journal of Education Studies, 13* (2), 117–135.

Landri, P. (2009). A temporary eclipse of bureaucracy. The circulation of school autonomy in Italy. *Italian Journal of Sociology of Education, 1*(3), 76–93.

Landri, P. (2012). Multiple enactments of educational research. *European Educational Research Journal, 11*(1), 62–67. Retrieved from http://www.wwwords.co.uk/rss/abstract.asp?j=eerj&a id=4907&doi=1

Latour, B. (2005). *Reassembling the social. An introduction to actor-network theory.* Oxford: Oxford University Press.

Latour, B. (2007). *La fabbrica del diritto* [The making of law]. Troina: Città Aperta Edizioni.

Latour, B. (2010a). *Cogitamus. Six lettres sur les humanités scientifiques* [Cogitamus. Six letters on scientific humanities]. Paris: La Découverte.

Latour, B. (2010b). Gabriel Tarde and the end of the social. In P. Joyce (Ed.), *The social in question. New bearings in history and the social sciences* (pp. 117–132). London: Routledge.

Mol, A., & Law, J. (1994). Regions, networks and fluids: Anaemia and social topology. *Social Studies of Science, 24*, 641–671. doi:10.1177/030631279402400402

Napoletano, D. (2008). La conferenza d'ambito come rete di organizzazioni [The conference of zone as network of organizations]. In R. Serpieri (Ed.), *Governance delle politiche scolastiche. La Provincia di Napoli e le Scuole dell'Autonomia* [The governance of schooling policies. Provincia of Napoli and School Autonomy] (pp. 125–136). Milano: Franco Angeli.

Provincia di Napoli, Napoli, & Dipartimento di Sociologia. (2004). *Per un modello di governance scolastica* [Towards a model of school governance]. Napoli: Euroffset 2000.

Rizvi, F. (2006). Imagination and the globalisation of educational policy research. *Globalisation, Societies and Education, 4*, 193–205. doi:10.1080/14767720600752551

Serpieri, R. (2008). *Governance delle politiche scolastiche* [Governance of school policies] (p. 224). Milano: Franco Angeli.

Serpieri, R., & Romano, T. (2008). Apprendere la governance delle politiche scolastiche [The Governance of schooling policies]. In R. Serpieri (Ed.), *Governance delle politiche scolastiche. La Provincia di Napoli e le Scuole dell'Autonomia* [The Governance of schooling policies. Provincia of Napoli and School Autonomy] (pp. 104–124). Milano: Franco Angeli.

Sørensen, E. (2009). *The materiality learning. Technology and knowledge educational practice.* Cambridge, MA: Cambridge University Press. Retrieved from http://www.cambridge.org/us/ academic/subjects/psychology/educational-psychology/materiality-learning-technology-and-know ledge-educational-practice#.UnDY2EOgCKw.mendeley

REVIEW ESSAY
Symbolic power, politics and teachers

Aspa Baroutsis

School of Education, University of Queensland, Brisbane, QLD, Australia

Symbolic power, politics, and intellectuals: the political sociology of Pierre Bourdieu, by David L. Swartz, Chicago, University of Chicago Press, 2013, 292 pp., US$27.50 (paperback), ISBN 9780226925011

Introduction

In the book, *Symbolic power, politics, and intellectuals: The political sociology of Pierre Bourdieu*, David L. Swartz (2013) frames his discussion around the notion of power while focusing on Bourdieu's 'political sociology', a 'largely neglected' aspect of Bourdieu's work. Swartz (2013) suggests that Bourdieu offers a 'sociology of politics' as well as a 'politics of sociology'. Therefore, sociology is a form of political engagement or as Bourdieu (2000a) suggests, 'scholarship with commitment' that enables a move towards 'more just and democratic life' (Swartz, 2013, p. i). This essay offers an outline of Swartz's reading of Bourdieu's political sociology using three of his 'thinking tools' and demonstrates the value of this book for analysing the cross-field effects of journalism and education (also see Lingard & Rawolle, 2004; Rawolle, 2005).

Swartz intricately and meticulously takes the reader on a historical and contextual journey through Bourdieu's life and works, focusing on the notion of power as a form of domination. He skilfully provides explanations, elaborations and examples of Bourdieu's writings and thinking, generating a detailed historical summary. In focusing on Bourdieu's political sociology, Swartz outlines Bourdieu's research agenda related to his politically oriented sociology projects, as well as areas of his political activism later in his career and his late polemical writings. Swartz masterfully develops critical understandings of Bourdieu's *oeuvre* by contextualising, comparing and analysing similarities and differences with the theoretical concepts of other scholars and theorists, in particular Max Weber. This enables readers who are both familiar and unfamiliar with Bourdieu's work to engage with his conceptual tools, what Bourdieu calls his 'thinking tools', as Swartz provides anchor points for developing deeper understandings. Equally commendable is Swartz's determination to identify tensions, critiques and gaps in Bourdieu's conceptualisations of the relationships between sociology and politics – something that Swartz often reconciles at the end of each of the analytic chapters.

Across the eight chapters, Swartz outlines the key understandings of Bourdieu's sociology through an overview of his key conceptual tools (Chapter 2) and an analysis of two of these tools – capitals and fields – in relation to the notion of power (Chapter 3).

These foundation chapters are augmented by more specific ones that develop Swartz's argument about Bourdieu's relevance for those interested in political sociology (Chapters 1, 6, 8) and Bourdieu's public interventions and political activism (Chapter 7). In two outstanding chapters of the book, Swartz specifically focuses on symbolic power as a form of domination (Chapter 4) and Bourdieu's analysis of the state (Chapter 5), again stressing Bourdieu's notions of power.

This review essay briefly outlines elements of Swartz's argument regarding Bourdieu's political sociology, using the concepts as they are structured throughout the book, and focusing on three key modes of analysis of power in the form of social domination: valued resources (capital), arenas of struggle (fields) and legitimation (symbolic power). This is followed by a discussion of symbolic power and how it operates in the journalistic and political fields, and across the education field, focusing in particular on symbolic power and violence associated with a number of media practices in the education field. Here, examples are drawn from the Australian print media, specifically *The Australian* which is a News Limited newspaper.

Power, domination and social order

Bourdieu was interested in power, particularly in the form of social domination, and the mechanisms and processes that are used to disguise, reproduce and perpetuate power in different societies (Swartz, 2013; Wacquant, 1996). Swartz (2013) explains that domination is 'systemic power embedded in the patterns of thought, basic assumptions, linguistic terms and categories, and social relationships that shapes how individuals go about their everyday lives though individuals are rarely aware of its influence' (pp. 30–31), thereby maintaining the social order. This order is not found in 'human reason', is not a 'naturally endowed right', or a 'social contract', or 'consent or reason', nor is it based on 'universal principles' (Swartz, 2013, p. 31). Rather, as Bourdieu (2000b) argued, 'there is nothing other than arbitrariness and usurpation' in relation to maintaining social order (p. 168). Additionally, social and political order originate in 'violence', are crystallised as 'custom', and are maintained and transmitted through 'bodily dispositions' (habitus) (Swartz, 2013, p. 33), a point that will be taken up later in this essay.

Specifically, Bourdieu analyses power in three distinct ways, each of which operates as a form of domination. The three modes of analysis are: power in valued resources (capitals); power in particular arenas or spheres (fields); and power in legitimation (symbolic power). First, power as a valued resource, which Bourdieu calls *capital*, includes the following forms of capital: 'economic (money and property), cultural (information, knowledge, and educational credentials), social (acquaintances and networks), and symbolic [resources] (legitimation, authority, prestige)'; these often become the objects and instruments of struggle (Swartz, 2013, p. 50). While these capitals can function to enhance economic worth, they are not always material or quantifiable, and often include social and symbolic capitals. For example, 'profits from education ... can be measured not just in income but in tastes, verbal style, [and] manners' (p. 53). The accumulation and exchange of capitals serve to maintain and enhance an individual's position in the social or political order (Swartz, 2013, p. 55). For example, Swartz explains, '[the] concept of cultural capital does not reduce to knowledge and skills directly related to productivity but represents a capacity to make individuals more effective actors within a particular social milieu' (2013, p. 53). As such, Bourdieu views capitals as both social and relational in character. Swartz explains, 'an object becomes a capital when it establishes a *social relation of power* that differentiates the holder from the nonholder, when it establishes some degree of social closure – a relation of inclusion and exclusion' (p. 51, emphasis added). Of interest here is the uneven distribution of capitals, which are a form of power across social groups, and the 'differentiating and stratifying effect' of such inclusions and exclusions (Swartz, 2013, p. 51).

Second, Bourdieu indicates that 'a capital does not exist and function except in relation to a field' (Bourdieu & Wacquant, 1992, p. 101). Consequently, power is analysed as specific *fields* of struggle. Bourdieu (1993) suggests:

> The structure of the field is a state of the power relations among the agents or institutions engaged in the struggle, or, to put it another way, a state of the distribution of the specific capital which has been accumulated in the course of previous struggles and which orients subsequent strategies. (p. 73)

Bourdieu also states, 'to think in terms of field is to think relationally' (Bourdieu & Wacquant, 1992, p. 96); that is, capitals, individuals, groups and institutions are all interdependent in networks of relations that shape the social order. Therefore, these networks are 'arenas of production, circulation, and appropriation of goods, services, knowledge, or status, and the competitive positions held by actors in their struggle to accumulate and monopolize different kinds of capital' (Swartz, 2013, p. 57). This field struggle is often over the 'distribution of capitals' within a given field, but also over the 'most legitimate form of capital', thereby becoming a struggle for symbolic power and the right to dominate and determine what is the most legitimate, and therefore, the most valued form of capital in a particular field (p. 35). The dominant groups distinguish themselves from the other classes by their 'sheer volume of capital', while also competing amongst themselves in order to 'impose their particular type of capital as the most legitimate claim to authority in the social order' (p. 36). As actors participate in the struggle, Swartz suggests they 'unwittingly reproduce the structure of power relations within and across fields ... misrecognising the arbitrary character of capitals by viewing them and the struggle over them as necessary' (p. 60). This he interprets as demonstrating how power is misrecognised because of the action of habitus, but also because of the actors' very participation in the struggle (p. 60).

Of all the fields, the field of power is considered a key feature of Bourdieu's thinking in relation to how power is dispersed in various societies (Swartz, 2013, p. 61). Bourdieu refers to the field of power as 'the relations of force that obtain between the social positions which guarantee their occupants a quantum of social force, or of capital, such that they are able to enter into the struggles over the monopoly of power' (Bourdieu & Wacquant, 1992, pp. 229–230). The field of power is the arena where struggle occurs between fields, for example the economic and cultural fields, for the 'right to dominate *throughout the social order*' (Swartz, 2013, p. 62, emphasis in original). Bourdieu (1996) indicates that this is the space where:

> These different forms of capital are themselves stakes in the struggles whose objective is no longer the accumulation of or even the monopoly on a particular form of capital (or power) ... but rather the determination of the relative value and magnitude of the different forms of power that can be wielded in the different fields or, if you will, power over the different forms of power or the capital granting power over capital. (p. 265)

Swartz (2013) identifies this struggle as being over the control of the state and therefore domination over institutional function, legitimation and the power to circulate political doxa that become naturalised in society (pp. 62, 138).

Symbolic power, a form of domination, requires *legitimation*, which is the final element of this analysis of power. Symbolic power extends beyond types of resources (capitals) and arenas of struggle (fields) to that which 'legitimates the stratified social order' of all social life (Swartz, 2013, p. 78). The notion of legitimation relates to commonly held, shared assumptions about the social order, or as Bourdieu (1990) suggests, a 'doxa' that is a 'kind of original adherence to the established order' (p. 127). Doxa is not equally shared amongst the dominant and dominated parties, with Bourdieu (1994) suggesting 'doxa is a particular point of view, the point of view of the dominant, when it presents and imposes itself as a universal point of view' (p. 15). Swartz (2013) states that symbolic power involves the 'capacity to impose symbolic meanings and forms as legitimate', thereby shaping a society's perceptions of social reality, but also involves the capacity to either maintain or transform social realities by shaping representations through 'inculcating classifications, schema of perceptions ... cognitive schemes and bodily expression'; therefore, symbolic power forms the 'dispositions of habitus' (pp. 83, 89). Symbolic power is often experienced as 'taken-for-granted, natural, [or an] inevitable state of affairs', making it a generative and 'imposed power' that is a 'cultural expression of dominance'; however, this also ensures that it is a 'contested power, being both the object and instrument of social struggle' (p. 83). Swartz adds that symbolic struggles occur for one of two reasons: 'to either maintain and reinforce public perceptions of existing social realities ... or to transform those perceptions and in doing so create conditions for social change' (p. 88).

Symbolic violence and symbolic capital are expressions of domination because they are used to stress the legitimation of power in a society. Symbolic violence is often disguised and Bourdieu (2001b) suggests that it is 'a gentle violence, imperceptible and invisible even to its victims, exerted for the most part through the purely symbolic channels of communication and cognition (more precisely, misrecognition), or even feeling' (pp. 1–2). Swartz (2013) suggests that symbolic violence is often 'misrecognised obedience,' where symbolic power is accepted as legitimate rather than arbitrary (p. 83). Additionally, symbolic capital, such as the 'esteem, recognition, belief, credit, confidence of others', often represents the perceived authority to exercise symbolic power (Bourdieu, 2000b, p. 166).

In the following section, following Swartz's (2013) understandings of Bourdieu's political sociology, this essay will draw substantially on notions of symbolic power and how it operates in the journalistic, political and educational fields. In particular, it will focus on the implications of symbolic power and violence on media practices associated with reportage about teachers and their work, drawn from the Australian print media.

Symbolic violence, media institutions and teachers

Symbolic power and violence circulate within the practices of media institutions, at times operating inequitably in relation to the ways reportage represents teachers and their work. However, symbolic violence also operates in relation to journalists, who are the agents of media institutions. That is, both teacher(s) and journalist(s) experience the effects of symbolic violence, albeit in different ways. The media institutions, as the dominant group, often through the actions of their agents, impose their ideology on other groups such as the readers of their newspapers, through their reportage of education-related issues. Such practices that influence public perceptions of teachers are maintained through symbolic power that exercises control over the circulation of ideas, thereby legitimating and naturalising the media institution's constructions of teachers. Therefore, symbolic power and violence often intersect.

Bourdieu conceives symbolic power through a 'power over' distinction that suggests it has the 'capacity to impose a social vision of the world as the most legitimate one' (Swartz, 2013, p. 119). That is, media institutions may exercise power 'over' their readers or those who they report on, by imposing their world view on their employees or the general public who view their publications and broadcasts. Media texts in newspapers may 'naturalise' certain negative understandings of teachers, thereby projecting a 'taken-for-granted' or 'commonsensical' perception of teachers and their work. Baroutsis (2014) has found that newspaper texts construct teachers as being in need of greater regulation, so as to improve teacher accountability, and greater transparency in their practices and therefore in need of auditing practices. News texts also suggest teachers across Australia are often poor 'quality' and incompetent, and privileged in terms of their conditions of service, but reckless in their execution of their duties. Symbolic power is formative of such realities (Swartz, 2013). Such reportage suffers from what Bourdieu (2011) refers to as 'structural amnesia', where media reportage fails to move debates forward, instead legitimating simplistic and narrow understandings, in this case, of teachers. Each news story under these conditions of structural amnesia is seen to be new, not linked to any past reportage. This orients in people's minds a particular version of 'reality', thereby maintaining power 'over' teachers and limiting their opportunities to voice alternative versions.

Symbolic power, therefore, operates in a hegemonic mode. In this example of the media, the dominant group is often the media institution, who may dominate journalists into producing stories that align with editorial perspectives and the sociopolitical views of media ownership (Baroutsis, 2014; Mockler, 2013). For example, journalists are delegated authority to speak on behalf of the institutional group; however, the group's interests often determine their individual actions and ways of speaking (Swartz, 2013, p. 108). At other times, the dominant agent of the group may be the editor of the media organisation, as was seen in the Leveson Inquiry (2012) in the UK, which heard that Rebekah Brooks, the former *News of the World* editor, levered politicians' cooperation through 'a fear of allegedly ... prying intrusively into their personal lives', including personal attacks in the press (p. 65). Such insidious practices operate as symbolic violence, involving the media agents 'bending under the weight of domination ... [and as] an assault against the personhood of the individual and authentic identity of the group' (Swartz, 2013, p. 97). Bourdieu (1996) explains this notion, stating that symbolic violence can involve an individual's predisposition to:

> Perform the institution's every wish because they are the institution made man (or woman), and who, whether dominated or dominant, can submit to it or fully exercise its necessity only because they have incorporated it, they are of one body with it, they give body to it. (p. 4)

Symbolic violence therefore secures 'compliance to domination through the shaping of beliefs' (Lukes, 2005, pp. 143–144) and actions or practices associated with the execution of such beliefs. Bourdieu (2011) suggests that this relates to the media policy of 'demagogic simplification', where media institutions and their agents are 'projecting onto the public their own inclinations and their own views' (p. 3).

Therefore, given such practices, trust becomes a key issue for media institutions and their agents. It can be argued that power operating in media institutions is largely symbolic, given that the agents within these institutions are dependent on symbolic capitals such as 'trust' or 'credit' that is extended to them from those groups they represent (Swartz, 2013, p. 106). Blackmore and Thorpe (2003) state that agents of media institutions are often considered with suspicion and characterised by mistrust and cynicism. As such, journalists engage in symbolic labour in order to maintain and develop their symbolic capital (Swartz, 2013, p. 106), at times with varying degrees of success.

Bourdieu (2001b) often referred to the notion of the 'paradox of *doxa*', which suggests that symbolic power and violence as forms of domination have a tendency to persist within the order of the world:

> The established order, with its relations of domination, its rights and prerogatives, privileges and injustices, ultimately perpetuates itself so easily, apart from a few historical accidents, and ... the most intolerable conditions of existence can so often be perceived as acceptable and even natural. (p. 1)

Elaborating on this paradox, it can be asked: Why would teachers, or groups such as teachers' unions that represent them, allow media institutions to persist with such symbolic violence through socially inequitable media constructs without powerful resistance (Swartz, 2013, pp. 37–38)? Bourdieu (1996) replies:

> The dominated always contribute to their own domination, it is at once necessary to recall that the dispositions that include them toward this complicity are themselves the effect, embodied, of domination. (p. 4)

This is a somewhat surprising statement that sounds like Bourdieu is 'blaming the victim'. However, Swartz (2013) suggests that the actions of the non-dominant groups are 'not out of choice or from external constraints but from the "fit" between the expectations of their habitus and the external structures they encounter' (p. 98). Habitus, therefore, plays an important role in perpetuating and reproducing injustices within various field struggles.

Media institutions and their agents operate within the journalistic field, but also across the education and political fields; for example, journalists interview politicians or teachers (educators) in order to obtain a story (Bourdieu, 2005). Politicians are often responsible for aspects of education policy and the circulation of information regarding teachers and schools. Bourdieu (2005) posits the hypothesis that the journalist and the educator occupy 'determinate positions in the field'; thus we see the journalistic and education fields speaking to each other (p. 31). This raises the question of the 'degree of autonomy' of fields (p. 33). The journalistic field is characterised by a 'high degree of heteronomy' making it a 'very weakly autonomous field', therefore it cannot be understood by its own '*nomos*, its own law of functioning' and 'the effects that the people engaged in this microcosm exert on one another' (p. 33). Here we see the cross-field effects, or the 'effects that result from the interrelations between fields' (Rawolle, 2005, p. 709), with Lingard and Rawolle (2004) suggesting these can be 'structural, event [related], systemic, temporal, hierarchical and vertical' effects (p. 368). While field struggles and cross-field effects are significant elements in understanding the practices of media institutions that perpetuate injustices, considerations must also be given to the habitus of the social agents.

Bourdieu (1990) suggests that in order for the agents in these fields to succeed, they need to develop a 'feel for the game' (p. 9). Swartz (2013) elaborates on this, stating that this can involve 'specific skills, competencies, sensitivities that are attuned to the particular conditions of the field' with many behaviours being shaped by the logic of the field (p. 106); that is, the habitus of actors, including embodied dispositions and schemes of practice (Lingard, Sellar, & Baroutsis, 2014). Swartz (2013) adds that symbolic power shapes habitus and 'the dispositions of habitus predispose actors to select forms of conduct that are most likely to succeed in light of their resources and past experience. Habitus orients action according to anticipated consequences' (p. 90). For example, newspaper editors hire opinion writers, whose writing aligns with the newspaper's ideologies. Journalists have a greater chance of having their articles published if they also align their texts with the perspectives of the editors and opinion writers (Baroutsis, 2014). Consequently, the effects of symbolic power are 'expressed through practices – a practical logic – rather than in sets of explicit beliefs or values', with these practices being 'unconscious and resistant to conscious articulation and critical reflection' (Swartz, 2013, p. 89).

Other journalistic practices that reflect the habitus of agents include the use of language in media reportage. Language is a central feature when exercising symbolic power, in that 'symbolic power is expressed through language' giving it a performative quality (Swartz, 2013, p. 86). Language in newspaper texts constructs a particular teacher identity. Take for example newspaper reportage about teachers, based on the actions of teachers' unions, that suggest teachers are 'militant' (Costa, 2009, 10 July, p. 12), 'ideological warriors' (*The Australian*, 2010, February 17, p. 13) who are 'waging a war' (Buckingham, 2009, December 15, p. 12) against society. They are identified as being 'on the fringes of the education debate, [and] out of touch with reality' (*The Australian*, 2010, February 17, p. 13). Consequently, teachers and their unions are characterised as having 'little credibility' (Albrechtsen, 2010, February 3, p. 12), being 'selfish and arrogant' (Bantick, 2009, July 29, p. 25), as well as 'unreasonable and reactionary' (Costa, 2009, July 10, p. 12). They are often accused of 'indulging in industrial thuggery' if they undertake industrial action (*The Australian*, 2009, July 24, p. 13). One commentator suggests, 'Teachers' unions care about protecting the jobs of teachers and the status quo of schools, no matter the performance of those teachers' (Albrechtsen, 2010, February 3, p. 12). Such linguistic choices demonstrate the 'relations of symbolic power in which the power relations between speakers or their respective groups are actualized' (Bourdieu, 1991, p. 37). Therefore, these specific word choices, rather than other choices, not only give insights into the opinions of the newspapers, their editors and commentators, but also constitute these social and public realities of teachers and their work. Moreover, teachers and their representatives have little recourse in terms of being able to write and publically circulate alternative versions of these 'realities' in media texts or outlets.

In closing

Unfortunately, the voices of groups that are most affected by dominant media politics, for example, teachers, are not always heard in media texts and broadcasts (Bourdieu, 2001a; Swartz, 2013). Bourdieu challenges all public intellectuals, in this case teachers, to 'expose the doxa of the fields of power', challenging the naturalisation of media assumptions that are circulated about teachers and their work (Swartz, 2013, p. 172). Consequently, teachers would 'enter the political arena not as political actors but as intellectuals who engage their specific authority of expertise' (p. 174). Sachs (2003) calls upon teachers to engage in greater activism. Here, she is not suggesting militant, extreme behaviour, but rather that teachers need to be 'responding publically' to the various issues, warning that this is 'not for the faint-hearted', as it 'requires passion, determination and energy' (p. 85). Bourdieu conceives this as 'anti-political politics', where intellectuals would 'be able to make their voice heard directly in all the areas of public life in which they are competent' (Bourdieu, 2001a, p. 9). Such calls towards 'acts of resistance' (Bourdieu, 2001a) constitute a generic capacity of action, working towards the non-dominant agents having a voice. Unlike the notion of the 'power over', these acts of resistance then become generative capacities of 'power to' act (Swartz, 2013, p. 119).

Swartz's (2013) book provides an outstanding account of the political component of Bourdieu's sociology. In particular, Swartz challenges the commonly held perception that symbolic power is just 'symbolic' in character; instead, he suggests that it permeates the practices of everyday life in both subtle and influential ways. The contribution of this book is to enable deeper and more transparent understandings of the power relations within a society. Swartz's analysis demonstrates the relevance of Bourdieu's thinking tools for education and education research. In the account given in this essay of practices across the fields of education and journalism, the book provides the impetus for challenging many of the undemocratic aspects in these fields. Swartz foregrounds Bourdieu's tools for confronting, disrupting or resisting many of the practices associated with these fields, especially when they cross over, so as to enhance democratic practices.

References

Albrechtsen, J. (2010, February 3). Carry on with this revolution, Julia. *The Australian*, p. 12.
The Australian. (2009, July 24). Lessons from the 70s. *The Australian*, p. 13.
The Australian. (2010, February 17). Taking a stand for mediocrity. *The Australian*, p. 13.
Bantick, C. (2009, July 29). Students, parents sacrificed on the altar of teacher greed. *The Courier Mail*, p. 25.
Baroutsis, A. (2014). *Troubling news: Challenging politics, perceptions and practices of newspaper constructions of teachers* (Unpublished doctoral thesis). The University of Queensland, Brisbane.
Blackmore, J., & Thorpe, S. (2003). Media/ting change: The print media's role in mediating education policy in a period of radical reform in Victoria, Australia. *Journal of Education Policy*, 18, 577–595. doi:10.1080/0268093032000145854
Bourdieu, P. (1990). *In other words: Essays towards a reflexive sociology*. Stanford, CA: Stanford University Press.
Bourdieu, P. (1991). *Language and symbolic power*. Cambridge: Polity Press in association with Basil Blackwell.
Bourdieu, P. (1993). *Sociology in question*. (R. Nice, Trans.). London: SAGE.
Bourdieu, P. (1996). *The state nobility: Elite schools in the field of power*. Stanford, CA: Stanford University Press.
Bourdieu, P. (2000a). *For a scholarship with commitment*. Profession, 40-45. New York, NY: Modern Language Association.
Bourdieu, P. (2000b). *Pascalian meditations*. Palo Alto, CA: Stanford University Press.
Bourdieu, P. (2001a). *Acts of resistance: Against the new myths of our time* (R. Nice, Trans.). Cambridge: Polity Press.
Bourdieu, P. (2001b). *Masculine domination*. Stanford, CA: Stanford University Press.
Bourdieu, P. (2005). The political field, the social science field, and the journalistic field. In R. Benson & E. Neveu (Eds.), *Bourdieu and the journalistic field* (pp. 29–47). Cambridge, MA: Polity Press.

Bourdieu, P. (2011). *On television*. Cambridge: Polity Press.
Bourdieu, P., & Wacquant, L. J. D. (1992). *An invitation to reflexive sociology*. Cambridge: Polity Press.
Bourdieu, P., Wacquant, L. J. D., & Farage, S. (1994). Rethinking the state: Genesis and structure of the bureaucratic field. *Sociological Theory, 12*(1), 1–18. doi:10.2307/202032
Buckingham, J. (2009, December 15). Teacher union still waging a war against transparency. *The Australian*, p. 12.
Costa, M. (2009, July 10). Teacher unions hold the future to ransom. *The Australian*, p. 12.
Leveson Inquiry. (2012). *Levenson Inquiry: Culture, practice and ethics of the press*. Retrieved December 16, 2012, from http://www.levesoninquiry.org.uk/
Lingard, B., & Rawolle, S. (2004). Mediatizing educational policy: The journalistic field, science policy, and cross-field effects. *Journal of Education Policy, 19*, 361–380. doi:10.1080/0268093042000207665
Lingard, B., Sellar, S., & Baroutsis, A. (2014). Researching the habitus of global policy actors in education. *Cambridge Journal of Education, 45*(1), 25–42. doi:10.1080/0305764X.2014.988686
Lukes, S. (2005). *Power: A radical view* (2nd ed.). New York, NY: Palgrave Macmillan.
Mockler, N. (2013). Reporting the 'education revolution': MySchool.edu.au in the print media. *Discourse: Studies in the Cultural Politics of Education, 34*(1), 1–16. doi:10.1080/01596306.2012.698860
Rawolle, S. (2005). Cross-field effects and temporary social fields: A case study of the mediatization of recent Australian knowledge economy policies. *Journal of Education Policy, 20*, 705–724. doi:10.1080/02680930500238622
Rawolle, S. (2005). Cross-field effects and temporary social fields: A case study of the mediatization of recent Australian knowledge economy policies. *Journal of Education Policy, 20*, 705–724. doi:10.1080/02680930500238622
Sachs, J. (2003). *The activist teaching professional*. Maidenhead: Open University Press.
Swartz, D. L. (2013). *Symbolic power, politics, and intellectuals: The political sociology of Pierre Bourdieu*. Chicago, IL: University of Chicago Press.
Wacquant, L. (1996). Foreword. In P. Bourdieu (Ed.), *The State Nobility: Elite schools in the field of power* (pp. ix–xxii). Stanford, CA: Stanford University Press.

Index

Note: **Boldface** page numbers refers to figures and tables, n denotes endnotes

AAS *see* Africentric Alternative School
actor-network (AN) perspectives 70
actor-network theory (ANT): and Deleuzian philosophy 26, 27; education policies 119; policy assemblages 72; policy enactments with 58–62; policy entanglements 73
Africentric Alternative School (AAS) 38–40, 44–5, 48–9
after actor network theory (after ANT) 84, 96n3
alcoholic liver disease (ALD) 60
AN perspectives *see* actor-network perspectives
ANT *see* actor-network theory
anti-political politics 139
Atwood school 11, 17
Australian school education 23
Australian, The 133, 138

Ball, Stephen 1, 2
behaviour management 12–14
BER programme *see* Building the Education Revolution programme
Bloch, Roland 4
Bottani, Norberto 101–2, 105, 115
Bourdieu's political sociology 132–3; capital 133–4; fields 134; symbolic power 135–6, 138
Braun, Annette 1, 2
Brooks, Rebekah 136
Building the Education Revolution (BER) programme 2, 22, 24–6, 33

Campion school 11, 15, 18
Canadian multiculturalism 39, 40
capacity law 85–6, **89**, 90
capital, Bourdieu's power analysis 133–4
Centre for Educational Research and Innovation (CERI) 105
CNW *see* curricular norm values
conference of education zone 124, 125, **126**
'containers-thinking' of social 120

contemporary learning spaces 33
curricular norm values (CNW) 85

Deleuzian philosophy 27
difference by degree 46–51
difference-in-itself 3, 40–2, 50
divergent policy enactments 9

Education at a Glance (EAG) 4, 100–1, 106
education policy: actor-network perspectives 70; enacting approach 25–6; in England 10; entanglements 72–3; meshworks 72–3; No Child Left Behind 71; policy and policy-guided practices 79–80; policy assemblage 72–3; rationalist approach 25; sociomaterial approach 119–20; turnaround plan 74–9
education zones (South Italy): conference of zone 124, 125, **126**; failure of 125–7; as fluid spaces 127–8; information system 124; intertextual associations 122; machines for deliberations 122–5, 130; preparatory works 125; Provincia di Napoli, map of 123, **123**; research groups 124; research programme 121; socio-technical analysis 122; statist legacy 120
ELA teachers *see* English language arts teachers
ELLs *see* English language learners
enacting approach, educational policy process 25–6
English as Second Language (ESL) teachers 72, 75–7
English language arts (ELA) teachers 77
English language learners (ELLs) 71, 72, 75
English (England) secondary schools: data collection 10–12; education policy in 10; high stakes policies 14–16; policy actors 8, 16–18; policy enactment 9–12; policy implementation 7–8; professional orientations 12–14
ESL teachers *see* English as Second Language teachers
evidence-based approach 70

INDEX

faciality enactments 38, 42–3, 48–50
fields, Bourdieu's power analysis 134
First Nation School 45
fluid spaces, education zones as 127–8
'free-range' learning **29**
free school meal (FSM) 11

GCSEs *see* General Certificates of Secondary Education
General Assemblies (INES) 113–14
General Certificates of Secondary Education (GCSEs) 15
George Elliot School 13, 15
German higher education: calculating teaching capacity 85–7; methodological remarks 83–5; new public management reforms 88–92; teaching without faculty 92–5
Gorur, Radhika 4–5
Gulson, Kalervo 3
Gum Park Primary School 31–3

heterogeneity and divergent enactments 9
Heyneman, Stephen 102
high stakes policy 14–16

ILP *see* individual learning plan
immutable mobiles 85
individual learning plan (ILP) 59
INES project *see* International System of Education Indicators project
intermediaries and mediators 119
International Journal of Educational Research (Bottani) 110
International Standard Classification of Education (ISCED) 102
International System of Education Indicators (INES) project: Centre for Educational Research and Innovation 105; challenges faced by 105–6; General Assemblies 113–14
ISCED *see* International Standard Classification of Education

Joyce, Patrick 130n1

Koyama, Jill 3–4

Landri, Paolo 5
Learning Spaces Framework 23
learning spaces in Victorian government schools **29**; analytic of assemblage in policy work 27–8; assembly practices 29–33; Building the Education Revolution programme 24; contemporary learning space 33; data and methods 28–9; enacting approaches to educational policy 25–6; 'free-range' learning **29**; policy assemblage 26–7; policy matters 24; practice of assembly 29–33; rationalist approach 25; re/assembling of 33–4; twenty-first century, notion of 23; types of 22–3
lesbian, gay, bisexual, and transgender (LGBT) 47

Maguire, Meg 1, 2
materialising process 24, 32–3
media institutions, symbolic power and violence 135–8
meshwork concept 3, 73
micropolitical learning space 28, 30
Mitterle, Alexander 4
Mulcahy, Dianne 2

NCLB *see* No Child Left Behind
neoliberal multiculturalism 39–40; difference-in-itself 40–2; faciality and policy enactment 42–3
newly qualified teachers (NQTs) 16–17
new public management (NPM) reforms 88–92
No Child Left Behind (NCLB) 3, 71, 74
NPM reforms *see* new public management reforms
NQTs *see* newly qualified teachers

OECD education indicators *see* Organisation for Economic Co-operation and Development education indicators
ontological politics 61, 63–5
Organisation for Economic Co-operation and Development (OECD) education indicators: Bottani, Norberto 101–2; calculation and critique 114–16; Centre for Educational Research and Innovation 105; design and function 104–5; *Education at a Glance* 4, 100–1, 106; growing influence of 111–12; INES General Assemblies 113–14; *International Journal of Educational Research* 110; International System of Education Indicators project 105–6; *A Nation at Risk* 105, 107; number of indicators 108–9; performance indicators 110–11; Sauvageot, Claude 102; Science and Technology Studies 103; science serving policy 107–8; sociology of measurement 103–4; *A System of Education Indicators to Guide Public Policy Decisions* 107

performativity and multiple ontologies: actor network theory 56, 58–62; classroom practice 62–3; enacting educational policy 57–8; material manifestations, policy and teacher learning 65–7; professional

INDEX

development meetings 62–3; socio-material assemblages 63–5
persistently low achieving (PLA) 71
PISA *see* Programme for International Student Assessment
PLA *see* persistently low achieving
policy actors 8, 16–18
policy enactment 42–3; definition 8, 9; heterogeneity and divergent 9; orthodoxies and stories 25–6; policy actors in 8, 16–18; study of 10–12
policy histories 44–8
policy implementation 7–8
policy work, analytic of assemblage in 27–8
poststructuralist theory 24, 26–7
power, Bourdieu's analyses: capital 133–4; fields 134; symbolic power 135–6, 138
problem-solving device 25
"problem-solving" mechanism 57
professional learning, enactments of policies 55–68
professional orientation (England) 12–14
professional ways of being 57
Programme for International Student Assessment (PISA) 100

qualitative and quantitative analysis (video data) 28

radical relationality 84
rationalist approach, educational policy process 25
Riveros, Gus 3

Sauvageot, Claude 102
school-based policy implementation 8
School Board Trustees 44
schools of recognition 37; difference and recognition 39–43; policy histories 44–8
Science and Technology Studies (STS) 103
7th International Conference on Interpretive Policy Analysis 1
Sheltered Instructional Observational Protocol (SIOP) Model 75

SIFE *see* students with interrupted formal education
SIOP Model *see* Sheltered Instructional Observational Protocol Model
Smyth, John 102
social constructivism 34n3
social domination 133–5
socio-material assemblages 63–5
sociomateriality of education policy: actor-network theory 119; containers-thinking of social 120; education space in South Italy *see* education zones (South Italy)
South Italy, education policy space in 120–2
staff planning charts 85–7, 90
STS *see* Science and Technology Studies
students with interrupted formal education (SIFE) 72
study place 86–8, 90–1
Swartz, David L. 132–9
SWS *see* weekly semester hours
symbolic capital 135
symbolic power 135–6, 138
symbolic violence 135–8
syncretism 33

TDSB *see* Toronto District School Board
territorialisation 27–8
territory 27–8
Toronto District School Board (TDSB) 38, 46
turnaround curriculum 74–9
twenty-first century learning 23

Victorian Department of Education and Early Childhood Development 28
Victorian government schools *see* learning spaces in Victorian government schools
Viczko, Melody 3

Wandering Spirit School 45
Wattle Park Primary School **29–30**, 29–31
Webb, Taylor 3
weekly semester hours (SWS) 85–7, 95, 96n9
Wesley school 11, 15
Würman, Carsten 4